The Management of Market-Oriented Economies:

A Comparative Perspective

The Management of Market-Oriented Economies:

A Comparative Perspective

Philip A. Klein

The Pennsylvania State University

Wadsworth Publishing Company, Inc.
Belmont, California

330.9
K 64

ISBN-0-534-00232-3

L. C. Cat. Card No. 72-93744

Printed in the United States of America

1 2 3 4 5 6 7 8 9 10———77 76 75 74 73

To the Memory of My Mother

    Rose Schaffer Klein

who had much to do with this book
by teaching her children through her
daily life that no nation, race, or
religion can claim a monopoly on virtue.

Preface

The economies of the world no longer fall neatly into two groups, one labeled free enterprise, or capitalist, and the other communist — and it may be questioned whether either system ever had the neatly distinguishable form we have all too often ascribed to the economic systems of the past. In recent years there has come into fasnion the convergence theory, which suggests that slowly but surely communist and capitalist economies are moving toward a meeting point: capitalist economies will have a large public sector and much direct government intervention in resource allocation, while the command, or communist, systems will resort to many of the resource allocation devices of the West — differential returns to factors of production, use of the profit motive, etc.

Although there is some evidence to support this view, it seems that many political and economic features will continue to differentiate market-oriented from command economies, to use the terminology which seems most appropriate, and which will be used in this book.

There has been much discussion in recent years concerning the increasing variation found among command economies: the diverse ways of allocating resources in the Soviet Union, China, the countries of Eastern Europe, and in that especially interesting hybrid, Yugoslavia, have been the subject of much analysis. This book is devoted to exploring the many differences among market-oriented economies as well as their similarities. It is designed to suggest that in the noncommunist world there can be many approaches to our common economic problems. Some of the differences among market-oriented economies are due to differences in the problems and diversity of the resources with which to meet them, but some differences are more due to diversity in institutions and in national predilections. Nonetheless, market-oriented economies have many problems in common and can learn much from each other. The principles of economics are not necessarily synonymous with how economic problems are approached in the United States.

It is hoped this book will be useful in enriching introductory economics courses by sketching in some of this diversity in economic approaches and policies to be found in market-oriented economies. The book may also be helpful in courses dealing with comparative economic systems by suggesting that just as command economies are showing greater variety so are market-oriented economies. In developing this theme, some chapters parallel many of the topics in microeconomic and macroeconomic policy found in conventional principles texts, and which form as well the areas for discussion in courses in comparative economic systems. The book makes no effort to be exhaustive, but uses various economies to illustrate the varieties of approach to current economic problems taken in market-oriented economies.

Acknowledgments

In writing this book I have incurred a number of debts to colleagues and friends who were kind enough to assist me in my research and writing. Professor Jan S. Prybyla of The Pennsylvania State University read the entire manuscript and made many helpful suggestions. And Professors John Sheahan of Williams College, and Harold Wolozin of the University of Massachusetts, Boston, both gave the manuscript careful attention, enabling me to make substantial improvements. Professor Will E. Mason provided invaluable advice on a number of questions on monetary and fiscal policies. Professors James Herendeen and George Brandow likewise helped me enormously with the chapter on agricultural policies and have my gratitude. Professor John T. Schmidman read the chapter on labor organizations and is responsible for my having avoided a number of errors. Professor Edward Budd provided me with extremely useful references for the discussion of income distribution.

The study depends very heavily, as the reader will discover, on the published documents of various national and international agencies for much of the basic data. In ferreting out this material I was privileged to have the assistance of a number of eager and helpful reference librarians in the Pattee Library at The Pennsylvania State University, particularly Mrs. Margaret LeSourd, Mrs. Joy Noble, and Miss Mina Pease. Mr. Frank Oreovicz is responsible for the index. I wish also to thank the Office of Research of the College of Liberal Arts at The Pennsylvania State University for its generous financial assistance. I acknowledge, too, my gratitude to Mrs. Wendy Benson who was in charge of much of the secretarial work involved in the book, and express my appreciation also to several of our departmental secretaries who assisted at various times with work on portions of the manuscript.

My wife, Margaret A. Klein, not only bore up womanfully under my virtual exile from home while I was writing this, but assisted me enormously in the task of proofreading and checking the manuscript for errors. For this and much else she has my gratitude and appreciation.

Contents

1

Introduction

Almost all American textbooks on the principles of economics concentrate on the economy of the United States until the last chapter, at which point the subject of "comparative economic systems" is broached. In this chapter one customarily finds brief discussions of contemporary communist or "centrally planned" economies typified by the USSR and China, and a discussion of "socialist" economies which might include Britain under the Labour government, the Scandinavian economies, and occasionally several others. Increasingly, Yugoslavia is put in a class by itself, France raises problems of classification, and Germany is seldom mentioned.

This book has two major themes. The first is that in many ways the word *capitalism* has lost much of its meaning (for a variety of reasons to be spelled out shortly). Nonetheless, it is still valid to claim that a large number of economies, here called *market-oriented economies,* have enough significant characteristics in common to justify viewing them as a group to be contrasted with the highly planned economies typified by the USSR, China, and most of Eastern Europe (the *command economies*). As we shall attempt to show, for the first group of economies above, *market-oriented* is a better descriptive term than *capitalist,* even though *market-oriented* too is far from perfect (Yugoslavia, for example, is in many ways a market-oriented economy, but it is not included in the group of economies considered here).

The second theme of this book is that despite the similarities there is also much diversity among the economies of the West, diversity which the typical American Principles of Economics text glosses over by focusing so narrowly on economic analysis appropriate to the U.S. economy. Thus, though not a full-fledged comparative study, the analysis below calls attention to the great diversity among market economies in the degree of their reliance on the market, as well as to how "free," by Adam Smith's definition, the markets really are. Similarly, despite whatever justification there is for the view (the *convergence theory*—to be discussed below) that "capitalist" and "communist" economies are "converging" toward some kind of part-market and part-planned economy, with aspects of both capitalism and communism but unlike either in its pure form, the comparative analysis of economic systems below should drive home the point that there is also much to be said for the contrary view. Moreover, there are good reasons for discarding the term *capitalist* as not really descriptive of any modern economy.

What Is an Economic System?

An economic system can be defined as the set of institutions adopted by society to decide—in light of existing natural resources, produced resources (capital), human resources, and technology—what goods and services should be produced for current consumption; what should be devoted to adding to the capital stock of the community so as to ensure added future production of goods and services (essentially, then, the growth rate of the economy); and how to distribute the fruits of economic activity among the participants.

Many years ago Robert Heilbroner pointed out that these fundamental economic problems can be resolved (1) by authority, in which case the community's leaders make the decisions and inform everyone else of them; (2) by tradition, in which case the decisions become buried in the past and are never questioned anew; or (3) by the market system using prices, in which case consumers are given "dollar votes" to which business firms presumably respond so that the decisions reached reflect the collective judgment of the community.[1] (The decisions are weighted, to be sure, in favor of the affluent because the principle of the market is "one dollar, one vote" rather than that of political democracy, "one man, one vote.")

While there may once have been a good deal to commend Heilbroner's classification of economic systems, it becomes increasingly too simple and possibly too neat in the modern world. And while there are examples of all three, even in the recent past, the commingling of other elements with "the

---

[1] Robert Heilbroner, *The Worldly Philosophers* (New York: Simon and Shuster, 1953), Chapter 2.

market" is an outstanding feature of the post-World War II world. Increasingly, economic systems have been forced to cope with the problems of how to provide "public goods"—those requisites of life in a modern economy to which the private sector, by prices, cannot properly allocate resources. National defense has always been the most commonly used example of such a public good, but as will be seen, the list is growing in all market-oriented economies. Indeed, the ways in which market-oriented economies differ from one another in how much each attempts to accommodate the requirements of the public sector, and in how successfully each meets its goals, are among the chief ways of distinguishing among market-oriented economies. We shall be exploring these differences in the chapters to come.

But note that while the growth of the public sector requires that the private sector's resource allocation, done by a price system, be supplemented by some central allocation mechanism—for example, incomes are taxed by Congress and the taxes allocated to executive and congressionally determined uses—Heilbroner's market system need not be infringed on by the category he labels *authority*. It all depends on those political arrangements that determine the scope and direction, the objectives, and the techniques utilized in the public sector. They can be democratic or dictatorial, responsive or unresponsive to the collective wishes of the participants in a given economy. In this book the term *market-oriented economy* means those economies which have chosen that private investment and consumption decisions shall continue to play a major role in resource allocation via "the market." But although this role is not equally large in all the economies we shall be concerned with, it is of sufficient prominence to differentiate these economies from those nonmarket-oriented economies often called *command economies*. In command economies, though a price system is invariably employed, it is manipulated largely through central decision-making bodies which do not necessarily aim primarily to reflect the public will (assuming they have ways of ascertaining it), either about production and distribution within the private sector or about the nature, scope, and direction of the public sector.

Is the Term *Capitalism* Obsolete?

Most observers agree that whatever is meant by *capitalism,* the prototypical capitalist state in the modern world is the United States. Andrew Shonfield wrote that "the United States is indeed one of the few places left in the world where 'capitalism' is generally thought to be an OK word."[2] What exactly does this OK word mean? There are, of course, many definitions, but one typical

---

[2] Andrew Shonfield, *Modern Capitalism* (London: Oxford University Press, 1965), p. 298.

definition is by David McCord Wright, an economist who all his life believed devoutly in the system:

> Capitalism is a system in which, on average, much the greater portion of economic life, and particularly of net new investment, is carried on by private (i.e. nongovernment) units under conditions of active and substantially free competition, and avowedly, at least, under the incentive of a hope for profit.[3]

How well does the United States economy, circa 1970, fit such a definition? In that year gross national product was approximately $974 billion. Of this about $616 billion was for personal consumption expenditures. Gross private domestic investment, excluding residential construction and changes in inventories—that is, gross private investment in plant and equipment—came to about $102 billion. This is not directly comparable to Wright's emphasis on *net* new investment, because it includes the investment necessary to maintain the private capital stock of the country at the level it had previously achieved—(that is, it includes expenditures for depreciation). Even so, the $102 billion scarcely compares to the $220 billion expended by all levels of government. If federal expenditures for national defense are excluded on grounds that, although crucial to the profitability of many sectors of the private economy (such as the aviation industry), they do not contribute to the production of consumer goods and services, one would still be left with a total of slightly more than $140 billion spent by all levels of government on nondefense projects. Some of these help provide public goods and services; others are transfer payments (relief, and so on). In any case, the critical point is that if one is to define *capitalism* in terms of the origin of "the greater portion of net new investment"—the wherewithal with which to produce consumer goods and services—it is clear that in dollar volume terms the "private sector" of the American economy, with its $102 billion of nonresidential fixed investment, did not equal, let alone exceed by any substantial amount, the contribution to the economy of the public sector.

This growth in the portion of GNP which originates in the public sector, both absolutely and relative to growth in the private sector, is one of the clearest trends in the postwar Western world. Why this has been the case will be one of our major preoccupations. The degree to which net new investment decisions are *not* made in the private sector—even in the United States—is, then, a statistical fact which vitiates the descriptiveness of Wright's definition of

[3] David McCord Wright, "The Prospects for Capitalism," in *A Survey of Contemporary Economics,* H. S. Ellis ed. (Philadelphia: The Blakiston Co. 1948), p. 452. Reprinted in Wright, *Capitalism,* Economic Handbook Series, Seymour Harris, ed. (New York: McGraw-Hill Book Co. 1951).

capitalism for the current American economy. That there are many who continue to view this change in economic structure with pessimistic dismay for the American future goes without saying.[4] Perhaps less obvious but equally important is that this view of what is essential to a "capitalist system" continues to color many efforts by economists to classify economic systems in the real world. We shall argue that the role of government is large in all countries in the modern world, but that how the government plays this role can help us differentiate among several types of economic systems.

What Is a Market-Oriented Economy?

What is distinctive about Western economies will be clearer if we consider the implications of the term *market-oriented economy*. J. K. Galbraith, for example, has commented,

> I have argued that capitalism, as a practical matter rather than as a system of theology, is an arrangement for getting a considerable decentralization in decision. An examination of the prospects for capitalism ... becomes in the last analysis an examination of the prospects for decentralized decision.[5]

We have here the basis of a redefinition of capitalism appropriate to the modern world, as a system which preserves insofar as it seems feasible the role of private decision-making in the allocation of resources and the distribution of income. If there is any validity to the convergence theory (mentioned above and considered later), it lies in the almost universal awareness today that whatever the role of decentralized decision-making, there must be increasing concern with centralized decision-making as well.

In part the concern with centralized decision-making springs from the

---

[4] Typical of this view is the following comment:

> It is all but universally agreed that socialism is the antithesis of the American way, that it infringes on human freedom, and that it should be avoided at all costs. ... But why a revolutionary manifesto? ... To point out that while no specter is haunting America, socialism in a variety of ways is coming in by the back door; to explain that capitalism—"pure capitalism" or capitalism unmixed with socialism—is the only economic system compatible with political democracy."

Louis O. Kelso and Mortimer J. Adler, *The Capitalist Manifesto* (New York: Random House, 1968), pp. 9-10.

[5] John Kenneth Galbraith, *American Capitalism* (Boston: Houghton Mifflin Co., 1952), pp. 206-7.

increasingly obvious fact that many critical economic areas lie in the realm of public consumption—or collective consumption as it is sometimes called—and that, because there is no clearly determined economic way for consumers to make their demands for public goods known, the market system of prices cannot possibly allocate resources to this sector. That there is therefore a legitimate role for government decision-making with respect to the allocation of resources even in market-oriented economies—a point stressed in recent years by many writers (Galbraith, Shonfield, Bornstein, and many others)—was recognized as long ago as 1907 by Alfred Marshall in his essay "Social Possibilities of Economic Chivalry":

> We are told sometimes that everyone who strenuously endeavors to promote the social amelioration of the people is a Socialist—at all events, if he believes that much of this work can be better performed by the State than by individual effort. In this sense nearly every economist of the present generation is a Socialist. . . . But I am convinced that, so soon as collectivist control had spread so far as to narrow considerably the field left for free enterprise, the pressure of bureaucratic methods would impair not only the springs of material wealth, but also many of those higher qualities of human nature, the strengthening of which should be the chief aim of social endeavor.[6]

It is, of course, efforts "to promote the social amelioration of the people" that have spawned child labor laws; social security; minimum wage laws; national health plans; and, only a bit less directly, antimonopoly legislation; stock market regulation; public utility regulation; consumer protection agencies; resource conservation programs; and more recently antipollution programs for air and water. That all this has significantly increased government intervention in today's market-oriented economies is self-evident. Equally self-evident is that all modern economies have felt the need to develop such programs and—equally significant—have recognized that in general there was no way in which the price system operating through the markets described in the typical American *Principles* textbook could accomplish these tasks.

A few have continued to argue that efforts in the West to achieve that "social amelioration" which Marshall saw as essential could only lead to disaster for a free society. John Chamberlain some years ago termed many of our professed national economic objectives mere "shibboleths" (for example, full employment, social security) and noted that none of these objectives was possible without becoming explicitly governmental objectives.[7] Chamberlain was writing

---

[6] A. C. Pigou, ed. *Memorials of Alfred Marshall* (London: Macmillan & Co., 1925), p. 334. Originally, *Economic Journal,* May, 1907.

[7] John Chamberlain, introduction to *The Road to Serfdom,* by Friedrich Hayek (Chicago: The University of Chicago Press, 1944), p. 111.

an introduction to Friedrich Hayek's book, *Road to Serfdom,* itself a major exposition of the thesis that once the central government intervenes in resource allocation, there is no stopping further intervention. "Socialism" was a species of "collectivism," and the latter meant "planning"—a notion that could in no way be made consistent with a free economy. As Hayek put it, "What our planners demand is a central direction of all economic activity according to a single plan, laying down how the resources of society should be consciously directed to serve particular ends in a definite way.[8] Hayek argued that this kind of planning was inevitably the "road to serfdom," but this is most distinctly *not* the goal of planners in any of the market-oriented economies under study in this book.

At the same time we must recognize that the development of a public sector has indeed spawned a gigantic bureaucracy, as Alfred Marshall predicted. But it is useful to recall that Big Government is only one of the institutional structures which has erected a vast bureaucracy in the modern economic world. In his *American Capitalism* J. K. Galbraith argued that in the United States conventional atomistic competition in the marketplace has given way to the "countervailing power" created by the conflicting objectives of Big Business, Big Labor, Big Farmers, and Big Government. He viewed it essentially as an economic system of "checks and balances" not unlike our political system, with the government in the role of umpire. Each of these units has become bureaucratized, however. Bigness itself breeds bureaucracy, in private organizations as well as in government. It seems clear that for many reasons bigness is here to stay, and a major challenge to modern market-oriented economies is devising ways of coping with it.

All market-oriented economies therefore have a good deal of centralized decision-making—that is, a considerable amount of real resources are allocated by governmental decision-making, but in varying degrees a significant role in the overall allocation of resources and distribution of income is still played by private economic units (frequently large on the producer side and almost invariably organized into larger structures representing primarily their own interests). Most modern definitions of *capitalism*, apply to this kind of economic organization in the real world, though the word is a misnomer to a purist. For example, Allan Gruchy was surely defining *market-oriented economies* when he wrote,

> Capitalism is an evolving economic system in which property, such as land, plant, equipment, and inventories, is mainly privately owned and is used for the pursuit of private gain or profits, and in which the major economic decisions relating to such matters as production, investment, and prices are privately made.[9]

---

[8] Hayek, ibid., p. 34.

[9] Allan G. Gruchy, *Comparative Economic Systems: Competing Ways to Stability and Growth* (Boston: Houghton Mifflin Co., 1966), p. 54. Morris Bornstein has characterized

Note his emphasis that the system is *evolving* (and can therefore have evolved today to different extents and in varying ways from country to country) and that the definition allows no absolute fixed characteristics. Note too the qualifying words: property is *mainly* privately owned, *major* economic decisions are privately made. In an evolving system these dividing lines could conceivably become blurred. One cannot say categorically how much property can be publicly owned or controlled before the system is no longer *mainly* private, nor can one be precise about what one means by *major* economic decisions. (Surely the $220.5 billion of 1970 GNP represented by government purchases could scarcely be thought "minor.") The degree to which market-oriented economies differ in these respects and the diversity of their evolutionary paths are among the major themes of the following pages. But one common factor among them all is that they preserve an important place for a market mechanism which is responsive to the wishes of the consumers. As J. M. Clark noted some years ago about the Western economies emerging after World War II, nowhere was competition, which he called "the chief organizing principle of the market system," accepted in unadulterated form. While competition was limited by the quest for the "social amelioration" mentioned above, "exploitative monopoly" was also generally condemned in the emerging market-oriented economies. He argued, moreover, that the organizations previously alluded to (unions, business organizations, and so on were an "inevitable and necessary protection for the common man: his alternative to serfdom."[10] In the end, he argued, modern market-oriented economies had no choice but to utilize the market, the state, and the other organized groups and develop a technique for coordinating them all. Said Clark, "This means a mixed system."[11]

Such systems defy the neat characterizations to which economists of another day might have been lured in their attempts to distinguish capitalism, socialism, communism, and other isms. But such a mixture is a good deal closer to what modern market-oriented economies have in common. To solve basic economic problems, all the economies we shall be considering do indeed mix in varying ways and degrees agencies of the state, business groups, labor groups, agricultural groups, and a market in which the preferences of consumers play a

---

modern capitalism in essentially the same terms, suggesting that its essential characteristics would include (1) private ownership and private enterprise with productive means, (2) "predominance of economic gain as the guiding force in production decision," and (3) reliance on markets and prices to allocate resources and distribute income. (Bornstein, introduction to the "Capitalist Market Economy," in *Comparative Economic Systems: Models and Cases,* Bornstein, ed. [Homewood, Ill.: Richard D. Irwin Co., 1969], p. 20.) Bornstein differs from Gruchy only in placing somewhat less emphasis on the significance of the public sector. Note, however, his concern with the "predominance" of the profit motive. As we shall see, he ends up attempting to distinguish "capitalist market economies" from "socialist market economies"—simply another way of indicating the growing importance in market economies of the public sector and government decision-making. Whether such a distinction can be meaningfully maintained, however, is a moot point.

[10] J. M. Clark, *Alternative to Serfdom* (New York: Alfred A. Knopf, 1948), p. 122.

[11] Ibid., p. 123.

significant role in resource allocation. This means that the results are determined partly by individuals who act independently and partly by organized groups of individuals who are associated by their economic function and who utilize the price system to allocate resources and distribute income through markets, but also partly by the state, through nationalization, taxation, government transfer payments, and government expenditures generally—all of which involves *collective* decision-making and *collective* determination of resource use (but usually through the use of the price system here also).

Significantly, what all market-oriented economies lack is a *single* comprehensive plan in which *all* decisions about resource allocation and income distribution are made centrally. As we shall find they have a good deal more in common. Andrew Shonfield summarized it very well:

> There are big differences between the key institutions and economic methods of one country and another. Yet when the total picture is examined, there is a certain uniformity in the texture of these societies. In terms of what they do, rather than what they say about it, and even more markedly in terms of the pattern of their behavior over a period of years, the similarities are striking.[12]

He then listed the similarities: (1) the public sector has become much more influential in the management of all these economies; (2) concern with public welfare has led to increased use of public funds to achieve Marshall's social amelioration; (3) in the private sector what he calls "the violence of the market" has been tamed; (4) all participants in economic activity—in both public and private sectors—have come to assume that GNP should increase each year, and these economies accordingly take what steps they can to assure such growth; and (5) increasing concern with longer run planning—that is, with some sort of effort, however crude, to match resources to economic requirements for longer periods into the future.[13]

Which Modern Economies Are Market-Oriented?

In considering modern capitalism, or market-oriented economies, various writers include lists of countries which differ somewhat from one another. Some of these differences result from efforts to subclassify economies according to the degree to which either planning or governmental direction has proceeded. (Others are based more simply on data limitations or on decisions to concentrate on a few economies.) These distinctions are necessarily somewhat arbitrary

---

12 Shonfield, *Modern Capitalism*, p. 65.
13 Shonfield, *Modern Capitalism*, pp. 66-67.

because the trends common to all economies that are not "command economies" represent, properly viewed, a continuum rather than clearly discernible groups.[14] Thus Morris Bornstein attempts a division of market economies into capitalist and socialist, ascribing to the United States and France "regulated capitalism," and to Yugoslavia "market socialism."[15] This distinction has some merit, but it glosses over, for example, the distinctions made by Shonfield, whose concept of "modern capitalism" excludes Yugoslavia but includes France, Britain, Italy, Austria, Sweden, and the Netherlands among the modern capitalist economies employing some type of planning, as well as the contrasting cases of West Germany and the United States, where formal planning is still eschewed. (We shall see, however, that there are many reasons for also distinguishing economic organization in West Germany today from that in the United States.) Joe Bain, to take yet a third approach, describes "capitalist economies" as those in which one finds "either free-enterprise. . . or economies with quite limited socialization of industries."[16] Under this rubric he includes the U.S., Britain, Canada, Sweden, France, Italy, India, and Japan. Other countries are excluded by Bain because of data limitations, but it is interesting to note that, like Bornstein, he puts the U.S. in the same category with the U.K., in contrast to Shonfield, who distinguishes them sharply (though both are "capitalist").

In the study to follow we have made no conscious effort to determine an exhaustive list of countries appropriately called *market-oriented*, nor would data be available for all countries on all the topics we have wished to discuss. We have decided that Jan Prybyla's distinction between "command economies" and "market economies" is the most meaningful and have therefore excluded China, the USSR, the Eastern European economies, Yugoslavia, and the under-developed or developing parts of the world. In effect, we view North America, Western Europe, and Japan as the prime geographic areas where market-oriented economies can be identified and have concerned ourselves with the management of these economies. The group of economies considered in each chapter is dictated generally by what information is available.

---

[14] Jan S. Prybyla, ed., *Comparative Economic Systems* (New York: Appleton-Century-Crofts, 1969). Gruchy has viewed these economies as representing a continuum also:

> The broad category of "capitalism" breaks down into a number of sub-types of capitalism, varying from the relatively unregulated and unplanned American Capitalism at one end of the scale to the planned French capitalism at the other end.

In the middle he places such economies as the U.K., Belgium, the Netherlands, and Italy. He provides a separate category, "democratic socialism," for Britain under the Labour government and for the Scandinavian countries. (Gruchy, *Comparative Economic Systems,* p. 882.)

[15] Bornstein, ed., *Comparative Economic Systems.*

[16] Joe S. Bain, *International Differences in Industrial Structure* (New Haven, Conn.: Yale University Press, 1966), p. 6.

Market-Oriented Economies,
Command Economies, and The Future

A major task of this book, as we have said, will be to indicate the great variety in management techniques presently employed in market-oriented economies, but an equally important task is to enumerate their essential similarities.

In recent years it has become fashionable to hold what is called the *convergence theory*—that is, the notion that market-oriented and command economies are gradually coming to more and more resemble one another. We shall be better able to appraise the validity of this theory after we have considered the aspects of managing modern market-oriented economies in the chapters to come. But it would be useful to know what the convergence theory is about at the outset, so that we can keep it in mind during the subsequent discussion. Bornstein, for example, distinguishes "regulated capitalist market economies" from "socialist centrally planned economies." In such a view the convergence theory could be based on the following changes among others in what we call here the market economies: (1) a larger public sector with greater government intervention in many aspects of economic decision-making, (2) higher taxes, and (3) broader social welfare programs. On the other hand, many writers have noted that the command economies are: (1) becoming more decentralized in some aspects of economic decision-making, (2) placing less ideological emphasis on their economic planning, (3) tending to emphasize international trade and specialization somewhat more heavily, and (4) putting a higher priority on consumption as opposed to producer goods in resource allocation.

The first list is, of course, made up of characteristics associated with command economies, whereas the second list is made up of traits associated with market-oriented economies. Finally, it has been suggested that both types of economies are to a greater degree utilizing mathematical models for decision-making and are placing greater emphasis on leisure in preference to greater output as work-weeks decline the world over.[17]

While all this may be true, other economists view the basic ideological positions of command economies and market-oriented economies as sufficiently different so that true convergence of these two types is not likely in the near future.[18] Gruchy, for example, feels that the Soviet Union is likely to remain "essentially authoritarian," with political considerations dictating the paths of both economic and social change—which will mean continued social ownership.

[17] This would appear to be the line of thought taken, say, by Tinbergen in "Do Command and Free Economies Show a Converging Pattern?" in *Comparative Economic Systems*, Bornstein, ed., pp. 432-41. Tinbergen's views fit with Bornstein's classification. While many economists have taken essentially this position in recent years, some, as noted, view the convergence hypothesis as both wrong and dangerous.

[18] See, for example, the argument of Prybyla, "The Convergence of Western and Communist Economic Systems: A Critical Estimate," in *Comparative Economic Systems*, Bornstein, ed., pp. 442-452.

On the other hand, he sees little likelihood that the American system will be anything but essentially privately owned for the foreseeable future and that hence American "affluence will be more private than collective."[19]

Some might argue that in recent years the United States has been forced to consider anew the division of its affluence between the public and private sector, but Gruchy's appraisal seems essentially sound. The American economy is the prototypical modern capitalist economy because it is in most respects less planned and more geared to market-determined resource allocation than any other economy in the modern world. In the chapters to follow we shall try to show just how varied the management of these market-oriented economies can be and also that they can all be reasonably distinguished from the command economies typified by the USSR, China, and the Eastern European bloc.

[19] Gruchy, *Comparative Economic Systems,* p. 890.

2

Basic Economic Objectives and the Role of Planning in Market-Oriented Economies

At the close of World War II the U.S. Congress passed the Employment Act of 1946. This landmark piece of legislation declared "that it is the continuing responsibility of the Federal Government to use all practical means consistent with its needs and obligations... to promote maximum employment, production, and purchasing power."[1] While the policy set down by the act reiterates the U.S. government's traditional commitment to "foster and promote free competitive enterprise,"[2] it was clear that out of the ashes of the Great Depression and the fires of the Second World War a new national commitment had been forged requiring our government to address itself squarely to national economic objectives which, the Congress recognized, could no longer be left to the vagaries of the market place.

A similar trend (frequently, as we shall soon see, far more extensive in its policy implications) was underway in Western Europe. In Britain, the birthplace of modern economics, there was recognition that Adam Smith's Invisible Hand could no longer guarantee that unfettered private self-interest operating in the market place would lead to that minimal required degree of "social amelioration of the people" that Alfred Marshall had long before recognised as unavoidable. This recognition led in the immediate postwar years to the election of a Labour

---

[1] Public Law 304 79th Congress, *Employment Act of 1946*, Section 2. Reprinted in *Readings in Unemployment*, 86th Congress, 2d Session, Prepared for the Special Committee on Unemployment Problems (Washington, D.C.: U.S. Government Printing Office), p. 12.

[2] Ibid.

government, which nationalized the steel industry and some other basic industries, adopted a comprehensive national health program, and in a number of other ways made clear that there were to be grave differences between conventional prewar capitalism and the postwar market-oriented economies.

In Canada, to take a final example, goals are spelled out quite like those of the United States. The Economic Council of Canada has listed the major goals of the Canadian economy to be: full employment, high economic growth rates, reasonably stable prices, a "viable" balance of payments, and "equitable distribution of rising incomes."[3] All but the last two are similar to the U.S. Employment Act of 1946.

Economic Objectives

By 1960 the market-oriented countries had organized in what is now known as the Organization for Economic Cooperation and Development (OECD), with its announced objective the promotion of policies to:

1. "achieve the highest sustainable economic growth and employment and a rising standard of living in Member countries, while maintaining financial stability. . . ."
2. "contribute to sound economic expansion in Member as well as non-member countries in the process of economic development."
3. "contribute to the expansion of world trade on a multi-lateral, non-discriminatory basis in accordance with international obligations."[4]

Thus, postwar concern with economic growth; the maintenance of full employment; and the taming of the business cycle, which had heretofore afflicted capitalist industrialized economies with periodic recessions, were all added to the social welfare obligations assumed by prewar national governments. In some countries, (for example, Austria, Belgium, Denmark, the Netherlands, and Spain) there was explicit concern with achieving more equitable distribution of income (and there were progressive tax systems in almost all of the market-oriented countries, though we shall see that their net impact was often

---

[3] Economic Council of Canada, *The Canadian Economy from the 1960's to the 1970's* (Ottawa: Roger Dahamel, Queen's Printer and Controller of Stationery, 1967), p. 2.

[4] This statement of objectives appears as the second page of all OECD publications. OECD countries include: Austria, Belgium, Canada, Denmark, Finland, France, West Germany, Greece, Iceland, Ireland, Italy, Japan, Luxembourg, the Netherlands, Norway, Portugal, Spain, Sweden, Switzerland, Turkey, the United Kingdom, and the United States. The OECD is therefore essentially coterminous with the world's market-oriented economies broadly defined.

limited).[5] Another general economic objective of many countries has been greater domestic economic stability against the impact of international trade. Balance of payments problems have continued to be troublesome, and all the major currencies, including by 1971 the dollar, have been subject to devaluation or revaluation one or more times. Difficulties with balance of payments equilibria notwithstanding, greatly increased international trade has been, in the view of many, a prime factor in achieving the other economic objectives noted earlier.[6]

Not only have these objectives become widely recognized, they have been so broadly accepted as governmental responsibilities that one can no longer distinguish among market-oriented economies (or separate them from command economies, for that matter) according to their devotion to the achievement of these objectives, or even according to governmental willingness to assist in their realization and unwillingness to leave such realization to the vagaries of the unregulated marketplace.

Similarity in Goals, Diversity in Means

Diversities among Market-Oriented Economies   The broad goals are reasonably similar for all the economies we call market-oriented, but the countries themselves and their means for achieving these goals are quite diverse. That the countries of the West[7] vary in size, wealth, natural-resource endowment, and other economically significant respects is obvious. Table 2-1 provides a convenient summary of three critical characteristics. There is an enormous range in per capita gross national product—from the $4,379 of the United States to India's $80. Although we shall concentrate on developed market-oriented economies and so shall have little to say about countries like India, the contrast is worth noting. Even among developed countries the differences in per capita GNP are large. Moreover, we shall see that facile explanations of the differences must be avoided. It is generally thought, for example, that declining percentages of the labor force involved in agriculture are a sign of industrialization, hence development. Yet, for example, Sweden shows

[5] See International Information Centre for Local Credit (hereafter IICLC), *Economic Policy in Practice* (The Hague: Martinus Nijhoff, 1968), p. 15.

[6] Andrew Shonfield, for example, views increased international trade as a prime factor in achieving the rapid rate of economic growth which has characterized many market-oriented economies in the postwar period. (See Shonfield, *Modern Capitalism* [London: Oxford University Press, 1965], p. 62.) The growing importance and magnitude of international trade is, of course, directly related to many of the difficulties with the system of settling international payments imbalances developed at the 1944 Bretton Woods Conferences (which set up the International Monetary Fund, among other things) and subsequently revised to augment the increasingly inadequate world supply of gold, which has always been the primary means used for settling international accounts.

[7] We shall adopt the simplification of including Japan among the market-oriented economies, even though occasionally we shall refer to them collectively as "the West."

Table 2-1
Three Measures of Economic Activity in
Market-Oriented Economies

Countries	Per Capita GNP (1968)[1] (1)	Percent of Labor Force in Agriculture (1967) (2)	Manufac- turing[2] (3)	Value of Exports as percent of GNP (1955-65)[3] (4)
United States	$ 4,379	5[b]	24[b]	6
United Kingdom	1.861	2	35	24*
Sweden	3,315	9[b]	31[b]	28
Canada	2,997	7[b]	22[b]	
France	2,537	15	25	15
Japan	1,404	20[b]	26[b]	9*
Italy	1,418	23	28	17
Netherlands	1,980	8	28	51*
Norway	2,362	NA	NA	40*
Belgium	2,154	5	32	38
Denmark	2,545	18[c]	NA	29*
Austria	1,544	32[d]	28[d]	25*
West Germany	2,206	10	36	22
India	80[a]	73	10	NA

Sources:
[1]   U.N. Statistical Office, Department of Economic and Social Affairs, *U.N. Statistical Yearbook, 1969* (New York, 1970), pp. 563-65. Current dollars.
[2]   U.S. Department of Labor, Bureau of Labor Statistics, *Handbook of Labor Statistics, 1969* (Washington, D.C: U.S. Government Printing Office, 1969), Table 151, pp. 388-90. Estimate for Denmark (col. 2) from Edward F. Denison, *Why Growth Rates Differ* (Washington, D.C.: The Brookings Institution, 1967), Table 16-4, p. 206.
[3]   OECD, *Fiscal Policy for a Balanced Economy*, December 1968, p. 26. * International Information Centre for Local Credit, *Economic Policy in Practice* (The Hague: Martinus Nijhoff, 1968), p. 14. The percentages are approximate and the exact year is not specified, but they reflect generally the situation in the 1960s.

Notes
[a]   Figure is for 1967.
[b]   Figures are for 1968.
[c]   Figure is for 1964.
[d]   Figures are for 1951.

a very high per capita GNP, although the percent of its labor force employed in agriculture remains, if not high, at least a great deal higher than that of, say, the U.K., which has a very low per capita GNP for a developed economy. And Denmark has a rather high percent of its labor force employed in agriculture, yet it manages to have one of the highest per capita GNPs. Nevertheless, the data in Table 2-1 for the United States on the one hand and for India on the other show that as a rough generalization there is indeed a clear relationship between the percent of a nation's labor force employed in agriculture and its per capita GNP.

One condition on the ability of any market-oriented country to attain its economic objectives is its dependence on international trade. In an ideal world all countries would specialize in the production of those goods and services in which they have the greatest relative advantage, but in the real world the ideals of free trade and specialization are constantly being advocated and sporadically advanced; the results still fall far short of what we would wish for, however. Thus, while world productivity might be advanced with greater trade and specialization, the figures in Table 2-1 give a crude measure of the degree to which economies have become self-sufficient. The United States, for example, has latitude in making policy choices to achieve its economic objectives which other countries, more dependent on international trade, simply do not have.[8]

In short, Table 2-1 suggests that even if all the postwar market-oriented economies were to adopt identical economic policies to attain those roughly similar objectives about which a fair degree of consensus has emerged in the post-World War II period, the results could hardly be expected to be identical, given the very important differences among these countries. (Other important differences will be considered in later chapters.)

The Role of Planning It is well known that even among market-oriented economies the policies utilized to achieve the objectives vary much from country to country. It is frequently asserted that many market-oriented economies have turned to planning in the last twenty-five years, the United States and possibly West Germany remaining the outstanding exceptions.[9] If one defines planning broadly enough, of course, there are no exceptions. One recent definition of planning (Peter Donaldson) states that "whatever its scope and form, planning involves alteration, in accordance with a central policy, of the pattern of output which would result from free enterprise."[10] If planning is so defined, it is difficult to argue that all market-oriented economies do not engage in some form of planning, and, indeed, Andrew Shonfield has commented that "economic planning is the most characteristic expression of the new capitalism."[11] He specifically exempts the United States and Germany from his view of planned economies, however, arguing that these two countries are outside what he calls the "mainstream" of modern economics and that they not only have no enthusiasm for tampering with the market but go so far as to show "ostentatious antipathy" to the whole process of planning.[12]

This view of planning can easily be pushed too far. Certainly in the United

---

[8] This does not mean that the impact of U.S. economic activities is not of great significance for other countries or that we can afford to be unmindful of this impact.

[9] This is a major theme in Shonfield's *Modern Capitalism*, for example.

[10] Peter Donaldson, *Guide to the British Economy* (Harmondsworth, England, and Baltimore, Penguin Books, 1965, p. 183. Reprinted in Jan S. Prybyla, ed., *Comparative Economic Systems* (New York: Appleton-Century-Crofts, 1969).

[11] Shonfield, *Modern Capitalism*, p. 121.

[12] Ibid., p. 239

States the area of collective decision-making has been enlarged, as it has been in all modern economies. The United States does not have a central planning bureau, nor do we adopt a five or ten-year plan, but we certainly consider resources as inputs to be allocated to public as well as to private outputs over a longer period of time than was the case before the Second World War.

If Donaldson's definition of planning seems too broad and Shonfield's view too narrow, it might be appropriate to offer a third, intermediate definition. John Hackett recently wrote:

> In essence, what is being attempted through planning can be seen as a move to give to economic policy-making an increasingly volitional coloring.[13] The idea that planning and market mechanisms are mutually exclusive alternatives appears unacceptable.[14]

In short, if by planning one means any deliberate effort to redirect resource allocation toward specific objectives and away from the results emerging from the interplay of free market forces, then all market-oriented economies plan. But if one means a formal statement of quantitative objectives by sectors, then many European market-oriented economies do plan, but the United States, at least, does not. It is worth noting that psychological, sociological, and political variations among countries may cause differing degrees of planning, as just defined, to be accepted in different market-oriented economies. A major theme in Shonfield's book is that the kind of planning which emerges in each modern capitalist country is strongly conditioned by its history and its long-standing traditions.[15]

In addition to differing according to how much it pervades the economy, planning among market-oriented economies can differ according to where it originates and who controls it. Politically, therefore, the crucial question, as Shonfield put it, is "Who controls the planners?"[16] One could conceive of economic planning in market-oriented economies which might be almost as

[13] John Hackett, *Economic Planning in France,* the Council for Economic Education (Bombay) (New York; Asia Publishing House, 1965), p. 53.

[14] Ibid., p. 54.

[15] Bela Belassa has made much the same point: "As a result of sociological and psychological factors, a free enterprise blueprint may work better in one and worse in another country. Similar considerations are relevant with regard to a socialist blueprint." (Belassa, *The Hungarian Experience in Economic Planning* [New Haven, Conn: Yale University Press, 1959]. Reprinted in Bornstein, ed., *Comparative Economic Systems*: *Models and Cases* [Homewood, Ill.: Richard D. Irwin Co., 1969], p. 18.) We are merely extending Belassa's point to suggest that the particular "free-enterprise—socialist" mix reflected in the degree to which market-oriented economies are planning is conditioned by noneconomic as well as economic factors, and that the same economic program is not equally appropriate to all modern capitalist economies.

[16] Shonfield, *Modern Capitalism*, p. 230.

pervasive as in command economies, provided that the planning process is subject to democratic controls.[17]

The famous Dutch economist Jan Tinbergen recently surveyed a number of economies, both communist and Western, developed and underdeveloped, in an effort to determine why they plan. The objectives sought through planning were usually approximately those objectives of virtually all market-oriented or "modern capitalist" economies—higher GNPs, less unemployment, balance of payments equilibrium, greater price stability, more equitable income distribution, and— Tinbergen adds—better balance in regional economic development. In achieving these objectives Tinbergen suggested that the main planning means employed included:

1. Investment expenditures by the government (both generally and for specific purposes);
2. Direct taxes (on profits, income, wealth, and for such specific items as death duties);
3. Indirect taxes (general turnover taxes, excise taxes, import and export duties);
4. Subsidies;
5. Wage rate controls;
6. Exchange controls;
7. Interest rate manipulation;
8. Credit restrictions;
9. Special permits (as for building);
10. Direct resource allocations (for example, land reforms);
11. Quantitative restrictions on imports;
12. Price regulations; and
13. Certain other special interventions, such as tariff protection for infant industries, technical assistance, tax relief for certain industries.

While he found evidence of virtually all of these techniques among one or more communist economies, many (but by no means all) of them are certainly

[17] In this connection the following definition of *planned economy* is instructive:

> Economic system in which the government, according to a preconceived plan, plays a primary role in directing economic resources for the purpose of deciding what to produce, how much, and possibly for whom. A planned economy may or may not be a command economy, depending on whether the government operates a substantially authoritarian or democratic framework.

(Milton H. Spencer, *Contemporary Economics* [New York: Worth Publishers, 1971], p. 699.)

anathema to the current U.S. view of appropriate governmental intervention. However, most of these techniques can be found in various combinations in the market-oriented economies of Western Europe.[18] Accordingly, the remainder of this chapter will attempt brief individual characterizations of the current approach to planning in several major market-oriented economies.

Approaches to Planning

Shonfield has classified modern capitalist planning into three broad types: (1) Indicative planning—the "intellectual approach." That is, in the presentation of their case to the private economic units and/or the legislative body, the planners compel acceptance of their objectives by the cogency of their arguments. Shonfield argues that in this approach the planners do what the market would otherwise do, only they do it "better." (2) Reliance on reinforced governmental power and economic intervention. In this approach the government owns or operates a sufficiently large percent of the economy so that it can achieve its objectives by sheer size and power. (3) A "corporatist" formula. The government eschews direct control and instead attempts to bring business, labor, and other groups together and help them to plan and coordinate their activities in ways the government views as appropriate.[19] The Western European countries that have experimented with planning (France, Britain, Italy, Sweden, Norway, the Netherlands, Belgium and Austria) represent various combinations of these "ideal-type" approaches. The three approaches represent various degrees of direct governmental intervention to achieve centrally planned economic objectives. As has recently been pointed out in another study, which includes West Germany as well in its consideration of economic planning policies, the least intrusive technique would be simply for the government to publish a plan and hope that each firm would act in an appropriate way to achieve the plan's objectives.[20] The authors suggest that planning techniques represent a continuum involving "methods of information, persuasion, influence, incentive, sanction, and pressure."[21] Indicative planning intervenes more "naturally" in the economic process and so is more compatible with a market economy than the second technique, which can approach the command-economy type of planning. The third technique is intermediate in impact.

We cannot describe all the planning techniques in detail, but it will be helpful to present a thumbnail sketch of those utilized in the more important market-oriented economies.

[18] Jan Tinbergen, *Central Planning* (New Haven, Conn.: Yale University Press, 1964), especially Table 8, pp. 120-21.

[19] Shonfield, *Modern Capitalism*, p. 231.

[20] Geoffrey Denton, Murray Forsyth, and Malcolm Maclennan, *Economic Planning and Policies in Britain, France, and Germany* (London: George Allen and Unwin, 1968), p. 409.

[21] Ibid.

Britain Like the United States in the Employment Act of 1946, the British in their 1944 White Paper on Employment Policy declared, "The Government accept as one of their primary aims and responsibilities the maintenance of a high and stable level of employment after the war."[22] As J. C. R. Dow comments, by accepting this responsibility for employment, the British government got involved with growth, balance of payments equilibrium, stable prices, and "management of the economy."[23] But ironically, despite the fact that the postwar Labour government nationalized much basic industry (coal, transport, electric power, iron, and steel) and adopted one of the most comprehensive and progressive national health services to be found anywhere, many observers have argued that Britain really made little progress in economic planning during this period. To the extent that this early approach to planning involved compulsory resource allocation and rationing, it was not very popular, although perhaps it was necessary to assist Britain in economic recovery from the war. Many decisions were short-run ad hoc, an approach which many have argued stemmed in part from a traditional British suspicion of public power.[24] Accordingly, planning in postwar Britain became blurred (industries such as steel were nationalized, denationalized, renationalized, and so on), and eschewed long-run coordination of resource inputs toward preselected outputs.[25]

In the 1960s, under the Tories (ironically), British concern with increasing its rate of economic growth by increased employment and productivity, both for domestic reasons and as a way to ease its balance of payments difficulties, had led to the establishment of the National Economic Development Council (Neddy) in 1962. This time planning was to be more comprehensive, was to involve cooperation among government, business, and the trade unions, and was to attempt longer-run projections of the country's needs and abilities to achieve the requisite progress to meet them. Selwyn Lloyd stated the objectives well in

---

[22] Quoted in J. C. R. Dow, *The Management of the British Economy, 1945-60* (London: Cambridge University Press, Students' Edition, 1970), p. 1.

[23] Ibid.

[24] In this connection Shonfield comments,

The striking thing in the British case is the extraordinary tenacity of older attitudes towards the role of public power. Anything which smacked of a restless or over-energetic state, with ideas of guiding the nation on the basis of a long view of its collective economic interest, was instinctively the object of suspicion.

(Shonfield, *Modern Capitalism*, p. 88.)

[25] That British planning in the postwar years was not particularly successful seems to be the view of most current writers, although much enthusiasm and interest in the British experiment was generated at the time. However, a major student of British planning in this period concluded an early analysis with the comment, "How much it contributes, or is capable of contributing, to the positive direction of the economy is still an open question." (Ben W. Lewis, *British Planning and Nationalization* [New York: The Twentieth Century Fund, George Allen and Unwin, 1952], p. 41.)

the debate over setting up Neddy in the House of Commons:

> I envisage a joint examination of the economic prospects of the country stretching five or more years into the future. It would cover the growth of national production and distribution of our resources between the main uses, consumption, government expenditure, investment, and so on. Above all it would try to establish what are the essential conditions for realizing potential growth.
>
> That covers, first the supply of labour and capital, secondly, the balance of payments conditions and the development of imports and exports, and thirdly the growth of income. In other words, I would ask both sides of industry to share with the Government the task of relating plans to the resources that are likely to be available.[26]

The revised National Economic Development Council set up in 1964 under the new Labour government included twenty-two members, with the minister of the newly created Department of Economic Affairs as chairman. Its members represented industry (both public and private), the trade unions, and independent members. Their purpose was to determine the maximum growth rate compatible with a "sound" British economy.[27] They maintained close liaison with some 100 technical specialists in various aspects of the British economy. The original (1962) NEDC had established a 4 percent growth target for the initial planning period (1961-66). With the return to power of the Labour party in 1964 there were some changes, and an amended total target of 25 percent increase in the 1964 gross domestic product was adopted for the goal to be achieved by 1970. The objective seems to have been to achieve a British growth rate which would be greater than that achieved in the previous decade—which had been considerably lower than that achieved on the Continent—but which would not be so fast as to threaten stability or strain the always precarious British balance of payments. In 1967 Britain ran into serious problems with inflation and a worsening of its balance of payments, and the second plan which was to have begun in 1967 was postponed. In November 1967 the pound was devalued 14.3 percent.[28]

The renewed British planning of the 1960s attempted to set quantitative targets for different sectors of its economy based on the target growth rate of 4 percent which seemed reasonable to the members of Neddy. It set up the Department of Economic Affairs to centralize and coordinate efforts to develop what may appropriately be called indicative planning (much British effort in this period was modeled on the French approach). It sought to modernize British

---

[26] House of Commons Debates, 7/26/61, col. 439. Quoted in Denton, Forsyth, and Maclennan, *Economic Planning and Policies*, p. 111.

[27] See Donaldson, *Guide to the British Economy*, p. 187.

[28] See Denton, Forsyth, and Maclennan, *Economic Planning and Policies*, p. 131.

industry through reorganization, manpower retraining, and research and development efforts; it took a sterner view of restrictive practices which could slow economic growth; it developed a regional policy to further economic development throughout the country; it set up the National Incomes Commission and subsequently the National Board for Prices and Incomes in an effort to achieve growth without inflation by use of an incomes policy. But ultimately the planning efforts failed to achieve their objectives.[29] Why? G. C. Allen argues that it is because the government failed "to infuse an expansionist spirit into the obstinately skeptical British industrialist"—that is, it failed to persuade the British entrepreneur that the growth rates targeted in the plan were attainable.[30] That the British economy was and is plagued with vexing difficulties is clear to all, and whether British economic failures in recent years to achieve their stated economic objectives could have been reduced by other means is one of those questions which must remain open. Allen argues that it is unfortunate that planning was introduced when it was, if only because the idea of planning may be discredited. Certainly, however, the British experience suggests that indicative planning cannot work unless the planners persuade the entrepreneurs and the trade unions that the planned targets are feasible.

In this connection, the "severe limitations" of pure indicative planning have been noted.[31] It has been argued too that indicative planning cannot succeed unless the government gets more involved in the processes of entrepreneurial decision-making than this approach customarily entails.[32] But this judgment of indicative planning, based on the British experience, may be too severe. In our view, the problems with which the British economy has had to wrestle in recent years have been so grave that the British probably could not have avoided difficulty. Indeed, difficulties might have been more severe in the absence of planning efforts, although we cannot, of course, be certain.

France　　Whereas the British are suspicious of public power, a number of observers have argued that planning came naturally to the French. That is to say, it grows out of what Shonfield has called the étatist tradition, which harks back at least to the French Revolution and means basically that efficiency requires that power be concentrated in the hands of the few people who are exceptionally capable and wise, and hence quite unlike the masses they govern. This means that even successful businessmen should generally not be given too much responsibility.[33]

But this view can be overdone. While French planning has most often been

---

[29] For a consideration of these efforts, see G. C. Allen, *The Structure of Industry in Britain*, 3d Ed. (London: Longman Group, 1970), pp. 141-44.

[30] Ibid., pp. 142-43.

[31] See Donaldson, *Guide to the British Economy*, p. 192.

[32] See Allen, *Structure of Industry in Britain*, p. 144.

[33] See Shonfield, *Modern Capitalism*, pp. 71-72.

called "indicative" rather than "imperative" (as encountered in command economies) it has been viewed by some as a combination of Shonfield's indicative planning and his second approach, in which the government throws its weight around more overtly. This is Shonfield's view; that is, French planning combines suggestions to specific sectors, based on overall determination of national economic objectives, and more coercive control. Others view French planning as essentially more compatible with democratic principles. Of this second view Shonfield says

> The typical form . . . expressed in the 1950s was to say that the Plan was "indicative" and never "imperative." But these simplified labels tended to blur an important issue of method; granted that the Plan was not imposed by direct compulsion, it was still open to the government to engage its greatly enlarged resources in an act of persuasion. If the government used all its considerable power, either to persuade the recalcitrants or to reward the obedient, the pressure behind the Plan could be well-nigh irresistible.[34]

This makes the plan sound more authoritarian than if it were evaluated solely, say, on the process by which it was drawn up. John and Anne Marie Hackett, in one of the more perceptive analyses of French planning in the early 1960s define the French plan simply:

> The Plan is a way of providing permanent arrangements for a collective and systematic reflection on the problems and prospects of the economy with a view to action.[35]

Shonfield argues that French planning is a bit more "imperative" than the Hacketts' definition makes it appear. It has recently been pointed out that despite the democratic and libertarian trappings of French planning (approval of the plan by Parliament, and so forth) the government can make its goals compelling targets for would-be laggards in two significant ways: (1) it maintains very strict control over the capital markets, so that businesses find it difficult to obtain loans except for projects that the government approves of, and (2) the sheer size of the public sector ensures that a large part of total investment will be under the direct control of the government.[36]

The French have been preoccupied of late with economic growth, like the

---

34 Ibid., p. 145.

35 John Hackett and Anne-Marie Hackett, *Economic Planning in France* (Cambridge, Mass.: Harvard University Press, 1963), p. 363.

36 Donaldson, *Guide to the British Economy*, p. 185.

British, but unlike the British, the French indeed have produced quite a remarkable record in this respect. In organization the French economy seems more complex, or at least more varied, than the British. Some industry is nationalized (for example, coal, electricity, gas); in some the government takes so active an interest as to approach regulation (for instance, petroleum); in some industries state-owned and privately owned firms operate presumably in competition with each other (in automobiles, however, the state-owned Renault signed an agreement to cooperate with privately owned Peugeot in 1966), and other industries are in private hands (for example, foodstuffs).[37]

Against this brief sketch of the truly mixed private-public character of the modern French economy we can attempt a rough characterization of French planning. At the close of the Second World War, France, like most European countries, faced enormous problems of reconstruction and modernization. By a government decree on January 3, 1946, France adopted the device, heretofore found largely in command economies, of embarking on a series of four- or five-year plans.[38] The father of French planning was Jean Monnet, a man who, like most of those who have developed French planning, has been European-minded rather than narrowly nationalistic.[39] All shared a desire to achieve rapid economic growth for the French economy, so that it could play a significant international economic and policial role in the postwar world as well as achieve higher standards of living at home. The decision to plan was not accepted without some opposition, however. The conservative Jacques Reuff, who continued to be influential in French economic thought throughout most of the deGaulle era, wrote a "letter to the Advocates of a Controlled Economy" in which he warned,

> You want both order and liberty at one and the same time. By fixing prices at a level different from that at which they would have spontaneously established themselves, you can have only disorder and disarray.[40]

[37] For a review of state intervention in French industry see Lionel Stoleru, *L'Imperatif Industriel* (Paris: Editions du Seuil, 1969), especially Chapter 3, "Les interventions de l'Etat dans le secteur industriel: un panorama," pp. 87-152. We shall consider French industrial organization in somewhat greater detail in a later chapter.

[38] *France* (Paris: La Documentation Française, 1969).

[39] Jean Monnet later became head of the European Coal and Steel Community. His successor, Etienne Hirsch, was chosen to head Euratom—the European Atomic Agency. The third commissioner general of the French Planning Agency was Pierre Massé, who held this position from 1959 until after the Fifth Plan was adopted in 1966, when he was succeeded by François-Xavier Ortoli.

[40] Jacques Reuff, *Epitre aux Dirigistes* (Paris: Gallimard, 1949). Quoted in *Essays in European Economic Thought*, Louise Sommers, trans. and ed. (Princeton N.J.: D.Van Nostrand Co., 1960), p. 136.

Friedrich Hayek could scarcely have put the case more forcefully. Nonetheless, the French experiment has now produced five plans, with the sixth scheduled to cover the period 1971-75.

The First Four Plans   The first three plans were usually referred to as modernization plans, and covered the periods 1947-52, 1954-57, and 1958-61, respectively. The First Plan concentrated on six basic sectors of the French economy—coal, electricity, steel, transportation, cement, fertilizers and agricultural machinery—to get these sectors functioning again after the devastation of World War II. Opinions vary, but most students of the subject feel that, all things considered, the French succeeded with the broad objectives of the First Plan.[41]

The Second Plan (1954-57) attempted to achieve by 1957 a 25 percent increase in total output over the level of 1952 and attempted to modernize the French economy on a broader front than did the First Plan. Emphasis was given to research and development to improve industrial efficiency, and to techniques to increase agricultural productivity, manpower retraining, and so on.[42] Once again, most French and American observers were impressed with French results under the Second Plan.[43]

Introduction of the Third Plan (1958-61) coincided with French entrance into the Common Market and more or less, with the chaotic birth of the Fifth

[41] It is important to note that *success* in this context is defined narrowly. The plan met the projected growth rates in the several areas in which industrial modernization seemed crucial to Monnet and his associates. But the plan abandoned efforts to increase housing, and it can be argued that the growth rates were based on pessimistic forecasts of what should be achieved or on how much demand could be expected to increase. Moreover, this plan, unlike subsequent plans, was much less ambitious in what it required by way of inter-industry coordination, etc. In some ways it was the least ambitious of the first six plans (though modernization was indeed essential to further development) and therefore it was the plan which could most easily achieve success. For diverse views of this and subsequent plans see John S. Harlow, *French Economic Planning: A Challenge to Reason* (Iowa City, Iowa: University of Iowa Press, 1966); Edgar Furniss, *France: Troubled Ally* (New York: published for the Council on Foreign Relations by Harper and Brothers, 1960); John Sheahan, *Promotion and Control in Post-War France* (Cambridge, Mass.: Harvard University Press, 1963); François Perroux, *Le IV Plan Français* (Paris: Editions "Que Sais-Je? " 1962); Warren Baum, *The French Economy and the State*, a Rand Corporation Research Study (Princeton, N.J.: Princeton University Press, 1958). Most of these writers are fairly approving of at least the First Plan on grounds that it assisted in the postwar recovery of basic French industry. Baum, on the other hand, tends to judge in terms of the appropriateness of the projected growth rates and concludes that they could have been higher, given demand growth. It is clear that this plan achieved its limited objectives to a considerably greater degree than the more extensive plans which succeeded it.

[42] For a summary of the Second Plan see Hackett and Hackett, *Economic Planning in France*, pp. 27-30.

[43] A summary of these views may be found in Harlow, *French Economic Planning*, p. 41. Exceptions to the favorable views, in addition, once more, to Baum, were the French Marxists, who disapproved of the whole enterprise of planning as undertaken in this first postwar decade on grounds that it was not sufficiently authoritarian. See the discussion below of the French planning techniques.

Republic under Charles de Gaulle. Coupled with the political crisis revolving around the Algerian problem (which was primarily responsible for returning de Gaulle to power), events produced a serious problem of external instability and led to yet another devaluation of the franc at the beginning of de Gaulle's presidency. In general, the Third Plan occupied an extremely difficult period in French history. Its growth objective of about 5 percent per year was in fact achieved—and some credit must go to the plan. This period also saw an innovation in the form of the Intermediate Plan (1960-61), a revision of the Third Plan designed to speed up growth because of the slowdown in economic activity which occurred during the first half of the Third Plan. This notion of revising relatively long-run targets in light of subsequent developments is an important feature of modern planning, and in the market-oriented world it was pioneered in France. The Third Plan also paid more attention to social objectives and explicitly projected growth in housing construction, expenditures in education, and so forth.[44]

The Fourth Plan (1962-65) decidedly enlarged the range and scope of French planning. Preparations for it started as far back as 1959, and along with targeting growth for the economy through 1965, attempts were made to project the development of the economy through the subsequent fifteen years. The Fourth Plan anticipated a growth rate of 22 percent from the end of the Third Plan to the end of the fourth and attempted more detailed sector forecasts and targets than had previously been attempted. It was also beset by great difficulties; not only did the Common Market present new difficulties as well as new opportunities but inflation (and the social unrest attendant upon the resultant deterioration in the real standard of living and the French balance of payments) led Valerie Giscard D'Estaing, the French finance minister, to embark in September 1963 on an unprecedented Stabilization Plan, which involved extensive and direct wage and price controls.

The French economy managed to meet its 5.5 percent per year growth rate during the Fourth Plan, but whether the plan can be considered a success must be in dispute. The Stabilization Plan had some success in curbing inflation, but only at a cost of greatly increased unemployment, and in the crucial area of productive investment the plan failed to meet its target, for public investment fared much better than investment in the private sector. Moreover, at this time France was suffering from great political, economic, and social turmoil. It is true that de Gaulle had brought an unprecedented degree of political stability to modern France, but the economic and social policies of the Fourth Plan also stored up problems which exploded in France during the Fifth Plan.[45]

[44] For more detailed discussion of the Third Plan, the reader is referred to Hackett and Hackett, *Economic Planning in France*, pp. 30-33, and to Harlow, *French Economic Planning*, pp. 44-52.

[45] Harlow provides one assessment of success during the Fourth Plan in *French Economic Planning*, pp. 52-62. For another see Stephen S. Cohen, *Modern Capitalist Planning: The French Model* (Cambridge, Mass.: Harvard University Press, 1969), pp. 179-84.

The Fifth Plan: How Planning Works in France—A Conventional View   The Fifth Plan was designed to last for five years (1966-71) instead of four. The plan represented a greater effort than heretofore to involve Parliament in its design and approval. Its targets were set for all the major sectors of the national economy and averaged out to a targeted growth rate of 5 percent per year. Because the Fifth Plan is the last for which detailed information is available, we may use it to illustrate the French technique for developing a plan.

French planning begins at the General Planning Commissariat, an administrative agency under the premier with no independent authority. It consults with many individuals and very early sets a preliminary growth target for the last year of each plan. (The target for the last year of the Fifth Plan, 1970, was originally set in 1963.) The projected growth target is then turned over to twenty-five Modernization Commissions,[46] each made up of representatives of government, business organizations, and the trade unions, as well as many technical specialists. Twenty of the commissions are "vertical"—that is, each represents a specific sector of the economy (agriculture, buildings and public works, energy, mines and metallurgy, steel, tourism, transport, television and radio, and so on). Five of the commissions are "horizontal" and cut across the entire economy, focusing on general economic problems (employment, productivity, regional development, scientific research, finance, for example). One of their functions is to attempt to synthesize the results of the other twenty-two. Each Modernization Commission develops a tentative target for its sector. The Fifth Plan introduced a new step in the planning process: the General Planning Commissariat was to develop the major options for the Fifth Plan, which had been developed during 1964 on the basis of the preliminary reports of the Modernization Commissions. In 1965 the General Planning Commissariat submitted the options for approval to the Economic and Social Council—a group designed to serve as liaison between the Modernization Commissions and Parliament; while it had existed for some time, its role under the Fifth Plan was enlarged and made considerably more explicit.

In the next stage the Planning Commissariat studied the reports of the Modernization Commissions and utilized statistical data on the status of the various sectors of the economy, which it obtained from the National Institute for Statistics and Economic Studies (INSEE). With this information the Planning Commissariat produced the first full, combined draft of the revised targets for each sector of the economy in 1965. The government considered the proposals,

---

46 Both the number of Modernization Commissions and the number of people working on these commissions have increased.

The number of commissions for each plan, according to Harlow, are:

First Plan, eight commissions: Second Plan, twelve; Third Plan, nineteen; Fourth Plan, twenty-seven; and Fifth Plan (in 1965), thirty. (See Harlow, *French Economic Planning*, p. 17.) On the other hand, the official release of the Service de Presse of the French Embassy (cited in footnote 47) states (p. 7) that twenty-five Modernization Commissions were involved in the Fifth Plan, twenty of which were vertical and five of which were horizontal. We have used these numbers in the text.

revised some aspects and submitted them to Parliament for discussion and approval. The Fifth Plan was approved in November 1965.

This brief sketch of the modern French planning process has indicated the role of all major agencies except the Regional Economic Development Committee, organized in 1965 and designed to elicit views regarding the proposed plan from a large cross section of local and regional economic interests, so as to both encourage wider participation in the planning process and to speed the economic development of all parts of the country.[47]

French planning therefore characteristically combines long-run and short-run forecasts, combines approval by the elected officials with widespread participation by both economic interest groups and technical specialists in developing the plan, and targets individual sectors on the basis of prior overall growth rates—which, however, are subject to revision before the plan is approved if the efforts of the Modernization Commissions to meet their part of the proposed growth rates suggest that the General Planning Commissariat has been unrealistic in its approach.

French Planning—Another View   Having described how French planning works on paper, we cannot leave the subject without suggesting the serious reservations which have been expressed about French planning, particularly by the leaders of the trade unions, or without noting that there has been increasing debate in France over whether or not French planning is accomplishing what is most necessary to the balanced growth and development of a viable French economy.

We have suggested that indicative planning, particularly in the work of the Modernization Commissions, encompasses the notion of triparite participation and cooperation (as indeed is also the case, at least on paper, in Britain). The French trade union movement, especially the communist CGT (Confédération Générale du Travail), has never been happy with the essential thrust of French planning. While conservative Jacques Reuff viewed French planning as a fatal interference with the free market, the communists not surprisingly viewed it as an expensive, frustrating, and ultimately futile effort to bolster capitalism, in the guise of "neocapitalism." The unions see the notion that the planning procedure in France is truly tripartite, involving big business, the government, and the trade unions, largely as a snare and a delusion. For one thing, the trade unions have been consistently underrepresented on the Modernization Commissions—representing about 10 percent of the total membership.[48] For another, as has already been suggested, because of the serious problem of strong class lines in France,

---

[47] This summary of French planning is based largely on *The Fifth Plan, 1966-1970* (New York: Ambassade de France, Service de Presse et d'Information, 1967).

[48] Cohen reports that there were fifty-seven trade union representatives out of 612 members on the nineteen Modernization Commissions involved in the Third Plan. While the number of members of these commissions increased to over 3000 in the Fourth Plan, trade

trade union representatives have never felt as included as the representatives of business and the planning commission have. The latter two are essentially of the same strata of society, having gone to the same schools, and so on. Thus problems of social distance have clearly colored the nominally tripartite planning process in France.[49]

All these factors have presented an ironic change in French attitudes toward planning. Whereas business was initially suspicious because of the kind of conservative fears expressed by Reuff, and the leftists applauded the efforts at planning, in recent years the tables have been partially turned. Because the conflicts between business and the plan have been somewhat muted, business no longer fears the plan, whereas the left, although as fragmented and disunited as ever, disapproves of the plan as a device which has thus far changed very little of the essential social and economic fabric of the country.

The early plans concentrated on advancing the national growth rate, and this has indeed been achieved. But have the distribution of economic power, the system of national priorities, the division of the economic pie been changed in any essential ways by indicative planning? There is reason to answer no, as does the left, both political and union. First, these groups argue that the plan needs to be more *democratic* (the role of Parliament has been perfunctory at best—at least until the Fifth Plan—and the unions, as we have noted, have felt isolated). Second, they argue that it should be more *normative,* with the General Planning Commissariat asserting itself more forcefully (after consultation with groups other than the business interests) concerning the priorities to be adopted in the development of the infrastructure (that is, the educational system, the transportation system, public housing and so forth).

Where does this leave us? We have seen that despite the elaborate machinery of tripartite interaction, there is a significant (though possibly minority) opinion that the plan is not democratic, that it represents chiefly the views of the General Planning Commissariat. The commissariat's views, it is argued, are virtually indistinguishable from those of the treasury, which controls much investment both through public spending and through loans via the capital markets. Even if they are not inconsistent with the objectives of business enterprise, these treasury plan views have nevertheless resulted in plans which have had little impact on business decision-making.[50] This has led to the conclusion, certainly

---

union representation was proportionally virtually unchanged. (Cohen, *Modern Capitalist Planning* pp. 193-94.) While the CGT refused to participate in the Second and Third Plans, it participated to a limited degree in the development of the Fourth Plan and ultimately participated, as discussed below, in the development of a counter plan in connection with the Fifth Plan. But there is no evidence that de facto trade union representation, as opposed to the participation on paper previously outlined, has increased significantly in the French planning process in recent years.

[49] See Cohen, *Modern Capitalist Planning*, Chapter 19.

[50] See, for example, the study by John McArthur and Bruce R. Scott, which concentrated on the relationship between business planning and the national plan and concluded: "We expected to find a close and important relationship between strategic

by the left, that the plan must first of all be democratized, so that it can then be normative in terms of the goals it sets for the economy. Finally, it has been argued that such a truly democratically produced plan should then be more imperative rather than merely indicative, as has in fact been the case thus far. If in fact the plans have produced growth, but little change in the economic power relationships or the basic thrust of the French economy, then of course this conclusion follows logically.[51]

In the face of all this the trade unions and indeed the left generally have been divided about how to proceed. Some have argued that only by direct confrontation with its goals and directions can indicative planning be diverted into the directions suggested above. Others have argued that direct confrontation will be futile and have advocated cooperation with the plan as a way of making a slow and possibly limited but nonetheless real impact on the national priorities implicit in the plan. Finally, a third position has advocated "contestative participation."[52] This position, advanced by a coalition of trade unionists when the Fifth Plan was being enunciated (1963-65), argued that the initiative should be seized from the big business-Treasury-Planning Commissariat power nexus by advancing a counter plan which would reflect the goals of trade unions. It advocated a higher growth rate than the Fifth Plan involved (recognizing that it could be achieved only by a larger degree of direct government participation in the planning process than had occurred in the past), stated measures to reduce income inequality, and increased spending in such areas as housing, health, transportation, and regional development. The trade unionists who advanced the counter plan acknowledged it as a bold new idea and hoped to rally the left around it in order, as they put it, to determine whether the future of France would reflect the values and goals of the CGT (the communist labor union) or of the Bank of France.[53]

It is clear that those who speak of "democratizing" the plan mean that a wider range of class and interest groups must be involved in the development of its objectives. In this connection it is interesting to note that Pierre Massé, who was for many years head of the Planning Commissariat, had himself been affiliated with Electricité de France, and this business orientation surely was not

---

planning by public and private enterprises and the activities of the [Planning] commission." They explicitly mention the major studies of French planning as the source of this expectation (Baum, Pierre Bauchet *[Economic Planning: The French Experience* (London: Heinemann, 1964)], the Hacketts, Shonfield, etc.) and conclude: "It became [early] evident that there was no such close and direct relationship as we had initially assumed between the national planning process and business planning." (McArthur and Scott, *Industrial Planning in France* [Boston: Division of Research, Graduate School of Business Administration, Harvard University, 1969], pp. 7-8.) Their study was based on extensive interviews with French business executives and is convincing on this point.

[51] See Cohen, *Modern Capitalist Planning,* Chapter 19, for a compelling discussion of this view.

[52] See ibid, p. 211.

[53] See Jean Ensemble (pseudonym), *Le Contre Plan* (Paris: Editions du Seuil, 1965), p. 123.

without impact in his administration of indicative planning. He recently wrote, "In a market economy guided by a plan, the principal responsibility for industrial development belongs to the heads of business."[54] In his entire discussion Massé does not mention trade unions or give any indication that his view of planning, French style, involves real tripartite participation in determining national priorities, basic resource allocation, and so on. Moreover, a significant number of observers argue that, with the exception of the First Plan, the plans have not significantly changed the force or direction of the French economy and that business firms do not significantly alter their goals and objectives because of the plans. There is considerable evidence to support this view.

Concluding Comments on French Planning   French indicative planning has been widely discussed and has been influential in Britain, at least. Indicative planning, *en principe*, as the French say, is perhaps an ideal compromise between an economy in which resource allocation is left to the vagaries of the unregulated market and a command economy in which democracy has little or no place. Whether French indicative planning is business-dominated is thus a question which must be faced. Certainly, any overall evaluation of planning in France would be incomplete without noting that the economy continues to be plagued by inflation, worker and student unrest, inefficient distribution systems, external instability which produces periodical downward pressure on the franc in exchange markets, and so forth. These continually festering problems can explode as in May 1968. Stephen Cohen has perceptively noted that the the de Gaulle response to that crisis was to seize upon a dramatic phrase, *worker participation*, to avoid the critical question—the future of democracy in France—and then to present in the name of democracy a program for dealing with France's problems which in the final analysis preserves "the existing distribution of power"[55] in all significant areas.

The comment is perhaps appropriate for indicative planning in general as it has been utilized thus far in France. Whether the problems that so dramatically erupted in 1968 exist in spite of or at least partially because of indicative planning as it has been developed is a question not easily answered. Certainly there is considerable evidence that in practice French indicative planning was not meant to alter the structure, the goals, or the essential nature of the French economy except insofar as it has encouraged rapid growth and to the degree that production has been somewhat coordinated by planning mechanisms. One of the most damning criticisms of French planning has come from a Frenchman, Lionel Stoleru, who has argued that the state tends to intervene most slowly in the sector in greatest difficulty, that state intervention often lacks an overall

---

[54] Pierre Massé, in his introduction to Cohen, *Modern Capitalist Planning* p. xxi.
[55] Cohen, ibid., p. 255.

strategy, and finally that the state intervenes in what he calls "noble" sectors (atomic research, space, aviation, and so on) rather than in "humble" sectors like agriculture, which ought perhaps to receive higher priorities. He concludes, "To dominate the world market for ravioli is not a goal that mobilizes the crowds...."[56] This is perhaps a criticism not so much of the French Planning mechanism as it is of the objectives to which the government in recent years has chosen to direct this mechanism (creation of a *force de frappe*, and so forth). As such it reflects criticism of national priorities like that often heard in the United States.

Trade unionists believe that indicative planning has underscored, but not resolved, the questions concerning national priorities with which other countries, including the United States, have been wrestling in recent years. Whether indicative planning does indeed offer an avenue down which genuine redirection of economic activity could be effected has not yet been demonstrated in France. We are left then with the conclusion that French indicative planning deserves our attention because in principle the approach possesses the *potential* for using tripartite participation to direct the economy toward collectively and democratically determined objectives and to coordinate microeconomic objectives and set them in a macroeconomic framework. That the level of accomplishment has fallen below the potential level need not detract from the value of the model in France and elsewhere.

Swedish Planning   We have devoted a good deal of attention to French planning because it is probably the most highly developed system of planning to be found today among the market-oriented economies. However, plans of one sort or another are utilized in a number of other countries, and one of the most interesting approaches is found in Sweden. Swedes view their planning efforts as less "programmatic" than the French, but the objective of growth plays as big a role in Swedish planning as it does in France. However, the Swedes insist that they have tried to keep their growth targets more realistic than have the French so as to avoid the inflation and other serious signs of economic imbalance which have plagued France. A second objective of Swedish planning is epitomized by the investment reserve—a manipulative device used by the government to stimulate investment in sectors of the economy it views as underdeveloped (such as highways and housing) and to retard investment in other sectors.[57]

The Swedes did not set up a permanent planning commission, as did the French, but instead established a Royal Planning Commission for each planning period. By the mid-1960s, however, they were considering a permanent planning

---

[56] Lionel Stoleru, *L'Imperatif Industriel*, p. 150.

[57] See Karl Jungenfelt, "The Methodology of Swedish Long-Term Planning," *Skandinaviska Banken Quarterly Review* 45 (1964): No. 4. 111-15. Reprinted in Prybyla, ed., *Comparative Economic Systems*, pp. 193-99. We shall also consider the Swedish investment reserve in a later chapter dealing with fiscal policy.

commission with a permanent secretariat to achieve more continuity. The Swedish plan would place this secretariat in the treasury. Jugenfelt has argued that French methods are somewhat more reliable in setting goals which can be met, partly because the French planning system is continuous rather than set up anew for each plan.[58]

The first long-run Swedish plan was set up in 1947 in connection with Swedish participation in the Marshall Plan. Subsequent long-term perspectives, as the Swedes call them, were developed by Royal Planning Commissions for the periods 1951-55, 1956-60, and 1961-65.[59]

Like the French Modernization Commissions, the Swedish Royal Planning Commissions have brought together civil servants, trade union officers, and representatives of employer organizations. However, the Royal Planning Commissions correspond more closely to the French General Planning Commissariat than they do to the Modernization Commissions, and although the Royal Commissions solicit advice and assistance from groups representing economic sectors and interest groups, the overall impression one gets is that planning has been a somewhat more centralized activity in Sweden than in France (although Svennilson and Beckman argue that Swedish planning is decentralized). Also, as befits a country which has played an important role in the development of modern economic theory and analysis, the Royal Commissions have employed academic economists to a much greater extent, it appears, than may have been the case in France.[60]

Swedish planners have devoted a good deal of attention to advice from and directives to units organized to represent particular economic interests. Thus in drafting a target for economic growth the Planning Commission will obtain information from the Agricultural Marketing Board about what seems realistic to expect in this sector. The representative organization for employers, the Svenska Arbetsgivareföreningen (SAF), provides information about trends in productivity, and in conjunction with the labor organization, the Landsorganisationen (LO), works out within the bounds of expected increase in output (via changes in both the labor force and productivity) what is known as the Central Wages Bargain. A crucial aspect of Swedish planning is the Labor Market Board, which can use direct control as well as control over investment funds to move economic activity in preferred directions.[61]

The Central Wage Bargain attempts to adjust distributive shares to the projected real growth in the economy, but the trade unions exert considerable pressure on the bargain struck. The trade unions feel that if they stick together

[58] Jungenfelt, "Swedish Long-Term Planning," in Prybyla, ed., *Comparative Economic Systems*, p. 197.

[59] A useful summary of Swedish long-term planning, on which this account has drawn heavily, is found in Ingvar Svennilson and Rune Beckman, "Long-Term Planning in Sweden," *Skandinaviska Banken Quarterly Review* 43, No. 3 (1962); 71-78.

[60] Academic economists have been involved in British planning efforts as well.

[61] Shonfield, *Modern Capitalism*, p. 209.

they will benefit in the long run because their pressure will augment natural market pressures, which tend to kill off the least productive firms and to strengthen the productive firms. This elimination process will, of course, reallocate some labor and other resources and in the unionists' view will ultimately benefit labor. As Shonfield has noted, the objective of Swedish planning insofar as trade unions influence it is to compel the economy to adjust to market forces (to the extent that the latter are reflected in the productivity of various firms and industries).

Closely related to the input received by the Royal Planning Commissions from groups representing labor, agriculture, and business are the input they receive from representatives of specific industries–the Steel Association, the Pulp Association, the Power Association, and so on. Ingvar Svennilson and Rune Beckman conclude, "The making of the perspective is thus a cooperative effort, in which private firms and their associations, public institutions, and specialized research units all take part."[62]

The planning procedure is therefore similar to the French system–an overall growth rate is selected initially by the Royal Planning Commission, and before the target is finalized many sectors have the opportunity to discuss and ultimately revise it. This approach has been called planning in stages; micro plans based on macro targets are reviewed at the industry level and at the macro level in order to achieve internal consistency and aggregate feasibility.[63] The ultimate targeted growth rate therefore attempts to coordinate what must be micro-economic targets with the aggregate growth rate set for the economy as a whole. However, the Royal Planning Commission, like the French Planning Commissariat, has no power of its own but serves principally to guide public policy. The Planning Commission suggests targets for individual sectors and attempts to achieve the targets through the investment reserve system and the Central Wage Bargain. Its direct control over investment, production, and employment is limited to nationalized sectors (railroads, hospitals, education, road construction, some power facilities, and so on).

Finally, a significant aspect of Swedish planning has been the development of long-term budgets as an adjunct of planning so that targets can be kept feasible. Both the growth targets and the budget estimates can then be subject to annual revision.

How successful has the Swedish "middle way" to the planned economy been? How the Swedes measure success is illustrated by the following summary, prepared at the start of the last year of the 1961-65 perspective. The overall targeted growth rate of 4 percent per year was being achieved, but some sectors were under and others over the Commission's targets. Specifically, comparison of actual with projected output for 1964 showed that at the end of the first four

[62] Svennilson and Beckman, "Long-Term Planning in Sweden," p. 71.

[63] Jungenfelt, "Swedish Long-Term Planning," in Prybyla, ed., *Comparative Economic Systems,* pp. 196-97.

years of the five-year planning period, mining, engineering, and foodstuffs had exceeded the projected targets, whereas iron and steel, timber, pulp and paper, and textiles and clothing were below their target output. Moreover, if gross investment is also considered more doubt is cast upon the likelihood that targeted capacity was being attained in the various sectors of the economy.[64] In general, however, the targets were being fulfilled. Johannson concludes:

> The development—as long as one confines oneself to a study of big aggregated items such as GNP, total gross investments, private and public consumption, etc.—seems on the whole to have been fairly well in line with, and in some areas even to have outstripped, the Commission's predictions regarding development tendencies.[65]

In sum, the Swedish "middle way" to planning is similar to the French system, although as of the mid-1960s it lacked the continuity of French planning. Moreover, the planning procedures give the impression of somewhat less coordination: the consultative procedures with economic sectors, even though highly similar to the French use of the Modernization Commissions, are less organized and more ad hoc. However, the approaches are quite alike. If one adds that French indicative planning served as a model for the renewed British efforts at planning in the early 1960s, when the NEDC and the little Neddies were set up, we see that there is indeed a common thread to planning techniques being developed for modern market-oriented economies.

Planning in Other Market-Oriented Economies   Space does not permit us to consider in any detail the planning techniques in other market-oriented economies, but the three cases we have examined set the tone for the others. Planning is an effort at coordination and cooperation between the government and the major economic sectors and industries. The plans lack the legal force and compulsoriness of those in command economies, but they can come closer to being imperative rather than merely indicative according to the moral and political force of the government and also to how directly the government participates in investment through nationalized industry, a subject we shall consider in greater detail later.

There are differences from country to country, but these characteristics would appear to apply to the planning of other market-oriented economies. Shonfield has commented that France, Britain, the Netherlands, Italy, Sweden,

---

[64] This assessment of the success of the Swedish Plan, 1961-65, was made by Osten Johansson, "Economic Development in Sweden during the 1960's: How Far Has the Long-Term Plan Been Fulfilled?" *Skandinaviska Banken Quarterly Review* 45 (1964); No. 4 115-23.

[65] Ibid., 123.

and Austria have broadly similar social objectives. He adds,

> And there is no overwhelming devotion to a market ideology which might get in the way of using the instruments of public authority to secure the aims of postwar economic policy—accelerating long-term economic growth and controlling business fluctuations.[66]

A number of other countries have planning bureaus. In Belgium the Economic Planning Bureau develops overall economic objectives; its first plan covered the period 1962-65.[67] Denmark has no formal planning agency, but the Economic Coordination Council gathers information and advises the government on overall economic policy. In Norway the minister of finance has a Planning Department which works out both a budget and a medium-term plan.[68] In Japan the Economic Planning Agency plays a similar role.

Modern planning in Italy began with the La Malfa Report of 1962, and an economist, Pasquale Saraceno, was vice-president of the Planning Commission, which is appointed by the minister of the budget and works out five-year plans. The Italian Planning Commission, like a number of other such commissions, is tripartite, with representatives of government, trade unions, and business organizations. However, in Italy the approach to planning is sometimes called *corporatist* because through the Istituto per la Ricostuzione Industriale (IRI), the state owns corporations in many sectors, and therefore directly determines policy for a vast amount of Italy's economic activity. Governmental control through IRI is increased through Ente Nazionale Idrocarburi (ENI), a national corporation set up in 1952 to administer fuel oils.

In the Netherlands the Central Planning Bureau had earlier contented itself with one-year plans, but in 1963 it developed its first five-year plan.[69] But the distinctive feature of Dutch planning is probably a reflection of the fact that, like the Swedes, the Dutch have long been leaders in the development of sophisticated economic analysis. In Holland particularly they have been at the forefront in the development of econometric models of the economy, whereby highly complex mathematical methods are applied to the rationalizing and coordinating of economic decision-making within the context of the growth and stability targets called for by the plan. Moreover, the Dutch have been prominent in "manpower planning" and have probably used direct wage and price controls to regulate inflation more than any other country. Shonfield

---

[66] Shonfield, *Modern Capitalism*, p. 176.

[67] IICLC *Economic Policy in Practice*, p. 182.

[68] Solomon Barkin et al. eds., *International Labor* (New York: Harper and Row, Publishers, 1967), p. 50.

[69] Shonfield, *Modern Capitalism*, p. 214.

comments, "Broadly, price control is to Holland what the system of investment reserves is to Sweden."[70]

Similar efforts at planning and coordination of aggregate economic policy with microeconomic activity are made in a number of other Western economies. In sum, overall setting of targets for growth and stability, efforts to coordinate microeconomic objectives, the use of planning bureaus, and direct government intervention in economic decision-making appear to represent a fair characterization of all the market-oriented economies on which we have thus far commented. The list is perhaps complete, with two notable exceptions—West Germany and the United States

Germany and the United States—Planning in "Unplanned" Economies

Among the world's market-oriented economies in the period since World War II, the United States has continued to be overwhelmingly the largest and most powerful, and West Germany (with the possible exception of Japan) by far the most dynamic. Both economies have continued to hold concepts viewed as slightly old-fashioned in other market-oriented economies. The Germans, who refer to their economy as a *social market economy* (Soziale Marktwirtschaft), and the United States, which refers to its economy as *mixed capitalism,* continue to talk a good deal about competition, free private enterprise, laissez faire, and other terms that have little current attraction in other market-oriented economies.

Although we cannot close this chapter on planning techniques without considering whether there are ways in which planning might enter these two economies—by the back door, so to speak—their real importance in the contemporary world will perforce not become apparent until subsequent chapters.

To describe postwar economic activity the term *social market economy* was coined in 1946 by Müller-Armack, a close adviser to Dr. Ludwig Erhard, German Minister of Economics during much of the postwar period (and later chancellor). Müller-Armack defined a social market economy as one having

> its origin in neo-liberal economic ideas ... which stressed the vital function of competition and at the same time sought to establish, in contrast to old-fashioned liberalism, a competitive order in accordance with the ideas of Walter Eucken and Franz Bohm.[71]

And what were the ideas of Walter Eucken? He stated that in the modern world there were a number of possible kinds of economic order, but the main

[70] Shonfield, *Modern Capitalism,* p. 215.

[71] A. Muller-Armack, *Studien zur Sozialen Marktwirtschaft* (Cologne: Institut fur Wirtschaftspolitik an der Universitat zu Köln, 1960), p. 10. Quoted in Denton, Forsyth and Maclennan, *Economic Planning and Policies,* pp. 34-35.

types were the centrally directed economy and the exchange economy, each of which had a variety of forms. But he stressed that if the market or exchange economy emphasized utilizing a free price system, there was a distinct role for the state, unlike the old laissez-faire system to allocate resources. The question was not so much the amount of state intervention as *how* the state intervened. Said Eucken:

> More or less State activity—this kind of question misses the point. . . . The basic principle does not simply require that certain measures of economic policy should be avoided, e.g., state subsidies, the establishment of state Monopolies, the freezing of prices, import restrictions, etc. It is also insufficient to forbid cartels. The principle is not primarily negative. Far more essential is a positive policy which aims at bringing the market form of complete competition into being, and which thereby fulfills the basic principle. It is here that the policy of the competitive order differs completely from the policy of *laissez faire* which, according to its own basic principles, did not recognize the need for a positive economic policy.[72]

One view is that "what is happening in Germany is a progressive synthesis and development of the theories of Keynes and Eucken."[73] The man who played the largest role in this synthesis was undoubtedly Ludwig Erhard. Most students of modern Germany have argued that the neoliberalism behind Germany's social market economy differs sharply from old-fashioned liberalism in that although it places great emphasis on letting the market perform basic allocative functions, the social market economy does have a place for government. Ideally, of course, the government should play its part by using the market mechanism.

From the beginning Erhard placed great importance on a stable money, and one early difference between Germany and other market-oriented economies was that stable money was given greater priority as an economic objective than full employment, equilibrium in the balance of payments, or economic growth.[74] Not until the 1950s did stability and growth receive top attention. This emphasis was understandable in light of the German experience with inflation, unstable money, and economic chaos following both world wars. The primary factors which gave postwar Germany a new direction and a new chance was the Currency Reform Act of 1948, which established the Deutsche mark and reestablished conditions in which sound money could prevail. As George Halm says, the Currency Reform Act was accompanied with a basic change in

[72] Euken's views are expressed in two books—one published in 1940 and the other published posthumously in 1952. The quotation is from the latter work and is quoted in Denton Forsyth, and Maclennan, *Economic Planning and Policies*, p. 39.

[73] Karl Schiller, "West Germany: Stability and Growth as Objectives of Economic Policy," in Prybyla, ed., *Comparative Economic Systems*, p. 168.

[74] IICLC, *Economic Policy in Practice*, p. 92.

philosophy—a "return to the principles of a market economy."[75] However, market principles in Germany must be viewed from a German perspective and with an awareness of German historical tradition, which includes much emphasis on individual self-discipline, a penchant for taking orders without question, and what Shonfield and others view as a natural tendency to concentrate authority and power.[76] Thus some of the system which emerged after the Second World War was based on an effort to Americanize German institutions—for example, the decentralization of the banking system by breaking up the three largest banks, the Deutsche Bank, the Dresdner Bank, and the Commerz Bank. This effort ultimately failed, and by the early 1950s all three had regrouped and reestablished essentially the previous, traditional structure.

In the postwar German economic institutions, therefore, one sees a no doubt sincere desire to break with the cartels, the concentration of power, and the authoritarianism that had characterized the economy of Nazi Germany, coupled with a historical tradition which emphasized authority and discipline. These latter ideas were essentially grafted onto the notion of the market system, which was viewed as a social instrument as well as a private instrument and hence subject to some government direction, if not control. From this combination the modern German economic system developed.

The question has been raised whether this system, despite its protestations to the contrary, is not after all "planned" either by the three large banks or by the state itself. It has been argued that the banks control (and hence plan) the German economy (1) by actual ownership of German corporations, (2) by the use of proxy votes at company meetings to benefit the customers whose stocks they vote, and (3) by the votes they control on special supervisory boards that are unique to the German economy called the Aufsichtsrat.[77] This question is complicated, but it seems reasonable to conclude that although the German economy is scarcely as competitive as it has sometimes been judged,[78] the banks, despite their considerable control over German industrial and commercial activity, probably do not have the unity of purpose that would be required to "plan" effectively for the economy. In this connection, Geoffrey Denton, Murray Forsyth, and Malcolm Maclennan conclude,

---

[75] George N. Halm, *Economic Systems: A Comparative Analysis*, 3d ed. (New York: Holt, Rinehart and Winston, 1968), p. 335.

[76] Shonfield speaks of the German "overwhelming instinct to centralize economic decisions." *(Modern Capitalism,* p. 240.)

[77] Shonfield discussed the use of the *Aufsichtsrat* in some detail. *(Modern Capitalism,* pp. 246-55.) The question of control of German industry through the banks is considered as well in Denton, Forsyth, and Maclennan, *Economic Planning and Policies*, pp. 28-72. We shall consider the question in greater detail in the chapter on industrial organization.

[78] But in this connection it is useful to remind ourselves that, as Shonfield puts it, "The last thing that German industrialists contemplated [after the war] was to establish a free market economy of many small producers in the Anglo-Saxon spirit." *(Modern Capitalism,* p. 240.)

The study of relationships between German banks and industry and commerce, although it reveals an oligopolistic structure, and although the bankers may work according to similar criteria, has not given support to the view that the banks act in concert to control credit and coordinate the economy.[79]

Does the state plan in Germany? Again, Denton, Forsyth, and Maclennan argue that while there were a number of specific economic interventions by the state in Germany during the period of Erhard's major influence, particularly in the public sector and in agriculture, "there was never any overall growth target toward which the planners attempted to guide the economy as a whole by means of specific interventions."[80]   More recently, a committee was established (in 1964) to forecast economic development in Germany, and since then efforts have been made in the direction of planning through a medium-term budget. The effects are not yet pronounced, but they reflect increased concern with economic growth, with utilizing some of the analytical concepts that planning and development make available, and with medium-term planning, which is being urged by the European Economic Community.[81]

In conclusion, while the German economy utilizes planning far less than any other European market-oriented economy, its resemblance to that of the United States may be more apparent than real. Important differences result from the vastly different histories and traditions of the two countries. (Shonfield has noted that "The Germans are equipped with both the business habits and institutions which would allow them to make an easy transition to a planned economy of the modern capitalist type."[82]) This brief consideration of the character of the modern socialist market economy in some ways isolates and differentiates the contemporary American economy from other market-oriented economies even more than might otherwise appear.

In an article entitled "Economic Planning in the United States,"[83] Gerhard Colm some years ago argued strongly that the United States did indeed use methods not unlike those of planned economies, but his argument seems somewhat strained. He contended that, although obviously there is no planning agency and

---

[79] Denton, Forsyth, and Maclennan, *Economic Planning and Policies*, p. 72. The study they refer to is, however, a German study undertaken to examine the relationships between German banking and industry *(Bericht über das Ergebnis einer Untersuchung der Konzentration in der Wirtschaft* [Bonn: Deutscher Bundestag, Drucksache IV/2320, 1964]) See also p. 68.

[80] Ibid., p. 73.

[81] This discussion has drawn heavily on Denton, Forsyth, and Maclennan, *Economic Planning and Policies*, pp. 72-75.

[82] Shonfield, *Modern Capitalism,* p. 260.

[83] Colm's article, originally published in *Weltwirtschaftliches Archiv* 92, Heft 1 (1964): 31-54, has been largely reprinted in Bornstein ed., *Comparative Economic Systems,* pp. 185-203.

no overall growth target set, there are at least four kinds of planning in this country. By the first, *program planning*, he meant the development of specific action programs to achieve desired results in certain fields—national defense, education, health, urban renewal, and so on. By the second type, *business planning*, he meant the efforts made by most modern businesses to project future trends and to estimate their own possibilities and needs within this projected range of future growth. By the third, *economic policy planning*, he meant stabilization planning, in essence, largely the province of the federal government, which he viewed as the current expression—in economic policy each year—of the responsibilities imposed on the government by the Employment Act of 1946. Finally, he referred to *priority planning* for natural resources—the notion that the federal government is forced to give thought to the relative importance of national security, elimination of poverty, resource conservation, urban renewal, and so forth. In a private-enterprise economy with a fairly large public sector these types of planning would in Colm's view be interconnected.

It is our view that Colm is correct in suggesting that all modern economies, including that of the United States, involve a large public sector and have assumed at the national level some responsibility for obtaining minimal economic objectives of the sort we discussed in Chapter 1, but he must strain to call what happens in the U.S. today planning in the sense that the countries considered earlier in this chapter plan. The U.S. does not set growth targets or make any consistent and coordinated effort to "plan" in the sense of coordinating microeconomic decisions with macroeconomic objectives. Wage-price controls are basically anathema to the economic policy-maker except in wartime, even though the persistent unemployment and inflation of the late 1960s forced the Nixon administration to adopt such a system. (But it was made clear that the wage-price "freeze" was to last no more than ninety days, and ironically it was adopted, under pressure, by the very groups which had looked with disfavor on the wage-price guideposts of the Kennedy-Johnson administrations.) So while this kind of interference with the economy may be with us for some time, its adoption was in a sense a desperation measure; at this writing its long run results are by no means clear, and it was evident that these measures could not be viewed as a conversion to a belief in the efficacy of planning per se by U.S. political leaders.

We have seen that although there is great similarity in the basic economic objectives of all market-oriented economies, West Germany to some extent and the United States to a much larger extent eschew planning of the kind that other market-oriented economies have embraced since the Second World War to achieve these objectives. In the next chapter we shall examine these differences more explicitly by considering the importance of public ownership as a means of achieving economic goals in market-oriented economies.

3

Governmental Control over
Resource Allocation: The Public Sector

In the previous chapter we noted that one way in which market-oriented economies can affect resource allocation directly, regardless of the degree of planning that may be employed, is through direct governmental ownership of resources. In fact, the two need not be related. Planning can be viewed as an effort to coordinate resource inputs to a rationally ("nationally") determined set of societal outputs rather than to the determination of such outputs entirely through the marketplace of laissez faire capitalism. We saw that to some extent the governments of all market-oriented economies today—whether "planned" or not—determine part of these outputs.

In this chapter we explore somewhat further several avenues by which the government can affect resource allocation directly. The first of these, as noted, is through direct ownership of (hence control over) resources—a device that is far more prevalent among market-oriented economies than is generally realized in the United States. But nationalism is only one way in which governments participate in resource allocation. The development of government expenditures and transfers—of taxing the economy (or borrowing from it) for the direct development of a public sector of the economy (in underdeveloped areas often called the infrastructure)—that is, in order to finance health programs, education, highway construction, urban renewal, resource conservation, and a host of other "public goods and services"— plus the ancient functions of running the

43

government and providing for national security have brought national governments into a more prominent role in resource allocation decisions in market-
oriented economies.[1]

Public welfare programs (roads, schools, hospitals, and so on) and the
nationalized sector (if one exists) are what is usually meant by the term *public
sector* of an economy, although, of course, expenditures for administration and
national security are also public expenditures. The public sector's direction and
character reflect the attitude of the government toward public versus private
allocation of resources. We shall be unable to review many market-oriented
economies in detail, but several examples will suffice to show the degree of
variation in the size and character of the public sector of market-oriented
economies.

Why Nationalize Industry?

"Except for the doctrinaire, nationalization of industry is not an end in
itself. Unless, on balance, its practical application increases efficiency,
productivity, stability, and net well-being, it must be regarded as a liability to
any nation."[2] Presumably, market-oriented economies, unlike command
economies, need not be doctrinaire about nationalization, and therefore when
market-oriented economies choose to nationalize an industry it is presumably
because they feel that some economic objectives can be better achieved with
nationalized industry than with private industry. At the outset it should be
noted that, unlike command economies, all market-oriented economies that have
nationalized any part of basic industry have first considered the merits of the
case for each particular industry.

We have suggested that one way in which governments can increase their
control over the economy, thereby furthering their planned objectives to the
greatest extent possible, is by owning or controlling industries directly. There
has thus always been a tendency to relate planning and nationalization,[3]

---

[1] We are here distinguishing between the deliberate manipulation of governmental tax
and expenditure programs to achieve greater growth and/or stability in the economy—
subjects considered in later chapters—and public programs which, like nationalization of
certain industries in themselves, give the government direct control over an increasingly large
percent of GNP in many countries to achieve allocative results which market-oriented
economies, in pursuit of social amelioration, increasingly find they cannot leave to the
market.

[2] William N. Loucks and William G. Whitney, *Comparative Economic Systems,* 8th ed.
(New York: Harper and Row, Publishers, 1969), p. 243.

[3] Ben W. Lewis, for example titles his study of postwar Britain *British Planning and
Nationalization* (New York: The Twentieth Century Fund, 1952). Loucks and Whitney
devote Part 5 of their book, *Comparative Economic Systems,* to "Types of Economic
Planning," and the first three chapters of this section are devoted to British nationalization.
They wrote, "Nationalization is an extreme form of central economic planning, one in
which those charged with formulating economic policy for the reaction and those who react
at the firm level are all employees of the state." (P. 258.)

although plans can obviously go astray even when the government owns the industries being planned.[4] The idea that nationalization can increase efficiency is based on several assumptions. If nationalization permits a larger scale of operations, it can lead to better systems for purchasing raw materials, obtaining funds for investment, organizing labor inputs, and distributing the final product, among other things. Moreover, it is sometimes argued that a nationalized firm or industry can act as a goad or challenge to related private firms or industries, thereby increasing efficiency in the private sector as well.

The argument that nationalization will increase stability involves the notion that government can use investment to further full employment, and that to the extent that nationalization means coordination, it will reduce the possibility of instability through miscalculation and poor forecasting.

Factors that promote efficiency ought also to increase productivity. In addition, nationalization might conceivably further productivity through programs of manpower retraining, capital expansion through long-run investment programs, and access to financial resources to carry out both manpower retraining and capital expansion programs, which private firms or industries might find more difficult to obtain.

The idea that nationalization can further "net well-being" undoubtedly refers to the British experience, considered briefly below, in which the British were convinced after World War II that a radical change might pull the economy out of physical, financial, and psychological chaos and depression. Change is not necessarily progress, but sometimes dramatic change can rejuvenate the spirit.[5]

On the other hand, it would be a great mistake to regard nationalization as an automatic route to greater efficiency, stability, or "well-being," let alone a panacea for the problems faced by industry in modern market-oriented economies. Indeed, nationalization may well be a hazardous path to the amelioration of the economic ills that beset modern economies. At the very least it involves the creation of a large bureaucracy—not yet proven to be an efficient organizational technique even when it is unavoidable for other reasons. If the British experience with nationalization has tempted some to credit it with "rejuvenating the British spirit," it should be remembered that in the years since World War II the British have vacillated in their attitude toward the merits of nationalizing basic industry, particularly steel. Moreover, the elementary notion on which modern capitalist economies were founded—that competition among private producers can yield social gains through rapid product and process improvement—is by no means to be discarded lightly.

[4] In this connection it is instructive to bear in mind that even in command economies it is by no means uncommon for plans to go unfulfilled. They can be too ambitious, they can be poorly coordinated, they might not bring forth the required level of performance from labor, they can leave consumers dissatisfied and hence less than ideally cooperative as factors of production, and they can reckon without the intervention of nature (particularly in agriculture but also in other areas—for example, construction, etc.).

[5] For a more detailed consideration of the advantages of nationalization, see Lewis, *British Planning and Nationalization*, pp. 43-45.

Finally, it is exceedingly difficult to judge the success of nationalization in any country in terms of the standards enumerated above. There is no controlled experiment; once nationalization has been achieved, it is difficult to estimate what a firm's or industry's performance would have been had it remained private.

The Extent of Nationalization in Market-Oriented Economies

Britain   Britain was one of the first Western economies to nationalize, and the British experiment after the war attracted interest in both command economies and other market-oriented economies. We cannot possibly consider the British program in detail, but we can offer some observations and a few conclusions.[6]

Interestingly, analysts do not even agree about how nationalized the British economy is, let alone whether it has been a success. George Halm comments, "In none of the developed market economies of the West has nationalization been carried to a considerable degree."[7] William Loucks and William Whitney, on the other hand, refer to the period "since the transition to a sizable segment of nationalized industries" in Britain.[8] Their estimate of the absolute size of the public sector is that 25 percent of the British labor force is employed by government, including the nationalized industries (an increase of 50 percent over 1945).[9] However, G. C. Allen has estimated that in absolute numbers the nationalized industries in 1963 employed 2,300,000 people—about one-tenth of civilian employees, or a sixfold increase over prewar employment in nationalized industry in Britain. One can easily forget that even before World War II railways, public transit, electricity, coal, part of the communications system, and air services were either nationalized or "semi-public undertakings" (as Allen calls them), so that the transition to nationalization under the Attlee Labour government after the war was not quite the dramatic change it is sometimes described as.[10]

Allen notes that even these figures do not adequately represent the importance of the public sector in British economic life, as two-thirds of all people with higher education work for the government in nationalized industries

[6] The interested reader is referred to the study by Lewis, already mentioned; R. A. Brady, *Crisis in Britain* (Berkeley and Los Angeles: University of California Press, 1950); and William A. Robson, *Nationalized Industry and Public Ownership* (London: George Allen and Unwin, 1960).

[7] George N. Halm, *Economic Systems,* 3rd ed. (New York: Holt, Rinehart and Winston, 1968), p. 339.

[8] Loucks and Whitney, *Comparative Economic Systems,* p. 244.

[9] Ibid., p. 218.

[10] See G. C. Allen, *The Structure of Industry in Britain: A Study in Economic Change,* 3rd ed. (London: Longman Group, 1970), pp. 128-29.

or elsewhere. Thus assessment of the importance of nationalization is difficult because: (1) considerable nationalization or near-nationalization existed before the war, (2) employment in nationalized industry must be separated from other public employment, and (3) a six-fold increase in employment in nationalized industry to approximately 10 percent of civilian employment can be considered either "significant" or "minor," depending on the viewpoint with which you examine that evidence.

How successful has nationalization been in Britain? The consensus seems to be that the areas already mentioned and natural gas needed to be nationalized. So-called natural monopolies, which become public utilities in the United States, tend to be nationalized industries in Britain (and for the same reasons). The coal industry was sick in Britain (as it has been in the United States), and although nationalization has not solved all the industry's problems, it has at least stopped its steady decline and disintegration. The Bank of England was nationalized when the war ended with little dispute and considerable facility. (Most central banks in Europe are nationalized. The U.S. Federal Reserve System is therefore unique.) Atomic energy, nationalized in Britain, has been essentially nationalized (under the Atomic Energy Commission) in the U.S. too.

The major nationalized sector of the British economy that became a political issue was the iron and steel industry. This basic sector of the economy was nationalized in November 1949 by the Iron and Steel Act, was denationalized by the Conservatives by a 1953 law repealing the Iron and Steel Act. The Labour party made the renationalization of steel a major political goal and succeeded in renationalizing the industry in 1967. The steel industry demonstrated that a market-oriented economy could take over a previously private industry and work out a suitable system for reimbursing its owners for the loss. It also showed that problems of organization, funding, investment, and modernization (a major goal of the original nationalization of steel) are not automatically solved by having the industry in government hands. Moreover, some critics have charged that a government bureaucracy is not necessarily preferable to a private bureaucracy in industrial decision-making. Allen insists that steel had been subject to extensive government regulation for a long time, so that nationalization made less difference than it would have, say to the operation of steel in the U.S.[11] Loucks and Whitney conclude that it is too early to say how successful steel will be in its renationalized form. Whatever the merits or demerits of nationalizing the steel industry are, everyone appears to agree that it cannot remain viable if it must go through this process again.

In general it has been argued (in Britain and elsewhere) that steel and many other industries need not be entirely nationalized in order to achieve government objectives. The nationalized sector can increase its capacity, alter its prices,

[11] This is Allen's view of all but a couple of relatively minor areas of the British economy which were nationalized. The results of nationalization "had little effect on the character of British industry." (*Structure of Industry in Britain*, p. 129.)

change its manpower policies, and so on. If it constitutes a significant percent of the entire industry, the private sector would have to go along or lose out.

Only recently have British nationalized industries come to grips with the fact that in addition to their concern with national policies they must also follow what Allen has called commercial policies—that is, policies based on decision-making which reflects some of the significant factors that enter into profit maximization considerations in private firms. In Britain access to loans, subsidies, and so on enable the nationalized industries to run for long periods on rates of return that are insufficient to cover operating costs, interest on debts, and depreciation. Recently the pricing and production policies of nationalized industry have become somewhat more realistic however.

In a White Paper published in 1967 the British Government stressed the need for greater flexibility in setting targets and in varying them from industry to industry, depending on circumstances. Moreover, the White Paper stressed that targets must be influenced "not only by considerations of a rational pricing policy and an acceptable rate of return on capital, but also the purposes of the prices and incomes policy. . . ."[12] The result is that the National Boards set up under the terms of most of the Nationalization Acts have increasingly followed sound operating principles along with their concern for the national interest.

In sum, the British have shown that nationalization is scarcely a panacea for economic problems (neither efficiency nor profitability are automatic results of nationalization), but it can be made compatible with democratic political institutions within a market-oriented economic framework.

Italy   Italy and Austria have been called the "most extreme" examples of governmental intervention and an enlarged public sector in Western Europe.[13] For this reason, and also because the Italian technique of intervention through nationalization is rather different from the British, it is instructive to look briefly at the organization of public participation in Italian industry.

Italian governmental participation in industrial activity through ownership and control is extensive, and in structure it is quite unique. Rather than owning an industry outright, the Italians pursue a corporatist formula; they use the Istituto per la Ricostruzione Industriale (IRI)—a chartered corporation which owns something like 130 joint stock companies, ENI (National Hydrocarbon Agency), ENEL (National Electric Power Agency), and similar state corporations which are involved in many aspects of the Italian economy. IRI was originally set up in 1933 to conduct "bank salvage" operations—it was a governmental

---

[12] The latter statement suggests that incomes policies may be easier to utilize in market-oriented economies with substantial nationalized sectors. We shall consider these policies in a later chapter dealing with stabilization policies. Quotation from Allen, *Structure of Industry in Britain*, p. 133.

[13] Andrew Shonfield, *Modern Capitalism* (London: Oxford University Press, 1965), p. 177.

program to rescue the three largest banks from disaster as a result of the Great Depression. Today IRI is involved in many diverse areas, but not necessarily through 100 percent state ownership. The IRI owns outright the three biggest banks, the airlines, and radio and television operations and percentages (the most recent figures available) of the following industries: passenger shipping, 60 percent; tin production, 70 percent; pig-iron production, 94 percent; shipbuilding capacity, 89 percent; steel production, 59 percent; mercury production, 65 percent; cement production, 10 percent; auto production, 8 percent; cargo shipping lines, 8 percent; and a host of other facilities as well.[14] In short, it owns transport, and communication facilities. In 1962 IRI accounted for an estimated 8.49 percent of gross domestic fixed capital formation in Italy—a percentage that has been rising.[15]

What is IRI? It has been called "the most characteristic expression of the Italian system of government holdings" by an Italian banker.[16] He has made much of the distinction between nationalized, or state-owned, enterprise and the formula of the IRI, which although it owns stock in the corporations (not necessarily all stock), nevertheless has turned over corporation management to public (as opposed to private) enterprise. IRI lays down general policies, but the public enterprises through their boards and so on determine policy for their firms, based presumably on principles similar to those which guide private corporations. Glauco Della Porta comments that although IRI firms had access to a certain amount of capital directly from IRI, between 1948 and 1964 they provided over 90 percent of their own capital requirements through normal market transactions, although IRI and finance companies may have helped them get the loans. Almost 10 percent of these loans was provided by IRI's endowment fund, which is, of course, unique to the Italian system.[17]

How successful has IRI been? That it has significantly contributed to modernizing parts of Italian industry and to increasing its productivity seems clear. How free Italian industry is to develop under the Italian system of mixed capitalism as compared to, say, the U.S. system of mixed capitalism is not so clear. The Italians make much of the competition which state-controlled or financed corporations can provide for private firms in the same industry. We noted that this point has also been put forth in Britain as an argument for income stimulation, and it differs from both the neoliberal effort to achieve

[14] These figures are taken from Shonfield, *Modern Capitalism,* p. 186: Robson, *Nationalized Industry and Public Ownership,* p. 495; and Business International Corporation, *Investing, Licensing, and Trading Conditions Abroad* (hereafter *ILT*) (New York: Business International Corp., January 1970), p. 507. They generally refer to the situation as of the late 1950s or 1960s. When there were discrepancies among the sources the most recent data were included.

[15] Computed from data in M. V. Posner and S. J. Woolf, *Italian Public Enterprise* (Cambridge, Mass.: Harvard University Press, 1967), Table 9, p. 146.

[16] Glauco Della Porta, "Planning and Growth under a Mixed System: The Italian System," *Banco di Roma, Review of Economic Conditions in Italy* 19, No. 6, November 1965. Reprinted in Jan S. Prybyla, ed., *Comparative Economic Systems* (New York: Appleton-Century-Crofts, 1969), p. 183.

[17] Della Porta, in Prybyla, ed., *Comparative Economic Systems,* p. 184.

perfect competition[18] and the Marxist view that outright ownership and control of all industry by the state is the only appropriate economic system. How one evaluates the IRI depends in part, of course, on what one expects of it. It has been termed "perfectly compatible" with an open economy by Della Porta, who declared it moderately successful because at least on paper there is no room for conflict between allocation of resources by the firm and the pursuit of national targets, for which the IRI system was developed.[19] This view of IRI's success revolves largely around the conflict which it has presumably avoided. On the other hand, William Robson criticizes IRI because he concludes that it has retarded economic and social equality in Italy.[20] Robson seems to stress noneconomic criteria as much as economic, but concentration on the latter does not weaken the validity of his conclusion. Italy has had special problems—the economic imbalance resulting from the concentration of industrialization in the north, the attendant poverty and the need to improve economic conditions in the southern Mezzagiorno, inadequate resources in some industries and consequent dependence on foreign imports, and so on. Moreover, the record of Italian growth in output and productivity has in general matched or even surpassed that of many other European countries in the postwar period. (M. V. Posner and S. J. Woolf say that national industrial production increased 270 percent from 1948 to 1962—an increase which they term "a remarkable performance by world standards." During this same period IRI output alone rose by 349 percent.[21]) Nevertheless, Italy today particularly in the south remains one of the poorer countries in Europe.

The IRI formula is similar to that developed for the petrochemicals industry in 1953 primarily to develop the oil and natural gas potential of the Po Valley. ENI (the National Hydrocarbon Agency) today operates through five wholly owned subsidiaries, which in turn own shares (not necessarily majority) in other Italian and foreign companies in the petrochemicals field.[22]

ENEL (National Electric Power Agency), organized in 1962, completes the structure and is unlike IRI and ENI in that it runs the electric power industry directly. It controls 67 percent of the shares; the rest are in municipal or private hands.[23]

The extent of these diverse forms of public intervention in the Italian economy can be summarized as follows: in 1968 IRI, ENI, ENEL, and related organizations constituted almost 20 percent of all capital investment in the

18 Note, however, that this definition of *neoliberal* is in marked contrast to Walter Eucken's definition considered in the last chapter. Eucken said that neoliberal never meant an effort to achieve perfect competition, but always had a role for the state.

19 Della Porta, in Prybyla, ed., *Comparative Economic Systems*, pp. 184-85.

20 Robson, *Nationalized Industry and Public Ownership*, p. 483.

21 Posner and Woolf, *Italian Public Enterprise*, p. 113.

22 Full information concerning ENI's far-flung activities is available in *ENI, 1961* (Rome: ENI).

23 Business International Corporation, *ILT* (January 1970), p. 507.

country and over a quarter of the payrolls in industry, transportation, communications, credit, and insurance.[24]

These agencies have all played a role in Italian economic development, and the conclusions concerning IRI would apply to the entire corporatist system in Italy, although it must be said that ENI has played a significant part in developing Italian oil resources, in modernizing the industry's facilities, and in freeing the industry from undue dependency on foreign petroleum interests. It has thus perhaps been the most successful of Italian endeavors. In general, Posner and Woolf suggest that the Italians have not yet developed their system fully (they call the public sector "a machine without a driver"[25]). In effect Italy has a four-stage system in the public sector—the appropriate ministry, the institute (IRI, ENI, and so forth), the financial holding companies, and the operating enterprise itself. However, the potential exists for an effective system of public-private enterprise in Italy, provided that state holdings are tied into the Planning Committee more closely and are expanded to many parts of the economy rather than concentrated—as they are now—in the "commanding heights" of the economy (a system found in Germany as well).[26]

Other Market-Oriented Economies   The British case, because it is the best known, and the Italian, because it is in some ways unique, are appropriate examples of nationalization programs to receive special attention. Here we shall simply try to indicate briefly the extent to which nationalization (usually along the lines of the British model) has been carried out in other market-oriented economies.

In Belgium there is no trend of significant size toward nationalization. The state owns (wholly or in part) the railways, some electric utilities, the national airline *(Sabena),* and some public services. In Denmark the state owns the railroads, the airlines (domestic), the airports, and communication facilities.

In France some 180 enterprises are state-owned; together they control about one-sixth of all industrial activity. The state has a monopoly in electricity, gas, atomic energy, coal mining, telecommunications, tobacco, match manufacturing, and the railroads. It has significant control in other areas by virtue of its ownership of the three largest banks, the biggest advertising agency, and large production facilities in automobiles, airplanes, oil producing and refining facilities, tractor production, coal-based chemicals, and fertilizers and chemicals.

In Germany the Eucken version of neoliberalism has not been found incompatible with state ownership or control of nearly 400 business enterprises. They vary in size, and some are large holding companies which in turn control

[24] Ibid.
[25] Posner and Woolf, *Italian Public Enterprise,* p. 118.
[26] Ibid., pp. 128, 131.

many other corporations.[27] German industry, particularly basic industry, was largely nationalized under the Nazis, and efforts were made to denationalize under American influence after the war, although these efforts have been slow. We saw in Chapter 2 that German banking has reestablished its pre-American-influence structure. The structure of German industry has also tended to remain what it was before we tried to revise German industry in our image. Today the German state owns the railroads, the postal facilities, over 76 percent of aluminum production, 49 percent of iron ore production, 17 percent of hard coal production, 27 percent of shipbuilding, 45 percent of passenger car production, between 5 percent and 15 percent of coke production, pig-iron production, electric power generation, crude oil production, and crude steel production, as well as some others.[28] This government investment in German economy has appropriately been termed a "remarkable percentage" of total investment in view of the announced German attitude toward interventionism.[29]

In the Netherlands the state owns the railroads and the coal mines as well as 51 percent of KLM (the Royal Dutch Airlines), "up to 50 percent" of the company that produces and distributes natural gas, and one-third of the Royal Netherlands Blast Furnaces and Steel Works. It has "substantial" interests in four airports, in the central bank of the Netherlands and four other banks, in a shipping company, and in postal services and telecommunications. In addition, it participates in approximately thirty industrial and commercial companies. Public utilities are owned at the local or provincial level rather than at the national level.[30]

Roughly comparable nationalization is found in other market-oriented ecnomies, such as Norway, Sweden, and Japan.

What can we conclude from this brief survey of nationalization in market-oriented economies? The extent of nationalization varies considerably from country to country. Many countries involve the state in a portion of industry and let the public firm compete with private firms. It is worth noting that Joe Bain, in his study of differences among eight market-oriented economies, found that the use of governmentally owned companies as "yardsticks" (that is, as pacesetters for the industry) is far less common than is sometimes asserted and that often their real function is to implement the planning goals.[31]

[27] Frederick G. Reuss, *Fiscal Policy for Growth without Inflation: The German Experiment* (Baltimore Md.: The Johns Hopkins Press, 1963), p. 232. Reuss notes that German investment by the state is concentrated in "key industries."

[28] Estimates based on Reuss, *Fiscal Policy,* p. 233; or Business International Corporation, *ILT* (January 1970), p. 450.

[29] Reuss, *Fiscal Policy,* p. 229.

[30] These estimates based on Reuss, *Fiscal Policy,* p. 545.

[31] Joe S. Bain, *International Differences in Industrial Structure,* (New Haven, Conn.: Yale University Press, 1966), p. 121. He adds: "Selective government ownership of manufacturing enterprise, vertically integrated super-control groups, and policies condoning cartelization . . . all tend to distinguish [Japan, France, Italy, Sweden, and India] from the

The extent of nationalization in Germany suggests that in this aspect, at least, Andrew Shonfield is misleading in distinguishing Germany so sharply from other European market-oriented economies and lumping it with the United States. The U.S. is clearly unique in the limited extent to which it has employed nationalization. The postal system was nationalized until President Nixon set up the postal corporation, which is still a rather public corporation. The recently established company to run the railroad system, Amtrack, should not be a surprise; ours was the only railroad system left in private hands among major market-oriented economies. The U.S. utilizes the concept and structure of the public utility, with the attendant state regulatory commissions, as well as a multitude of national regulatory commissions (the Federal Trade Commission, the Security and Exchange Commission, the Interstate Commerce Commission, the Federal Power Commission, the Atomic Energy Commission, and so on). However, the assessment that "the laws of the U.S., the policies of the Administration and Congress, and public sentiment all oppose nationalization of private enterprise,"[32] seems appropriate and serves also to indicate the gulf which separates this country from other market-oriented economies in this regard.

Extent of the Public
Sector in Market-Oriented Economies

A crucial aspect of state intervention in economic affairs in all market-oriented economies today involves not direct government ownership or control over resource allocation through nationalization but the preempting of resources through taxation or other means in order to provide the goods and services we call collective consumption. Increasingly, as we saw in chapter 1, all economies— whether market-oriented or command—have been forced to realize that the price system cannot function effectively to allocate resources to those economic requirements which we need as an economy but which we do not "buy" as individuals. Government administration and national defense were, of course, the first such areas which market-oriented economies exempted from the allocative dictates of the market system—indeed, they did this from the start. Because it scarcely constitutes a means for distinguishing market-oriented economies from command economies, we say little about national defense in the public sector (although we shall note its magnitude in passing). However, a host of public goods and services—schools, highways, housing, pollution control,

---

United States, Canada, and the United Kingdom" (p. 121). We should point out that it is the other activities mentioned after "selective government ownership of manufacturing enterprise" which forms the basis for Bain's division of these countries into two groups, and that the role of government ownership is essentially similar in all the countries, with the single exception of the United States. Bain's sample did not include Germany.

[32] Business International Corporation, *ILT* (January 1970), p. 973.

resource conservation, and welfare programs such as unemployment insurance, health and accident insurance, old age and retirement security, and poverty relief programs—have gradually been added to the public sector. Governments tax incomes or borrow to provide these goods and services and others to the private sector. They are an increasingly important part of all market-oriented economies, including our own, and as such they should be assessed along with nationalized industries in analyzing the extent to which government has replaced the marketplace in basic resource allocation. We find that although there are still significant differences between the United States and other market-oriented economies in this area, in the last thirty-five years (since the New Deal) the U.S. economy has taken on some of the aspects of a "welfare state," so that the differences here are far less striking than in the degree of nationalization.

Table 3-1 provides a convenient point of departure for consideration of the extent of the public sector into areas not included in nationalization. The expenditures, output, and incomes earned in nationalized industry are not included in the government sector of the OECD national income accounts but appear in the appropriate sections relating to domestic fixed asset formation or

Table 3-1
Relationship of Government Expenditures to Gross
National Product, Eleven Market-Oriented
Economies, 1962[a]

	1962 GNP	Total government expenditures[b]	Government expenditures as a percent of GNP
	(Millions of current dollars)		
	(1)	(2)	(3)
United States	556,190	150,704	27.1%
Canada	37,332	10,396	27.8
Belgium	12,743	3,469	27.2
France	71,631	23,425	32.7
West Germany	88,700	26,241	30.0
Italy	39,509	11,111	28.1
Netherlands	13,133	3,880	29.5
Austria	7,190	1,982	27.6
Denmark	7,361	1,726	23.4
Sweden	14,543	4,390	30.2
United Kingdom	79,066	24,550	31.0

Source:
Bernard Mueller, *A Statistical Handbook of the North Atlantic Area* (New York: Twentieth Century Fund, 1965): column 1 from Table III-2, p. 66; column 2 from Table V-3, p. 121; column 3 computed by author.

Note:
[a] All foreign currencies converted into U.S. dollars at affixed 1962 exchange rates.
[b] All levels of government included.

production of consumer goods and services. Thus the official accounts include largely what we refer to as collective consumption in government expenditures. The most striking finding of Table 3-1 is that there is remarkably little variation now in the total percentages of gross national product represented by the government expenditures in market-oriented economies. While the absolute amounts of course grow all the time, the percentages are quite stable (although there is a slight increase in government expenditures as a percent of GNP over time). The United States (along with Denmark) not surprisingly has the smallest percentage, as befits a country that professes to believe in letting the market do the bulk of the resource allocation, but it is not very much smaller.[33] At the other end, the United Kingdom and France show the highest percentages of GNP accounted for by government expenditures.

Table 3-2 provides more detailed information on how these expenditures in the public sector are allocated to different purposes. Not surprisingly, even in this pre-Viet Nam period the United States spent a percent on national defense which was almost double the percent any other country spent. Bear in mind that the absolute amount represented by U.S. Government expenditures dwarfs those of any other country—indeed, U.S. expenditures were and still are greater by a considerable amount than those of all other governments shown in Table 3-2 combined. All this makes the 36 percent of its GNP that the U.S. was spending on defense in peacetime even more striking.

In order to grasp the significance of the information in Table 3-2 it should be noted that government expenditures for goods and services include expenditures on goods such as military equipment; government buildings and equipment, such as hospitals, schools, and so on; and expenditures on services such as law enforcement, the legal system, defense, and general administration. (The data of Table 3-2 cover federal, state, and local government in the United States and comparable subunits in other countries). Government transfers refer to the welfare programs involving payments for illness, old age, unemployment, dependency allowances, and other social services. Subsidies involve mostly payments to farmers, which we shall consider in the chapter devoted to agriculture.

In general, the figures speak for themselves. While the U.S. spends a far larger percentage of its total GNP on defense, its percentage expenditures for

[33] However, there is some reason to believe that Mueller's data, taken from OECD sources (which means, among other things, converting the monetary values for other countries into dollars at their official exchange rates) have somehow managed to give a slightly exaggerated picture of the relative size of the government sector in the United States. Mueller's estimates of GNP in the U.S. are close to those presented in *The Economic Report of the President,* which presents the official Department of Commerce data. However, according to the Department of Commerce data the percentage share of government purchases in GNP has risen from 20.8 percent in 1962 to 22.5 percent in 1970, bearing out our statement that the percentages change very slowly over time. We have kept Mueller's estimate in order to present comparable data on all countries in these tables. (See *Economic Report of the President* [Washington, D.C.: U.S. Government Printing Office, February, 1971], Table C-1, p. 197.)

Table 3-2
Government Current Expenditures, by Type of Transaction, 1962

Country	Total amount (in millions of dollars)	%	Goods and Services			Current Transfers		Interest on public debt	Current transfers to rest of world
			Total	Defense	Civil government	To households	Subsidies		
					(Percentage Distribution)				
United States	$150,704	100.0	71.5	36.3	35.2	20.4	1.1	5.3	1.7
Canada	10,396	100.0	53.3	16.4	36.9	32.5	2.6	11.3	0.3
Belgium	3,469	100.0	45.9	12.0	33.9	39.8	4.5	9.7	0.1
France	23,425	100.0	40.6	15.8	24.8	45.2	6.1	3.5	4.6
West Germany	26,241	100.0	50.4	14.3	36.1	42.6	2.5	1.9	2.6
Italy	11,111	100.0	52.6	9.7	42.9	35.4	5.6	5.9	0.5
Netherlands	3,880	100.0	50.1	14.1	36.0	35.9	3.2	9.3	1.5
Austria	1,982	100.0	47.2	4.0	43.2	42.2	7.4	3.1	0.1
Denmark	1,726	100.0	57.5	12.6	44.9	33.1	4.3	3.9	1.2
Sweden	4,390	100.0	60.2	15.5	44.7	29.5	4.4	5.3	0.6
United Kingdom	24,550	100.0	55.9	20.6	35.3	22.6	7.1	13.0	1.4

Source:
Bernard Mueller, *A Statistical Handbook of the North Atlantic Area* (New York: Twentieth Century Fund, 1965), Table V-3, p. 121.

other public goods and services is one of the lowest. Only France spends a smaller percentage for schools, highways, public housing, general government operations, and the like. (And this situation goes a long way toward explaining why the French had a serious political, social, and economic crisis in the spring of 1968. Grossly inadequate provision of these public goods and services breeds severe discontent among the people.) The British percentage is also smaller than most in this category.

The relative size of U.S. governmental expenditures on these public needs has been the root of much concern in recent years. When John Kenneth Galbraith wrote of "public squalor" in the midst of "private affluence," he had this in mind. He and others have been at the forefront of the drive to encourage the United States to devote more of its resources to schools, hospitals, housing, resource conservation, and pollution control (among other things) and to do it through taxation, so that in effect we would spend less on frequent automobile style changes and other expenditures which from some social points of view seem unnecessary. The Galbraithian argument runs into stiff opposition in this country because it suggests that some socially conscious elitist group knows what is "best" for the rest of us and can therefore justify interfering with the market. The reply, of course, is that even assuming we can collectively know what is "best," our politicoeconomic system is a clumsy instrument for reallocating resources to these public uses. (It can be done, of course, if Congress will raise taxes, a big *if* in a country in which Congress must get itself reelected and in which people often welcome public services only when *others* pay for them.[34])

Current transfers to households provide an idea of the extent of welfare programs in market-oriented economies. The U.S. figures represent the pre-Medicare period, but it is nevertheless clear that this is an area in which programs in the United States are far less extensive than they are in other countries. The *New York Times* estimated that 2.7 million women get assistance from the Aid to Families with Dependent Children program, which they termed "the vast federally assisted program at the heart of the American welfare problem."[35] The

---

[34] The Galbraithian position is set forth clearly in John Kenneth Galbraith, *The Affluent Society* (Boston: Houghton Mifflin Co., 1958). In connection with this argument that a reallocation of resources from the private sector to the public sector can be done in this country only with difficulty because of the opposition to higher taxes, it is interesting to note that, while we often hear comments about an incipient "taxpayers' revolt" in the United States if taxes are raised any higher, the United States in fact has one of the *lowest* tax rates in the Western world. The figures representing total taxes as a percent of GNP at market prices (based on averages of 1963 and 1964) for the countries we are considering are as follows: the U.S.,-24.5 percent; Canada,-26.6 percent; Belgium,-28.7 percent; France,-37.6 percent; West Germany,-34.8 percent; Italy,-29.7 percent; the Netherlands,-32.8 percent; Austria,-34.4 percent; Denmark,-28.6 percent; Sweden,-37.1 percent; the U.K.,-28.8 percent. Indeed, among all OECD countries only Ireland, Greece, Switzerland, Japan, Portugal, and Turkey indicated total taxes representing a lower percent of GNP than was the case for the U.S. (See OECD, *Border Tax Adjustments and Tax Structures* [Paris: OECD, 1968], Table 14, p. 196.)

[35] *New York Times,* July 4, 1971, p. 1, col. 8.

Table 3-3
The Structure of Social Security Benefits in Western
European Countries, 1960
(Percentages)

Country	Health and welfare[a]	Employment injuries	Family allowances[b]	Unemploy-ment	Pensions	War victims
United States	21.6	4.6	—	9.5	48.9	15.4
Canada	30.3	3.7	16.9	13.2	27.6	8.3
Belgium	35.1	4.6	17.6	7.1	29.8	5.8
France	24.8	5.4	28.6	0.2	33.0	8.0
West Germany	27.6	3.6	3.1	1.5	55.7	8.5
Italy	19.1	3.0	18.8	50.1		9.0
Netherlands	29.6	2.5	18.0	1.6	47.4	0.9
Austria	23.2	2.8	12.4	3.7	51.8	6.1
Denmark	36.2	3.1	5.8	4.6	49.9	0.4
Sweden	42.7	1.1	14.1	1.3	40.6	0.2
United Kingdom	49.7	1.9	5.2	1.3	38.3	3.6

Original source:
  ILO, *The Cost of Social Security 1958-1960* (Geneva, 1964).

Source:
  Secretariat of the Economic Commission for Europe, *Incomes in Post-War Europe: A Study of Policies, Growth, and Distribution* (Geneva: United Nations, 1967), Chapter 6, Table 6.9, p. 13.

Notes:
a. Including sickness insurance, public health, public assistance, school meals.
b. Includes household help, mothers' pensions, rent allowances.

program may be "vast" in absolute terms, but it is scarcely comparable to the outlays of European national governments. For the fiscal year ending June 30, 1970, the total amount expended in the public assistance program in the United States was $14,346,912,000. This represents 52.3 percent federal funds, 36.5 percent state funds, and 11.2 percent local funds. The total represents 6.4 percent of total government expenditures at all three levels during the calendar year 1970 and a scant 1.4 percent of 1970 GNP. This includes the public assistance programs for the aged, the blind, and the disabled, Aid to Families with Dependent Children, medical assistance generally and for the aged, and several other types of public assistance.[36]

---

[36] Department of Health, Education, and Welfare, National Center for Social Statistics, "Source of Funds Expended for Public Assistance Payments and for the Cost of Administration, Services, and Training, Fiscal Year Ended June 30, 1970," Report No. F-2 (FY 70) (Washington, D.C.: U.S. Government Printing Office, 1970). Care must be exercised in making international comparisons because many U.S. programs are federal, state, local, whereas many European programs are national only. In the text Tables 3-1, 3-2, and 3-3 refer (insofar as we can ascertain) to all levels of government.

Two other observations are worth special attention. First, despite the widespread attention given to the British National Health Service, the *total* British expenditures on welfare programs are only slightly larger than the United States figure. Second, it is clear that this is the area in which France has chosen to expand the public sector most rapidly. The French pay more than 80 percent of almost all medical expenses for their citizens and have made payments to families based on the number of children to encourage net population increases and so on.

Finally, we note in Table 3-2 that despite the attention paid to the large *absolute* sums which U.S. foreign aid has amounted to in many postwar years, compared to our gross national product our foreign aid has constituted a smaller percentage than that of either France or West Germany, and that many countries spend amounts which, in proportion to their GNPs, are not much different from that of the United States.

We should examine the welfare expenditures which constitute transfers to households in more detail. It is often said that the expansion of expenditures for welfare in the years since the Social Security system was first established during the Roosevelt New Deal period threatens to turn this country into a "welfare state." We have already seen that our total expenditures represent the smallest percentage of GNP of any of the market-oriented economies included in Table 3-2. Table 3-3 indicates that we in fact devote a larger percentage of welfare expenditures to unemployment insurance[37] than many other countries, and the same can be said for payments to veterans. However, the percentage devoted to health and welfare is one of the smallest. Moreover, the "family allowances"— common as a part of the total welfare program in other countries—are not utilized in the United States except at the state or local level. And the figures in Table 3-2, as indicated, refer only to federal family allowance plans. This kind of program was suggested for the U.S. by President Nixon early in his term of office.

Conclusions

We have considered the growth of the role played by the public sector in market-oriented economies by examining three ways in which it has been expanded: by direct participation in economic activity through nationalization of industry, by compulsory allocation or reallocation of resources (through taxation plus borrowing) to public goods and services, or by direct expenditures (again through taxes plus borrowing) by the government for welfare programs. All three forms of expansion have been used by market-oriented economies in the years since World War II.

---

[37] Many programs in the U.S.—and elsewhere—involve contributions to such programs by employers, employees, and the government. The figures in Table 3-3 clearly refer to governmental contributions to such schemes.

The United States is the major exception to the statement that significant parts of basic industry (sometimes referred to as the "commanding heights" of the economy) have been nationalized in a large number of market-oriented economies. Atomic energy, the postal system, the railroads—these are the major forays into nationalization which have been tried here (and now the postal system is in a "public corporation"). The U.S. also devotes a smaller part of economic resources to the health and welfare programs than do many other market-oriented economies, although the differences among market-oriented economies with respect to these expenditures are great. (Needless to say, the absolute amount spent in this category by the U.S. is the largest.) The U.S. also has one of the lowest percentages of GNP devoted to government expenditures on civilian goods and services—our relative expenditures for construction (housing, hospitals, schools, and so on), health, education, resource conservation, pollution control, and so forth are not high in comparison with other market-oriented economies. Only in defense expenditures does the U.S. have a vastly larger "public sector" than do other countries in the West.

Thus we can conclude that the private sector is still a more important aspect of the U.S. economy, proportionately, than it is in most other market-oriented economies. The U.S. has an important public sector, but the area of discretion left to market forces is still larger than is the case in most other industrialized economies, and in studying how mixed capitalism works, it is well to remember that other economies outside the communist world are far more mixed than that of the U.S.

It must be stressed that nationalized programs to achieve progress in the areas enumerated may not be the only appropriate or viable avenues down which modern economies can move. There are great virtues to fundamental reliance on a market mechanism, but no system—market or otherwise—can survive in the modern world unless the areas mentioned are provided for in some fashion. That would appear to be a fundamental lesson to be learned from the last thirty-five or forty years of economic history.

4

Income and Its Distribution
In Market-Oriented Economies

A basic aspect of the conventional description of a market system is that relative prices allocate not only goods and services but also the factors of production. The distribution of income is, of course, one of the by-products of the latter. Even in an ideal world in which all individuals would have the equality of opportunity implicitly guaranteed in our Declaration of Independence, in which technological development would be at the most advanced level everywhere, and in which educational systems would be developed to bring out fully the abilities of all of each country's citizens, one would expect differences in income among nations and among men. The total income generated in different countries would reflect differences in their endowment of natural resources; differences in personal income, depending on current economic factors only, might reflect individual differences in intelligence, educability, talents, and motivation.

Factors Affecting Income Levels

Resource Distribution and Technology   As we all know, the real world is far from ideal. If we look at per capita gross national product of some market-oriented economies (Table 4-1), we see immediately that the differences among countries reflect a great deal more than differences in real resources per capita. Differences in real resources are reflected to some extent—the United States, for example, had a per capita GNP of $3,520 in the late 1960s, whereas the Japanese figure was only $860. This comparison reveals at least partly the fact that Japan is a relatively small country (see column 3) with a population (in 1966) of 102.1 million people, whereas the United States, a far larger country, had a population of a little less than twice Japan's (203.1 million). The man-land ratio is very much in favor of the U.S. Part of the explanation for the great disparity in per capita GNPs noted in Table 4-1 thus involves these man-land ratios and the unequal distribution in resources per capita that they connote.

But not all the differences can be so easily explained. The United Kingdom, France, West Germany, and Italy have roughly equal populations and their geographic sizes are at least in the same range, but Italy's real per capita GNP is much lower than that of the other three countries. Japan's population is twice as large as the four countries just mentioned, but if we could make Japan's population comparable to those of its geographically larger West European counterparts (that is, cut the population in half), its real per capita GNP would be about $1,720. Thus, despite its greatly smaller size, its income per capita would compare favorably with that of the U.K., France, and West Germany, and would far exceed that of Italy.

Table 4-1
Population, Size, and Per Capita Gross National Product,
Twelve Market-Oriented Economies, Late 1960s

Country	Per capita GNP (in current dollars) (1)	Population (in millions) (2)	Size (in square miles) (3)
United States	$3,520	203.1	3,675,547
Sweden	2,270	8.0	173,666
Canada	2,240	21.3	3,851,809
Netherlands	1,930	12.9	13,961
Denmark	1,830	4.9	16,629
France	1,730	50.0	210,039
Norway	1,710	3.8	125,182
West Germany	1,700	58.1	95,959
Belgium	1,630	9.7	11,781
United Kingdom	1,620	55.7	94,214
Italy	1.030	53.1	116,316
Japan	860	102.1	142,772

Sources:
    Per capita GNP and population from *Distribution of Population and Wealth in the World* (New York: Committee for World Development and Disarmament, 218 East 18th Street). Population estimates originally from Population Reference Bureau. GNP data originally from International Bank for Reconstruction and Development, 1968. Geographic size from Edward B. Espinshade, Jr., *Goode's World Atlas*, 13th ed. (Chicago: Rand McNally, 1970), p. 189.

Part of these differences in per capita GNP have little to do with the size of the country. The U.K., West Germany, France, and Italy all have some natural resources, although many of Italy's resources are somewhat less abundant and what Italy does have has tended to be less developed than the resources of the other three countries. Many resources in all four of these countries are as well developed as those of Japan. The U.K. has a disproportionately large resource base for an iron and steel industry, which historically has been the bedrock of the British economy.

Resource Exploitation and the Role of Technology   The differences in per capita GNP cannot therefore be entirely explained by the fact that people and natural resources are not evenly spread over the face of the globe;[1] Some variations must be explained by differences in the degree to which resources and technology have been developed and exploited. For example, the role played by England throughout the nineteenth century was based on its ability to triumph over resource limitations by developing the most impressive technology of its time. The postwar "miracles" in West Germany and in Japan are not due only (or even primarily) to superior resources or favorable man-land ratios (Japan, we noted, has a large population for its size). But both these countries have adopted modern technology and have set about to exploit their resources with great zeal. Thus the Japanese growth rate is one of the highest in the world.

To be a "developed country," which all the market-oriented economies under review definitely are, means in the final analysis to develop one's resources by utilizing existing technology as well as by contributing to the advance of technology. These economies have all been part of this process, but in varying degrees, and the variations can account for differences in GNP levels among countries with similar resource endowment and comparable populations. Some differences in income levels may be explained, therefore, by differences in economic efficiency.

Factors Affecting Income Distribution

Inequality in the Distribution of Wealth   Wealth (all assets which can produce income) is highly unevenly distributed throughout Western populations. James Meade has commented, "An unequal distribution of property means an unequal distribution of power and status even if it is prevented from causing too unequal a distribution of income."[2] (It can only be prevented from so affecting

---

[1] We could drive this point home by noting that the USSR (the major command economy) has an enormous land mass, is generously endowed with resources, and has a population of only 241.0 million people. Nonetheless, its real per capita GNP in 1966 was only $890. (Source same as for Table 4-1.)

[2] James E. Meade, "Determinants of Inequality in a Property-Owning Democracy," in Edward C. Budd, Ed. *Inequality and Poverty* (New York: W. W. Norton and Co., 1967), p. 105.

income distribution by a progressive income tax, but as we shall see later in this chapter, that is rarely, if ever, the case.) Figures reflecting the distribution of wealth are hard to find. Robert Lampmann studied this question for the United States and discovered that the top 1 percent in the United States held about 26 percent of all personal wealth in 1956, compared to 31.6 percent in 1922. Thus there is a slight tendency toward equalization of wealth holding, but it is still concentrated and will undoubtedly remain so.[3] With the possible exception of the Scandinavian countries, the distribution of wealth is at least as unequal in other market-oriented economies as it is in the United States, though we have little evidence to prove this.[4] What is significant for our purposes is that wealth distribution is invariably more unequal than income distribution.

Distribution of Innate Human Characteristics   Wealth is not the only factor affecting the distribution of income, however. Most physical, mental, and motivational traits are distributed among the population according to what statisticians call a normal distribution curve (See Figure 4-1). Such a curve has a number of important characteristics, but for our purposes it will suffice to note that the bulk of the population falls in the middle of the distribution (the average or mean) and that the rest of the population is distributed symmetrically around this central concentration. There are thus as few idiots as there are geniuses in the population, and one would find the same percentage of lazy fellows and hard-driving go-getters.

In a price-determined system we would expect income distribution to follow the distribution of mental, physical, and motivational traits, but in all the market-oriented economies the distribution of income does not follow the normal distribution curve. Instead, the income distribution is highly unequal, and highly divergent from the normal distribution (see Figure 4-1). Why is this? We cannot fall back on the unequal distribution of resources or technology in various countries, because this explains only low *levels* of total or per capita income. And the unequal distribution of wealth explains only part of the unequal distribution of income.

Barriers to Equal Opportunity to Develop Human Economic Potential
Some of the differences between the normal distribution curve and the income distribution curve in Figure 4-1 can be explained only by other factors—often

---

[3] Robert J. Lampmann, *The Share of Top Wealth Holders in National Wealth*, National Bureau of Economic Research (Princeton, N.J.: Princeton University Press, 1962), Tables 93 and 94. Reprinted in Budd, ed., *Inequality and Poverty*, p. 84.

[4] Paul A. Samuelson has suggested that while many market-oriented economies have distributions in income which are basically not very different from that in the U.S., the distribution of wealth in a country like the U.K. is a good deal more concentrated in a relatively small part of the population. In pre-industrial economies the inequality in the distribution of wealth is often even more marked. (See Samuelson, *Economics*, 8th Ed. [New York: McGraw-Hill Book Co. 1970], p. 112.)

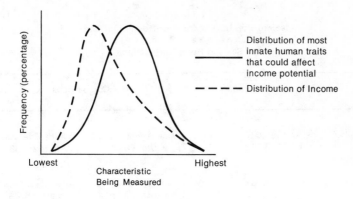

Figure 4-1. Distribution of Incomes and a Normal Distribution Curve.

noneconomic factors that nevertheless have profound economic consequences. In all the countries considered in Table 4-1 there are differences in the openness of the society, in access to first-rate education, and the myriad cultural and social factors that cause differences in the degree to which potential manpower development is realized.

The concentration of wealth in relatively few hands is partly a reflection of class and status, and the class lines in most European countries, as well as Japan, have been hardened for many centuries. (Certainly from this perspective the United States has been an open society.) Educational and other opportunities which affect earning power are far from equal in all these countries. All Americans do not have equal potential access to Harvard or Yale or Englishmen to Cambridge or Oxford or Frenchmen to the Sorbonne, or the Ecole Polytechnique. Discrimination on the basis of race, religion, and sex adds to the impact of wealth and class in the creation of inequality in opportunity. All these factors would make the distribution of income unequal even if resources and technology were evenly distributed (which they are not), because some individuals are not given equal opportunity to develop their income earning potential.

Let us take an example from the United States. In 1968 the median family income was $5,359 for black families and $8,936 for white families. This means that black income was only 60 percent of white income.[5] There are also

---

[5] One can approximate the international impact of differences in resources and wealth, discussed earlier, by looking at regional differences in the U.S. The median family incomes in the West were $7,706 for blacks and $9,462 for the whites, whereas in the resource-poor and relatively underdeveloped South the comparable figures were $4,278 for blacks and $7,963 for whites. So clearly the resources and technology labor has to work with affect the laborer's income, but that racial discrimination in many ways is a factor as well—the topic of this section—is clear both from the national figures and from the fact that in each

Table 4-2
Median 1968 Income for Year-Round Full-Time
Workers 14 Years Old and Over,
by Sex and Race, United States

	Median incomes	Comparisons	
Males			
White	$8,047	Male: % black to	White: % female
Black	5,518	white: 68.6%	to male: 58.2%
Females			
White	4,687	Female: % black to	Black: % female to
Black	3,625	white: 77.3%	male: 65.7%

Source:
    U.S. Bureau of the Census, *Current Population Reports,* Series P-60, No. 69, April 6, 1970. "Income Youth Rates in 1939 to 1968 for Persons By Occupation and Industry Groups, for the United States," p. 81.

differences between the median income earned by women workers and that earned by men workers. One can combine these factors as is done in Table 4-2 and see the effect of both kinds of discrimination for 1968. Black females clearly have the lowest median income, while white males have the highest. Many factors contribute to these differences. Undoubtedly there are differences in productivity, but these are probably explained not by differences in innate abilities but rather in the discriminatory way in which individuals are given access to the home life, education, nutrition, cultural stimuli, and all the countless other factors which enable an individual to achieve his full potential for productivity in society.[6]

region of the country, blacks' median family income is lower that of whites. (Data from U.S. Department of Labor, Bureau of Labor Statistics, *The Social and Economic Status of Negroes in the United States, 1969,* Report No. 375; and Bureau of the Census, *Current Population Reports,* Series p-23, No. 29, p. 15.)

  [6] There have been studies designed to correlate the basic intelligence, the scholastic attainment, and the physical characteristics of identical twins reared together and those reared apart, of nonidentical twins reared together, of siblings reared together and apart, and of unrelated children reared together. The measures themselves may well be faulty, but there is considerable support for the hypothesis that basic intelligence may well be a matter of heredity—identical twins reared together have a high correlation in their basic intelligence, whereas unrelated children reared together have a relatively low correlation in their basic intelligence. Correlation in scholastic attainment, which is a better measure of what a person has managed to accomplish with his basic intelligence, is much higher for identical twins reared together than for those reared apart and likewise for siblings. It is actually somewhat higher in one study for unrelated children reared together than it is for siblings reared apart. The studies, carried out by C. Burt and J. Conway and by Newman, Freeman, and Holzinger, are reported in Harold F. Lydall, *The Structure of Earnings* (London: Oxford at the Clarendon Press, 1968), Table 4.1, p. 74. They were originally summarized in an article by C. Burt, "The Evidence for the Concept of Intelligence," *British Journal of Educational Psychology* 25: 158-77.

Other market-oriented economies might not have the severe problem of racial discrimination which faces the United States, but they do have sexual discrimination: the Women's Liberation movement is not confined to this country. Moreover, class and caste lines, as we have noted, are more rigid in European countries, and they affect the distribution of income in those countries in similar ways. In short, all economies appear to have erected barriers which would not exist in an ideal economic world. These barriers give differential opportunities for different groups to develop the innate abilities which would allow them to make their optimal contribution to economic productivity. They not only keep down the *levels* of income and output but are a significant factor in skewing the *distribution* of income away from the "normal."

How Unequal Is Income
Distribution In Market-Oriented Economies?

Let us now consider briefly exactly how unequally income is distributed in market-oriented economies. The most common method for examining the inequality in the distribution of income is to employ what is known as a Lorenz curve—a simple graphic device which indicates the deviation from equality in any income distribution. In Figure 4-2 we have shown two Lorenz curves—one for Britain and one for France in the 1960s. If incomes were distributed equally, twenty percent of the population would receive twenty percent of the income, forty percent would receive forty percent of the income and so on. The deviation for each twenty percent (called quintiles) from twenty percent of income is a measure of the inequality in income distribution.[7]

The distribution of income is not radically different from one market-oriented economy to another.[8] Table 4-3 shows the percent distribution of income for fifths of the population in nine market-oriented economies for which data were available. All data (except for Denmark) are before tax and refer, with two exceptions, to the early 1960s. In Figure 4-2 we show the Lorenz curve for

[7] It is important to bear in mind that the use of a Lorenz curve does not suggest that equality in income distribution is necessarily "good" or that adopting policies to achieve equality are at all recommended. Equality is simply a convenient point from which to compare income distributions. Remember that we have already seen that those physical, mental, and motivational traits which are measurable and which we think would affect income earning potential are *not equally* but *normally* distributed, and the resources which individuals or countries have to work with are highly *unequally* distributed, accounting partly for differences in *levels* of national income among countries.

[8] It is not even very equally distributed in command economies, where there is some doubt about whether it is distributed according to either ability or need. The former criterion is the Marxist criterion for contributing to output, the latter the conventional Marxist distribution criterion. Income distribution in a country like the Soviet Union would appear to have some elements of distribution by power, class, status, etc., just as do the distributions in market-oriented economies.

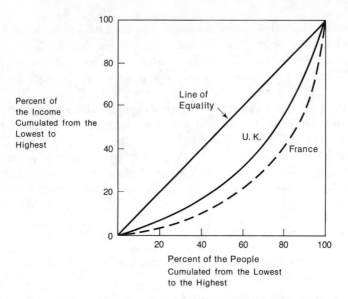

Figure 4-2. Percent of Gross Personal Income Received by Each Fifth of the People in the United Kingdom and France, Early 1960s.

the "most unequal" country (France) and for one of the "most equal" countries (the U.K.) to give the reader some idea of the differences in income distribution among market-oriented economies. The French distribution reflects strongly the hardened class lines in that country; indeed, one is tempted to conclude that class discrimination in France has a greater effect on income distribution than racial discrimination has in the United States, but such conclusions should not be attempted without more information about both the determinants of income distribution and the measures themselves. (Sweden's distribution is quite similar to Britain's.) One conclusion which is probably fairly safe is that the *differences* in inequality in income distribution are remarkably small among market-oriented economies.

H. F. Lydall has attempted to rank 25 countries by the degree of "dispersion" in their distribution of income, which is a very rough effort to measure the degree to which income distribution is unequal. He ranks the countries we are concerned with in the following order, from "most equal" to "most unequal" (the dates in parenthesis indicate the year for which he had data): first, Denmark (1956); second the United Kingdom (1960-61); third, Sweden (1959); fourth, West Germany (1957); fifth, Canada (1960-61); sixth, Belgium (1964); seventh, United States (1959); eighth, Austria (1957); ninth, the Netherlands (1959); tenth, France (1963); eleventh, Japan (1955). Because Lydall feels his estimates are quite crude, he suggests that it is probably safer to view the inequality in income distribution for groups of countries. Interestingly, when he does this none of the countries under our study appears in either the most equal or the most unequal distribution group. In the second most equal

Table 4-3
Percent of Gross Personal Income Received by Each Fifth
of People, Ten Market-Oriented Economies

	U.K.		West Ger.		Netherlands		Denmark	
	%	Cum.	%	Cum.	%	Cum.	%	Cum.
Lowest fifth	5.1	5.1	5.3	5.3	4.0	4.0	5.0	5.0
Second	10.2	15.1	10.1	15.4	10.0	14.0	10.8	15.8
Third	16.6	31.9	13.2	29.1	16.0	30.0	16.8	32.6
Fourth	23.9	55.8	18.0	47.1	21.6	51.6	24.2	56.8
Highest Fifth	44.2	100.0	52.9	100.0	48.4	100.0	43.2	100.0
	1964		*1964*		*1962*		*1963*	

	Sweden		France		U.S.		Canada	Italy	Japan
	%	Cum.	%	Cum.	%	Cum.	%	%	%
Lowest fifth	4.4	4.4	1.9	1.9	4.6	4.6	4.3	5.5	7.5
Second	9.6	14.0	7.6	9.5	10.9	15.5	–	–	–
Third	17.4	31.4	14.0	23.5	16.3	31.8	–	–	–
Fourth	24.6	56.0	22.8	46.3	22.7	54.5	–	–	–
Highest Fifth	44.0	100.0	53.7	100.0	45.5	100.0	36.4	48.4	39.4
	1963		*1962*		*1962*		*1955*	*1948*	*1954*

Sources:
    For all countries except the United States, Canada, Italy, and Japan data are from United Nations, *Incomes in Post-War Europe: A Study of Policies, Growth, and Distribution* (Geneva: United Nations, 1967).
    The figures represent the number of taxpayers, except for France, where unit is the household. (The non-French figures therefore understate the lowest fifth: persons with incomes too low to pay taxes are excluded.) Danish figures are after-tax figures and hence indicate greater equality (to the extent that the tax system is progressive) than would be the case if the data were comparable to that of the other countries. For details of data and calculations see original source.
    For the United States the data are from Edward C. Budd, ed., *Inequality and Poverty* (New York: W. W. Norton & Co., 1967), Table 1, p. xiii. They refer to families.
    For Japan, Canada, and Italy the data are unfortunately much older and are taken from Irving B. Kravis, *The Structure of Income* (Philadelphia: University of Pennsylvania Press, 1962), Table 7.2, pp. 245-46.
    Italian data refer to families and unattached individuals. The Canadian data refer to the aggregate non-farm distribution. The Japanese data refer to urban families of two or more and exclude families headed by the self-employed.

income distribution group he places the first eight countries on the list just presented. The Netherlands is in the third group, and France and Japan are in the fourth (next to the most unequal) group.[9]

[9] He puts Czechoslovakia, New Zealand, Hungary, and Australia (two command economies, two mostly nonindustrialized market economies) ahead of Denmark in the "most equal" in his group of 25 countries, and in the "most unequal" group in income distribution he places Brazil, Chile, India, Ceylon, and Mexico (all below Japan)—hardly the leading "capitalist" economies in the world. (See Lydall, *The Structure of Earnings*, Table 5.5 and 5.6, pp. 153, 156.)

This classification is of interest in connection with our discussion in Chapter 2 of the goals of economic policy in market-oriented economies. We listed Austria, the Netherlands, Belgium, Denmark, and Spain as countries which have adopted more equality in the distribution of income as an explicit goal. All of these countries are in Lydall's second most equal group, the same group in which one finds the U.K. and the U.S.

Table 4-4
Percent Distribution of Family Personal Income,
by Fifths, U.S., 1929 and 1967

Fifth	1929	1967
Lowest	3.5%	5%
Second	9.0	12
Third	13.8	18
Fourth	19.3	24
Highest	54.4	41
	100.0	100

Sources:
1929 data from Budd, *Inequality and Poverty,* Table 1, p. xii.
1967 data from Samuelson, *Economics,* 8th ed., p. 111.

Are Income Distributions Becoming More Unequal?

Over the years there has been some tendency for incomes to move toward greater equality in the United States. The latest data for quintile distribution in this country is for 1967 and can be compared to 1929 as shown in Table 4-4. The differences are noticeable, although not spectacular. The biggest change has occurred in the top 5 percent, which now gets about 20 percent of the income compared to 30 percent in 1929. Evidence concerning changes in other market-oriented economies is scanty and does not cover as long a period as that for the United States.

Developing uniform and consistent methods for measuring the distribution of income to facilitate international comparisons has lagged far behind comparable developments in, for example, the field of national income accounting. The problems involved in international comparisons have been particularly noted by the United Nations study from which most of the data in Table 4-3 were obtained.[10] Moreover, what comparisons they have managed to

[10] United Nations, *Incomes in Post-War Europe* (Geneva: United Nations, 1967), Chapter 6, p. 14.

make are mostly between the 1950s and the 1960s—too short a period to be very significant. Nonetheless, what information there is seems to suggest that inequality in income distribution has been clearly reduced "only in Norway." It has remained unchanged, or possibly been very slightly reduced, in the U.K., the Netherlands, and Denmark. West Germany is difficult to interpret in the view of the U.N. study, although they feel there was an early tendency for income inequality to be reduced, a tendency which had "practically ceased" in the 1960s, however.[11] There was some decrease in inequality, nonetheless, between the mid-1950s and the mid-1960s. Inequality in income distribution actually became greater in Finland, Sweden, and France. In almost all cases where there were significant changes, the middle income groups appear to have been the gainers. The U.N. study concludes, "The poor have become poorer in relation to the middle groups, whether the rich have become, by the same measure, richer or not."[12] This suggests that the pattern of redistribution in market-oriented economies outside the United States has not been a transfer from the top income groups to the other income groups, as has been the case here.

Finally, one subject of continuing interest is the comparison of the changes in income distribution in market-oriented economies with those in socialist or command economies. Unfortunately it is extremely difficult to get reliable data with which to make these comparisons. However, a recent study has considered the available data for the U.K., Poland, the U.S., and the USSR. The general conclusion was that all four had moved toward greater equality in the distribution of income in the past twenty years. Moreover, the distribution of income was closer to equality in Poland than in the U.K., which in turn was closer to equality than the U.S. The authors found that the greatest movement toward equality between 1946 and 1966 occurred in the Soviet Union, although the distribution of income in that country still exhibited inequalities which they termed "surprising." In the final analysis, the greatest difference between capitalist and socialist distributions was the fact that the capitalist distributions revealed a small percentage of income recipients who are very rich in comparison to the highest incomes received under socialist systems.[13]

---

[11] Ibid., p. 17.

[12] Ibid.

[13] Techniques of comparison include the use of Lorenz curves, Gini ratios, and similar methods customarily used to compare income distributions in the West. See the two-part article by P. J. D. Wiles and Stefan Markowski, "Income Distribution under Communism and Capitalism," *Soviet Studies* 22, Issue 3 (January 1971); 344-69, and Issue 4 (April 1971); 487-511. The conclusions above are from p. 344. Lydall, in his *Structure of Earnings*, previously cited in connection with the relative dispersion of income in twenty-five countries, includes the United Kingdom (1960-61), Poland (1960), and the U.S. (1959) and in this order, although he finds the differences small—they are all in the middle of his rank order, and in his "second most equal" group (Tables 5.5 and 5.6, pp. 153, 156).

Effect of Taxation on Income Distribution

Reasonably reliable information on the effects national tax systems have on the distribution of income is extremely sketchy and also now somewhat dated. Table 4-5 presents information for the U.S. and the U.K. and suggests that income taxes have a greater impact toward equality on the British distribution of income than is the case in the United States. In the U.S. the tax *rates* tend to be progressive, but the system of exemptions and the treatment of nonwage income are both regressive, which nullifies a good deal of the progressivity in basic rates. It has been suggested that in general the U.K. and the Netherlands have the most progressive tax programs in Western Europe. Norway and Sweden have fairly comparable rates in the highest income groups, but their tax rates fall much more rapidly in lower income groups, thus affecting the total distribution relatively less. West Germany has a less progressive tax system than the four countries just mentioned, and Denmark has the least progressive of all.[14] It seems fair to conclude that whatever the announced goals, the tax systems of market-oriented economies have only modest effects on the distribution of income.

Conclusions

We have seen that the vagaries of nature are such that one would not expect equal per capita national income or output even among the industrialized market-oriented economies we are primarily concerned with in this book. As a group they are the occupants of land as resource-laden per capita as any on the earth. This, along with their relatively small populations, their technology, and their ability to exploit it, goes a long way toward explaining why they are among the richest countries in the world, both in absolute levels and in per capita GNP. They probably have more equal income distributions than underdeveloped countries, where the barriers class and caste create are even more rigid. In general, the distribution of income is fairly similar among the countries we have considered, and in all of them it deviates from what a normal distribution curve might lead us to expect. These deviations can be explained in part by the barriers to equal opportunities for developing full individual productive potential. As such they are economically important because they keep aggregate levels of output as well as growth rates (to be considered in a later chapter) below the optimum. As a society we might wish to choose more leisure rather than more goods and services, but such a choice would be deliberate.

[14] These conclusions were reached by the U.N. study, *Incomes in Post-War Europe,* Chapter 6, p. 24.

Table 4-5
Percent of Total Income Received by Lowest and Highest
Fifth of Spending Units, Before and After
Taxes, Two Market-Oriented Economies

	Lowest fifth		Highest fifth		
	Before tax	After tax	Before tax	After tax	Year
United Kingdom	5.0	6.0	44.0	40.0	1951-52
United States	4.9	5.3	44.0	41.8	1950

Source:
Irving, R. Kravis, *The Structure of Income* (Philadelphia: University of Pennsylvania Press, 1962), pp. 245 and 250.

We find little relationship between income inequality and whether market-oriented economies plan or do not plan or nationalize or do not nationalize their basic industry. (Compare the U.K., West Germany, France, and the U.S., for example.) As yet there is little to suggest that the countries which have announced greater equality in income distribution as a major economic goal (Austria, Belgium, Denmark, the Netherlands) have made significant headway. Both Denmark and the Netherlands have slightly more equal distributions in the 1960s than in the 1950s, but the differences were scarcely significant. For some countries no data exist.

Finally, it is well to remember that most of the figures cited in this chapter probably understate the percent of the population in the lowest income group. To the extent that we have had to use tax information this is clearly the case. Even where information on families or spending units was available, it is not certain that all welfare cases, considered at the end of Chapter 3, would be included. In this connection it is useful to remember that even in the United States, the richest country in the world, many people live in abject poverty. Michael Harrington, whose book *The Other America* is widely credited with having been a major factor in launching President Kennedy's war on poverty, has written, "Somewhere between 20 and 25 percent of the American people are poor. They have inadequate housing, medicine, food, and opportunity. From my point of view, they number between 40,000,000 and 50,000,000 human beings."[15]

Herein lies the crucial link between our discussion of welfare programs in Chapter 3, and the lower income groups considered in this chapter. Other factors which many feel significantly affect the distribution of income are the degree to which monopolies or cartels are present in the industrial sector and the significance of labor organizations. Many argue that these concentrations of

[15] Michael Harrington, *The Other America* (Baltimore, Md.: Penguin Books, 1962), p. 178.

economic power affect inequalities in both opportunities and the emergent income distribution. Industrial structure generally and monopolistic elements and programs to control them in particular are the subject of the next chapter. Labor organizations are considered in the following chapter.

5

Industrial Organization—Patterns of Structure, Conduct, and Control

A vast gulf separates purely competitive economies from market-oriented economies or capitalist economies from mixed capitalist economies. "The classical market of the textbooks in which firms struggle with one another and disregard any possible effect that their actions may have on the market as a whole has become more remote than ever."[1] These changes are what Joan Robinson, the well-known English economist, had in mind when she commented that Adam Smith's Invisible Hand had become the Paralyzed Hand. An important theme we are trying to develop in this book is that *all* modern market-oriented economies have been forced to cope with these changes and that the diverse ways in which they have coped have created many different patterns. We have already seen some of the differences in the varying degrees and ways in which the market itself has been narrowed through nationalization, which in effect allows the state to perform a significant part of the allocative and distributive function originally conceived of as the appropriate role of the free market. All the states use prices, but they are not set as they would be in a free private enterprise economy; nor do the economic consequences of the price-determination process necessarily connote what they were presumed to signify in the simple world of Adam Smith.

---

[1] Andrew Shonfield, *Modern Capitalism* (London: Oxford University Press, 1965), p. 66.

In this chapter we are not concerned with nationalized sectors per se, nor shall we be studying the American solution to the problem of the "natural monopoly," which is to declare such industries public utilities and subject them to governmental regulation (at the federal, state, or local level), as we saw in Chapter 3. Rather, we shall look at the sector still literally oriented toward the market and consider the diverse ways in which Western economies have coped with the changes which time has forced on the simple textbook marketplace. (It is by now a commonplace to note that the differences between a perfectly competitive economy and the mixed capitalist economy we are here calling market-oriented are at least as great as those between market-oriented and command economies.[2])

What Happened to Laissez Faire and Why

In all the countries of the Western World public policy has had to come to grips with the same general set of factors, producing a quantitative divergence of market operations away from the competitive norm so large that it has often been viewed as qualitative as well. These factors are a result of the absolute *size* of producing units and the *extent of the market* in which they operate. Ironically, the factors have probably been most pronounced in the United States because of its advanced industrial development, but in many ways it adheres in principle as well as in practice to the tenets of competitive market policy to a larger extent than any other major economy.

Carl Kaysen and Donald F. Turner, in the well-known book *Antitrust Policy,* expressed the customary American view in these words:

> We assume that the sectors of the economy in which government monopoly, or private monopoly controlled in more or less detail by government (to which antitrust policy is not applicable) are limited, and are not growing rapidly relative to the rest of the economy.[3]

Other market-oriented economies either view the government-owned and/or controlled sectors as necessarily more extensive than we do, or as we shall see in this chapter, they tend to view public policy toward big business as having more limited objectives in *principle* as well as in *fact.*

---

[2] However, it is only fair to note as well that the differences between an orthodox Marxist economy and a modern command economy such as one finds in China or the Soviet Union are extremely large also, whether or not one subscribes to the convergence theory briefly touched on at the end of Chapter 1.

[3] Carl Kaysen and Donald F. Turner, *Antitrust Policy* (Cambridge, Mass.: Harvard University Press, 1959), pp. 3-4.

Technology and the Economies of Large-Scale Production   All agree that modern technology, particularly in the manufacturing sector of a modern economy, requires that the producing units be large if production is to be efficient and modern technology used. How large? The answer will vary from industry to industry, depending on the most advanced technology in each, but two conclusions are probably safe. In almost all plants in any industrialized economy, the absolute size required for efficiency will be greater, relative to the extent of the market, than would be permissible in a world of textbook perfect competition, which would have a large enough number of buyers and sellers of essentially the same product so that no single buyer or seller could affect market prices by his own actions. This condition cannot be met in the United States economy in most sectors in which the products are produced by companies familiar by name in every household. It is not true in steel, in automobiles, in cigarettes, in meat processing, in tin cans, in rubber tires, in mail-order retail sales, in national food processing and distribution, and so on. The same conclusion is probably valid in comparable areas of other market-oriented economies. The second conclusion is that large as these economies of scale are, there are undoubtedly many plants in the U.S.—and probably in other economies as well—which are a good deal larger than production technology alone might require.

The Drive to Bigness: Nontechnological Factors   This leads to the complex question. Why, except for production efficiency, do *firms* get big? Multiplant firms allow managerial efficiencies: there are potential efficiencies in raw materials purchased and in the establishment of distribution systems and dealerships, and there is often access to more favorable terms at bank and other credit facilities. These advantages of large size are undoubtedly present in all industrial economies utilizing modern technology and managerial systems, but they vary in extent among production units and are also probably sufficiently limited so that our second conclusion is probably valid with respect not only to plant size but also to firm size. Why then do plants and firms grow larger than their "optimal" size?

Two reasons seem of paramount importance. The first is the classic motive behind any economic system based on entrepreneural decision-making—the quest for maximum profits. While economic literature, particularly in the past few decades, has been full of discussions of the extent and character of the modern profit motive, it seems clear that in many production areas in market-oriented economies, firms in a position to reap "monopoly profits" by increasing market control will do so. Questions can be raised about whether firms seek maximum long-run profits or short-run profits, about whether they attempt to determine the absolute maximum profit for each market period or simply settle for tacking a healthy percentage of their production costs on as profits, and so forth. But that firms seek bigness (relative to the extent of the market) in order to have control—primarily, if not exclusively—over price and hence profit rates seems clear.

The second reason firms seek bigness is more complicated but is related to the first factor. As a rough generalization it seems fair to say that all economic units created by man exhibit an urge to grow as a way to avoid decay. This "onward and upward" aspect to the psychology of any economy, including those based on private entrepreneurial decision-making, was well understood by Austrian economist Joseph Schumpeter, who wrote in *Capitalism, Socialism and Democracy,*

> Economists ... think that they have understood what there is to understand if they interpret the behavior of ... firms by means of the principle of maximizing profits. ... The problem that is ... being visualized is how capitalism administers existing structures, whereas the relevant problem is how it creates and destroys them.
>
> In capitalist reality as distinguished from its textbook picture it is not that kind of competition which counts but the competition from the new commodity, the new technology, the new source of supply, the new type of organization (the largest-scale unit of control, for instance). ... [4]

The drive for bigness, growth, and control is an inherent part of the motive force that makes an enterprise system function. In the simple world of Adam Smith the Invisible Hand may have functioned to produce public good out of private self-gratification; in no modern economy could this possibly be the case. So market-oriented economies require public regulation and control, and as we have already seen, they necessarily limit the scope of the market even in that most market-conscious of all market economies—our own.

Accordingly, our task here is (1) to ask how big firms absolutely are in market-oriented economies, (2) to consider size in relation to efficiency, (3) to relate bigness to the extent of the market—that is, to consider how "concentrated" modern market-oriented economies are, (4) to consider the public policy which various countries have adopted along the lines of our antitrust laws, and (5) to appraise the results of these efforts.

How Big Are Firms in Market-Oriented Economies?

One can measure size by a number of criteria. Economists have employed total assets (or net assets), total volume of annual sales, net income of a firm, the number of employees, value added to total industry income or output, and so

---

[4] Joseph A. Schumpeter, *Capitalism, Socialism, and Democracy,* 2nd ed. (New York: Harper and Brothers, Publishers, 1947), p. 84.

on. Each of these measures (and there are others as well) tells us something different. We shall use total sales by the largest firms to get an initial idea of the absolute size of industrial firms in various countries, because these data are readily available. Table 5-1 indicates the total sales by the five biggest (and where possible the ten biggest) firms in eleven market-oriented economies in 1968. Although there are a number of problems in so simple a measure, the results seem clear. Firm size in the United States is much larger than in any other market-oriented economy; British firms are the only ones that are even close to the U.S. norm.[5] If one adds the total of all the top ten firms (or as many firms as are included in the list of 200 largest non-U.S. industrial firms for those countries with fewer than ten on the list), one finds that the 1968 total sales for all non-U.S. top ten firms was $109,977,761,000, compared to 1969 sales of $99,595,312 for the top ten U.S. firms. More precise figures would not seriously affect the order of magnitude on which the rankings for these eleven countries is based. If one included consideration of *all* firms on the list of 200 non-U.S. firms, possibly somewhat greater importance would be given to Japan, West Germany, France, and Canada (in that order) than is suggested by the ranking in Table 5-1.

Another way to note the disparity between firm size in the United States and in other market-oriented economies is to compare the single largest non-U.S. firm (by sales), which is the Royal Dutch Shell group (jointly owned by Dutch and British interests) to U.S. firms. Royal Dutch Shell had 1968 sales of $9,215,772,000. General Motors and Standard Oil of New Jersey were both larger, the former by more than two and one-half times. The largest non-U.S. firm (by sales) wholly owned by one country was British Petroleum (sales were $3,260,160,000 in 1968), and at least fifteen U.S. firms equaled or surpassed this level. That size is related to technology is shown by the fact that the same industries appear on the list of biggest firms in all countries: petroleum products, iron and steel, automobiles, chemicals, electrical and electronic equipment, telecommunications, and pharmaceuticals, all areas in which large plants are

[5] This relationship can be confirmed by examining size as measured by assets, which indicates that in the early 1960s the ten biggest British firms had assets of approximately $27,506.8 million, compared to figures (for 1957) in the U.S. of $39,205.8 million. The four-year difference gives the British a decided advantage, but even so, the top ten U.S. firms were 1.4 times larger. British data, converted by the author at official exchange rates, is from Peter Donaldson, *Guide to the British Economy* (Harmondsworth, England, and Baltimore, Md.: Penguin Books, 1965), p. 83. U.S. data from Martin L. Lindahl and William M. Carter, *Corporate Concentration and Public Policy*, 3d. (Englewood Cliffs, N.J.: Prentice-Hall, 1969), pp. 79-85.

A similar comparison between the absolute size by assets of French and U.S. companies in industries has been made by Lionel Stoleru. The U.S. firms were bigger than the French firms in all cases, and frequently the third largest U.S. firm was bigger than the biggest French firm. Stoleru used the *Fortune* magazine data also. (Lionel Stoleru, *L'Imperatif Industriel* [Paris: Editions du Seuil, 1969], p. 50.) Comments Stoleru somewhat ruefully, "Do you know that the net profits realized by the *totality* of French industry, with its 8 million employees, are lower than those of General Motors *alone*, with its 745,000 employees?" (p. 18.)

Table 5-1
Total Sales for the Largest Firms in Eleven
Market-Oriented Economies, 1968

Country	No. firms in the 200 largest non-U.S.	Total sales ($000)			
		Top five firms	Rank	Top ten firms	Rank
United States[a]		$69,625,850	1	$99,595,312	1
Britain	46	23,603,996[b]		33,111,321[b]	
		23,201,282[c]	2	30,471,361[c]	2
		12,051,452[d]		17,547,222[d]	
Netherlands	8	18,866,324[e]	3		
		4,917,447[f]			
West Germany	27	10,437,278	4	17,133,477	3
Japan	44	9,116,847	5	15,683,668	4
Italy	8	7,731,844[g]	6		
		6,435,573[h]			
France	21	7,041,553[i]	7	11,908,337[i]	5
		6,283,467[j]		10,791,963[j]	
Switzerland	8	4,808,955	8		
Canada	12	3,914,936	9	6,213,372	6
Sweden	6	2,799,884	10		
Belgium	4[k]	2,372,440[k]	11		

Source:
Fortune, May 1970, p. 184, for U.S. data; data for other countries, August 15, 1969, pp. 107-11.

Notes:
a. U.S. data for 1969.
b. Includes Royal Dutch Shell and Unilever—owned jointly with the Netherlands. Includes the government-owned British Steel (top five) and the government-owned National Coal Board (top ten).
c. Includes the two companies owned jointly (but privately) with the Dutch in the top five; excludes two companies owned by the state and substitutes two private companies next in order of sales for the top ten.
d. Excludes two companies owned jointly with the Dutch and two government-owned companies in top ten. Hence the figures represent the five or ten largest all-British, all-private firms.
e. Includes two companies owned jointly with British.
f. Excludes two companies owned jointly with British and substitutes two next largest (by sales) wholly Dutch owned. In ranking we have adopted the rough rule of including half the jointly owned companies' sales, putting Dutch sales for the top five around $19 billion. This is crude, but it puts the Netherlands at a level reflecting Dutch strength by one meaningful criterion.
g. Includes ENI and Italsider, both government-owned companies.
h. Excludes the two government-owned companies and substitutes the next two largest private companies.
i. Includes Renault, the largest (but government-owned) French firm and (in the case of the top ten) ELF (ERAP), also government-owned.
j. Represents only private firms by substituting the next largest companies (two for the top ten, one for the top five).
k. Only three firms included among the 200 largest industrial firms outside the U.S. are wholly Belgian-owned firms. The fourth, Agfa-Gewaert, is half German-owned.

productive. (It is at the plant level rather than the firm level that technological factors are most prominent.) The other advantages to bigness help explain why so many firms in these industries are multiplant firms.

That the size of firms is related to industrialization is also clear. In his study of eight market-oriented economies, Joe Bain concluded that the percent of the labor force devoted to manufacturing, commerce, and services was the best single measure of industrialization. On this basis he ranked the degree of industrialization in his eight countries as follows: the U.S. 70.4 percent; the U.K., 69.0%; Sweden, 61.5%; Canada, 61.3%; France, 56.4%; Japan, 47.7%; Italy, 42.3%; and India, 24.7%.[6] Bain's conclusions on absolute plant size (for which we have little evidence) corroborate our conclusions about firm size. He concluded that U.S. plant size was clearly larger than that of the other seven countries he studied, with the U.K. closest to U.S. size (see Table 5-2). In the other countries plants tended to be considerably smaller than in the United States.[7]

How Efficient Are Big Plants and Firms?

The question of the relationship between size and efficiency, both at the plant level and the firm level, is very complicated. A number of studies in the U.S. of these relationships[8] appear to suggest that at the plant level the economies of scale produced by modern technology require large plants, in some cases too large to permit any approximation to textbook competition even if we restricted these industries to one-plant firms. In other cases plants may be larger than is required by technology.

At the firm level there are considerable managerial and operational efficiencies connected with multiplant firms, but there is also evidence that firms frequently get larger than these economies would justify and that there are also diseconomies connected with large firms in the U.S. and quite possibly elsewhere. Little is known about the efficiency of firms in other economies, except that their smaller general size would suggest that whatever the diseconomies of large-scale firms may be, they might be less evident in other market-oriented economies. Bain assumes that technology should be exportable and has attempted to measure the level of efficiency in "typical" plants in

[6] Joe S. Bain, *International Differences in Industrial Structure* (New Haven, Conn.: Yale University Press, 1966), p. 18. His data refer to the 1960s, and since then industrialization has undoubtedly increased in several of these countries, particularly in Japan.

[7] Ibid., pp. 38-39.

[8] A classic study of plant size and efficiency, now quite old, is John M. Blair, "Technology and Size," *American Economic Review 38,* (May 1948): 121-52. More recently Bain studied the percentage of national industrial capacity in one optimal-size plant and one optimal-size firm in a variety of industries. Bain, "Economics of Scale, Concentration, and the Condition of Entry in Twenty Manufacturing Industries," *American Economic Review 44* (March 1954): 15-38.

countries outside the United States. He concludes that the U.K. is the only country other than the U.S. in which more than half the employees worked in plants which he terms "reasonably efficient" by U.S. standards. He based this conclusion on a study of twenty-four industries, in which at least 70 percent of the U.S. workers were employed in "reasonably efficient plants," so his comparisons were in terms of this standard. In none of the comparable industries in other countries were as many as 70 percent of the workers employed in reasonably efficient plants.[9]

Concentration in Market-Oriented Economies

Absolute size of plant or firm, although very important (Bain felt it was a crucial factor), is only one determinant of market power for a firm. Another major determinant is the extent or size of the market. The percent of the total market that a relatively small group of large firms controls determines what is called the market concentration, and it is a primary determinant of market power. How concentrated markets are in the manufacturing or industrial sector of market-oriented economies is therefore a critical factor. In the only careful study of intercountry concentration which has been done, Bain found several countries in which concentration was greater than in the United States, not because plants or firms were larger but because the market was so much smaller. The results of his efforts, with respect to the eight market-oriented economies for which he found reliable and comparable data, are summarized in Table 5-2. This table is complicated, but it will reward careful study.

Plant Concentration by Country We can begin with Bain's finding, already noted, that average plant size is larger in the United States than in any other country. He has expressed the median size (to minimize the effect of very small or large plants) for the twenty largest plants[10] in thirty-four industries relative to the median size plant in the United States. Thus the fact that all the plant size relatives in column 2 are less than 100 indicates that the median size was smaller in all seven countries than in the United States, the divergence from 100 indicating how much smaller.

But the extent of the market in the United States is also very large, while for some countries—notably India, Canada, and Sweden—it is very small. Thus plant size and concentration ratios (here measured by the percent of total industry employment accounted for by the twenty largest plants) can diverge sharply. Again using the United States plant concentration ratio as a yardstick, Bain has compared plant concentration in the other seven countries to that in

---

[9] Bain, *International Differences in Industrial Structure,* Table 3-9, pp. 62-63.

[10] Or less than twenty plants for countries in which one of the thirty-four industries considered had less than twenty plants in all.

Table 5-2

Plant and Company Concentration Comparisons for Eight Market-Oriented Economies, 1950s

| | Plant concentration | | | | Company concentration | | | | | Company/plant concentration Multiple | |
| | Based on percent of industry employment accounted for by 20 largest plants (U.S. percent = 100) | | | | | Top-level seller concentration (compared to U.S.) | | | | | |
Country	Median size plant relative	No. of comparable industries	Plant concentration relative (median)	Rank	No. of comparable industries	Lower	Same	Higher	Rank of average company concentration	No. of Industries	Mean Multiple
(1)	(2)	(3)	(4)	(5)	(6)	(7)	(8)	(9)	(10)	(11)	(12)
United States	100	34	100	1	42	–	–	–	1	19	3.6
Japan	34	31	109	2	25	9	5	11	2	12	3.9
Italy	29	32	122	3	19	1	4	14	4	5	3.6
France	39	31	129	4	19	4	4	11	3	9	4.3
United Kingdom	78	32	131	5	32	12	9	11	1	17	2.6
India	26	22	189	6	16	2	1	13	6	3	4.3
Canada	28	14	221	7	22	0	6	16	5	5	2.0
Sweden	13	27	234	8	7	0	1	6	7	6	1.7

Source:

Bain, *International Differences in Industrial Structure.*

Notes:

Col. 2 is based on the average size of the twenty largest plants in thirty-four U.S. industries; the median size plant in the U.S. equals 100 (Table 3-3, p. 39). Col. 3 indicates the number of these thirty-four U.S. industries for which data were available in other countries (p. 39). Col. 4: median plant concentration data for comparable industries in the list of thirty-four U.S. industries; median plant concentration ratio in the U.S. equals 100 (Table 3-5, p. 47). Col. 6: concentration data available for forty-two U.S. industries and for the indicated number of comparable industries in other countries (p. 71). Cols. 7, 8, and 9 taken from Chapter 4; Col. 10 from p. 119. Col. 11 indicates the number of direct comparisons of company and plant concentration which could be made between the U.S. and at least one of the other countries. Of the nineteen U.S. industries utilized, the numbers of comparable industries for each other country is shown in this column (p. 132). Col. 12 is taken from p. 132. For explanation see text.

the United States. Once more he relies on medians to reduce the impact of extreme values. Column 3 indicates for how many of the thirty-four U.S. industries he was able to obtain comparable plant concentration ratios for the other countries. If the median plant concentration ratios in other countries were equal to that in the U.S., the plant concentration relatives in column 4 would be 100. The fact that all seven exceed 100 indicates that plant concentration was larger in all the other countries—significantly so in India, Canada, and Sweden.

It is at the plant level that technology will exert its largest impact and produce what we call the economies of large-scale production. Since we have seen that the U.S. has the largest typical plant size but the lowest plant concentration ratio, it is clear that the extent of the market is the dominant factor in determining plant concentration ratios. It is not plant size alone, but *plant size relative to the size of the market* which is decisive. We shall see that this has serious implications for public policy. It may be true, as we have seen, that some plants in the U.S. are larger than technology requires for optimum efficiency, but this is not so clear for other countries. It is not clear, therefore, that public policy could or should reduce plant concentration in other countries, especially in view of the limited size of their markets. (Plant concentration is not likely to be reduced in the U.S. either.)

Company Concentration by Country   What about company concentration ratios? If each firm consisted of only one producing plant the two ratios would be the same. But we all know that General Motors produces Chevrolets in several plants. Hence the percent of total automobile output produced by the three biggest plants in the U.S. would be much smaller than the percent of total output produced by the three biggest firms. Public policy must be directed at firms—producing companies—and a major question is whether significant incremental efficiencies arise from having a single management operate several plants. These questions cannot be considered, however, until we have examined the evidence concerning company concentration in various countries. Once again Bain has utilized company concentration in forty-two industries in the United States as the norm and has compared company concentration ratios for as many of them as he could find comparable data in other countries. The number of industrial comparisons is indicated in column 6.[11]

Among the comparable industries he found cases in which company concentration, as measured by the share of the top sellers, was greater than column 7, less than column 9, or about the same as column 8, as it is in the same industry in the United States. Column 10 indicates his conclusions that on the average the degree of top-level seller concentration is about the same in the United States and the U.K. and that the other countries have increasingly large

---

[11] The comparisons deal with "top-level seller concentration" because sometimes he had to compare the percent of industry output produced by the Big Three, the Big Four, or the Big Twenty, etc. There were also differences in the unit used to measure concentration—it could be output, value of shipments, etc.

company concentration ratios, in the order indicated by the rankings in that column.

Column 10, therefore, indicates Bain's ordering of these countries in terms of company concentration, and it is his view that company concentration *alone* is sufficient to account for "the greater degree of monopoly power" found in Italy, Canada, India, and Sweden.[12] Bain adds,

> This impression is reinforced by the findings that as we ascend the concentration ladder past Japan, we must find in France, Italy, India, and Sweden a significant minor fraction of industries in which all or almost all industry output is supplied by one, two, or three firms, this phenomenon being very rare in the United States, the United Kingdom, and Japan.[13]

Importance of Multiplant Companies by Country   Before turning to the public policy questions which such concentration ratios involve, one other piece of information that Bain provides us is worth considering. If all companies were one-plant companies, the plant concentration ratio would be the same as the company concentration ratio, as previously suggested. Thus, by taking the ratio of the company concentration ratio to the plant concentration ratio, he is able to give a very crude indication of the extent of multiplant firms. For nineteen U.S. industries for which he had both plant and company concentration ratios, he found that the former was on average 3.6 times greater than the latter. If all plants were of equal magnitude (they are not, of course), this would suggest that the "average U.S. firm" contains 3.6 plants. However, the estimates are included only as indicative of international comparisons and should not be interpreted in any more precise manner than as a crude indication of the comparative extent of multiplant firms in these countries relative to the U.S. Bain's conclusion from all this is

> that in all eight countries except Canada and Sweden (unpopulous countries with small domestic markets) multi-plant development by leading firms is on the average a very important factor contributing to observed degrees of top-seller concentration in manufacturing industries.[14]

Here is a crucial finding for public policy considerations, because the efficiencies multiplant firms can achieve are quite different than the economies of scale which large plant size brings.

[12] Bain, *International Differences in Industrial Structure.*, p. 119.
[13] Ibid., p. 120.
[14] Ibid, pp. 132-33.

We must at least mention one other kind of concentration before we try to relate this discussion of plant and firm concentration to public policy in market-oriented economies. The United States has a long history of investigating the degree to which a small number of wealthy families or large banks or other concentrations of wealth (for example, holding companies) were able to exercise economic power over many companies in diverse fields.[15] Bain makes it clear that while the degree of seller concentration in Japan (measured in terms of the twenty-five industries for which he secured comparable data) is not very different from concentration in the U.S. today, the situation for public policy in Japan is very different. In Japan one must still contend with the zaibatsu, each of which may be described for the prewar period as a financial, industrial, and commercial unit which is controlled or held by a family or small group of families that use the formal device of a holding company plus a complex of subsidiaries to achieve great concentration of decision-making authority in relatively few hands.[16] Despite the efforts of the occupying Americans to disband the zaibatsu, it is clear that they have reemerged, and at the time Bain wrote he estimated that the three major zaibatsu (Mitsubishi, Mitsui, and Sumitomo) together controlled something like 40 percent of all "big business" in Japan.[17] We mention this because such a control network is vastly tighter than any comparable phenomenon in the U.S., and it creates public policy problems in Japan. In these circumstances, to suppose that because the company concentration ratios in the U.S. and Japan are similar, similar policies could achieve similar results is most misleading.

Moreover, the zaibatsu system in Japan is similar to the situation in West Germany, the major country for which Bain could not obtain comparable data and which he therefore excluded from his intercountry comparisons. Andrew Shonfield has reported that a government study in 1960 showed that 70 percent of the capital of a sample of companies which in the aggregate represented three-fourths of the nominal value of all shares quoted on the German stock exchange was controlled by the German banks—presumably the Big Three (the Deutsche, the Dresdner, and the Commerz).[18] These huge banks, like the

[15] See, for example, A. A. Berle and Gardiner Means, *The Modern Corporation and Private Property* (New York: The Macmillan Co., 1932); National Resources Committee, *The Structure of the American Economy* (Washington D.C.: U.S. Government Printing Office, 1939); and Temporary National Economic Committee, "The Distribution of Ownership in the 200 Largest Non-Financial Corporations," Monograph No. 29 (Washington, D.C.: U.S. Government Printing Office, 1940), for three classic studies of the lines of control over American corporations. These efforts have been brought up to date by Robert J. Larner, "Ownership and Control in the 200 Largest Non-Financial Corporations, 1929 and 1963," *American Economic Review* 56, No. 4, Part I (September 1966): 779-87, and Peter C. Dooley, "The Interlocking Directorate," *American Economic Review* 59, No. 3 (June 1969): 314-23.

[16] Bain, *International Differences in Industrial Structure*, p. 86.

[17] Ibid., p. 88.

[18] In comparison, the National Resources Committee in the 1930s considered the control over manufacturing exercised by the fifty largest non-financial corporations, and more recently Larner was concerned with the control by the 200 largest nonfinancial corporations.

zaibatsu in Japan, were presumably dismantled after the Second World War, and again like the Japanese zaibatsu, they have put themselves back together. We have seen that the Big Banks exercise much control through the operation of the Aufsichtstrat, that unique form of German corporate supervisory boards. These boards must approve all major investment decisions, employment decisions, and so on. The banks collect proxies from stockholders and thus can obtain significant control over the decisions of the Aufsichtsrat. The Big Three Banks, moreover, exchange proxies under a system called *Stimmenleihe* (loaned votes) to increase their influence individually at particular Aufsichtsrat meetings.[19] Clearly such arrangements complicate the public policy problems and make the social market economy of Germany not quite the modernized version of a laissez faire competitive system that it is sometimes pictured as.

In short, both absolute plant size and absolute firm size are clearly greatest in the United States, but the degree of both plant and firm *concentration* is smaller (though not always very much smaller), however one measures them, than in all the other countries we have considered except Germany, for which no data are available. The German banks may exercise significant control over market decisions, however.

What is the current state of public policy toward bigness and the market power it may convey in market-oriented economies? We will shortly turn to this important question, for which the discussion just concluded is an indispensable background.

How Firms Get Big—A Necessary Digression

We have seen that both plants and firms are largest in the United States, but that concentration—the relationship of size to the relevant market—is probably larger in all the other market-oriented economies we have examined, with the possible exception of Germany, where other forms of market control have been developed. Before this discussion of size and concentration can be related to problems in public policy it is necessary to recognize that modern manufacturing firms get large, and hence acquire significant market power, in different ways.

The discussion in the first section of this chapter suggested the absolute size levels which have been achieved in a number of market-oriented economies. The first way in which firm size can increase is through an increase in the absolute size of the plant or plants which make up the firm. This type of firm growth is most closely related to modern technology and the large minimal size which is required in many basic industries for firms to be efficient. A small Bessemer converter, hence a small steel plant, is simply an inefficient way to produce steel. Moreover, in many industries there are some advantages (that is, managerial efficiencies) related to the operation of several plants by one firm. Both these factors produce size through *internal growth* of the firm. It is clearly possible to

[19] Shonfield, *Modern Capitalism*, pp. 246-50.

exaggerate the importance of both these kinds of economies, but they do exist and explain a significant part of firm size.

A second kind of firm growth occurs through what economists call *vertical integration*, which means that a producing firm might acquire facilities to provide raw materials necessary in its operations, and at the other end of the production process it might acquire distribution facilities or dealerships to make its products available to the consumers. Vertical integration can be accomplished through the purchase of existing facilities, in which case we call the result a merger. (If the firm in question develops the facilities on its own, this growth is part of the internal growth process referred to above, not a merger.)

A critical public policy problem in any market-oriented economy is to distinguish vertical integration that allows various kinds of managerial efficiencies, such as more coordinated production techniques throughout the production process (and so presumably lower consumer prices) from vertical integration that simply enhances market power and control for the firm. In the latter case integration through merger might be more easily dealt with than development of such facilities by the firm.

A second kind of integration is not vertical but horizontal—the acquisition of plant at the same stage of the production process. If a steel company acquires a second plant that duplicates converter facilities, it would represent horizontal integration. (Once again, if the steel firm builds the plant itself it is internal growth; if it acquires the assets of an existing independent plant, we call it a merger.) The public policy questions are similar to those involved in vertical integration, except that the economies of multiplant operation are limited to more efficient purchasing, financing, and distribution systems. The dangers involve obtaining greater market power and hence control of a single output. Vertical (and more especially) horizontal mergers have played an important part in creating the present structure of industry in the United States.[20]

A third kind of merger—one that has been increasingly important in the United States—is the *conglomerate merger*, in which firms acquire other firms producing totally unrelated products in an effort to diversify. Cigarette companies, fearing that the crusade against cancer would spread and cut into their sales and profits, acquired companies producing nontobacco products. DuPont in the United States and Unilever in Europe, to name two, have long been conglomerates. In the United States companies like Ling-Temco-Vought (airplanes, steel, car rentals, sporting goods, meat packing, and so on) and Monsanto Chemicals have recently emerged as giant conglomerates. Clearly they create quite a different public policy problem. The technology of diverse production processes makes efficiencies through economies of large-scale production difficult to justify. Some economies undoubtedly can be shown in knowledgeable and efficient management, which can be transferred from one

[20] For a thorough review of the history of American mergers, see Ralph L. Nelson, *Merger Movements in American Industry, 1895-1956,* National Bureau of Economic Research No. 66, General Series (Princeton, N.J.: Princeton University Press, 1959).

area of production to another, but that the urge to obtain market control through large size is a significant factor in conglomerate mergers seems equally or more apparent.

Public Policy toward Big
Business in Market-Oriented Economies

Section 1 of the Sherman Antitrust Act, passed by the United States Congress in 1890, declares, "Every contract, combination in the form of trust or otherwise, or conspiracy in restraint of trade or commerce among the Several States, or with foreign nations, is hereby declared to be illegal."[21] This is the bedrock of American antitrust policy. It has its basis in economic theory which derives from the conclusion that a monopoly can take special advantage of its market position. All firms attempt to maximize profits by the price and quantity decisions they make, but the monopolist can take advantage of the degree of elasticity in his demand curve, with the result that his set price is customarily higher and the quantity produced is smaller than would be produced by competitive firms with the same cost functions. Thus economists argue that monopoly per se malallocates resources. It may be inevitable on technological grounds (what economists call a natural monopoly), in which case it is accorded the status of a public utility and regulated by a public commission in return for its monopoly position, or it may develop through the kinds of growth just considered.

In general, antitrust laws, their enforcement by the Department of Justice and their interpretation by the U.S. judiciary have had a checkered history, but as we have already seen, despite the enormous size of much basic industry in this country, the U.S. generally has the lowest concentration ratios among market-oriented economies. And while U.S. growth rates have lagged behind those of most other market-oriented economies in the postwar period, our economy has been and continues to be enormously productive, and at the same time it has maintained a larger and more vigorous private sector than perhaps any other market-oriented economy. What role have antitrust laws played in this record? Specifically, should we attribute lower concentration ratios in U.S. manufacturing industry to the fact that our markets are so huge that concentration has been held down despite the great size of our firms or to the positive accomplishments of antitrust policy in keeping the size of American firms from getting even larger?

The answer to this important question is complex. One important aspect, however, involves distinguishing among market *size,* market *conduct,* and market *behavior.* Public policy toward big business has become involved in all three of

---

[21] Commerce Clearing House, *The Federal Antitrust Laws* (New York: Commerce Clearing House, 1949), p. 7.

these in all market-oriented economies, because any one or a combination can be used (or rejected) as a basis for public policy.

Many believe that Section 1 of the Sherman Act suggested that market size should be the standard for public policy. Subsequent court cases suggested that mere size might not be an offense against the antitrust laws—that what was illegal was *unreasonable* size. Thus was born the famous "Rule of Reason," first enunciated by the Supreme Court in the 1911 Standard Oil case.[22] In that decision the high court declared that "mere size is no offense" no matter how large a share of the market a firm might constitute. Only "unreasonable" behavior, involving the use of monopoly power to perpetrate "unfair practices," is outlawed by the Sherman Act. This view of the antitrust laws in effect substituted a standard of behavior for a standard of structure.

In the 1940s the courts seemed to deny the validity of the Rule of Reason and in a series of cases declared that "mere size" could be an offense provided it was big enough and carried with it sufficient market control. Thus in the famous Alcoa case Judge Hand declared that size large enough to produce control of 90 percent of virgin aluminum production "is enough to constitute a monopoly; it is doubtful whether sixty or sixty-four per cent would be enough; and certainly thirty-three per cent is not enough."[23] Apparently mere size, if it carries with it sufficient market control, can be illegal in the U.S. We shall shortly consider whether this is true in other market-oriented ecnomies. (It is worth noting that little significant change in the structure of the American economy has resulted from antitrust prosecutions under this "New Sherman Act.")

The market conduct standard for public policy toward bigness has tended to judge big firms by how they behave: Do they set prices arbitrarily, divide markets geographically (market-sharing), allocate quotas through either tacit or express agreements? Do they try to drive out small business through "price wars" or use the device of letting one firm always initiate price increases (price leadership)? Do they try to sell the same product to different buyers at different prices when the differences do not represent cost differences (price discrimination)? Do they require customers to agree to buy only from them (exclusive dealing)? Do they attempt to erect barriers to keep potential new firms from entering the industry? All these are examples of market behavior which the antitrust laws and their interpreters in the United States have at least frowned on, though not necessarily uniformly and consistently.

In the United States and in other market-oriented economies there has been a tendency to pay increasing attention to the market *performance* of various industries and to judge the success or failure of public policy by pragmatic results rather than by either structure or behavior criteria alone. Thus one can

---

[22] *U.S. v. Standard Oil Co. of New Jersey,* 221 U.S. 1 (1911); *U.S. v. American Tobacco Co.,* 221 U.S. (1911).

[23] *U.S. v. Aluminum Co. of America,* 148 F. 2d 416 (1945). Quoted in Richard Caves, *American Industry: Structure, Conduct, Performance,* 2d ed. (Englewood Cliffs, N.J.: Prentice-Hall, 1967), p. 62.

ask: Are most plants of reasonably efficient size? Is there an acceptable level of excess capacity in plants? Are price-cost margins such that profits can be considered "normal" rather than "monopolistic" or "excessive"? Are there pressures producing unremitting efforts to improve both production processes and products, with subsequent benefits passed on at least partly to consumers? Are advertising and other selling efforts considered "reasonable"? These questions are designed to determine if the price system is being utilized in the market to enable consumers to express preferences which producers are sensitive to and to allow consumers to benefit from progress along with producers. These are central problems for any economy, and market-oriented economies can be distinguished from command economies in part by the fact that they consider these factors dimensions of economic performance at least equal in importance to economic growth, the development of basic industry, and other economic objectives.

We have thus far tended to concentrate on the development of public policy criteria in respect to industrial organization and performance in the United States, because antitrust laws appear to be most highly developed in this country, and it is against the standard developed in the U.S. that we shall compare public policy toward industry in other market-oriented economies.

Laws against Monopoly and Market Dominance   Several other economies have laws against monopolization which are patterned very much after Section 1 of the Sherman Act. Section 2 (f) of the Canadian Combines Investigation Act defines monopoly as "a situation where one or more persons either substantially or completely control throughout Canada or any area thereof the class or species of business in which they are engaged."[24]

The Japanese enacted the Anti-Monopoly Law of 1947 to keep the zaibatsu from reestablishing themselves as agents of control and to deconcentrate Japanese industry generally. However, in the view of at least one thoughtful student of recent Japanese economic developments (Bain), their antitrust policy is becoming more and more *pro forma* and in fact a good deal more pro-cartel, with decreasing efforts to control either monopolies or restraints of trade.[25] This has been the result of amendments to the law and the attitude of the government. One observer concurred with Bain's judgment:

> Neither the Japanese Government nor the business world accepts the concepts of free competition as they are understood in the U.S. and in Europe. Japanese traditions are for a high degree of collusion and collective action, often under the leadership of the State.[26]

[24] Quoted in Organization for Economic Cooperation and Development (OECD), *Market Power and the Law* (Paris: OECD, 1970), p. 40.

[25] Bain, *International Differences in Industrial Structure*, p. 86.

[26] Business International Corporation, *Investing, Licensing, and Trading Conditions Abroad* (New York: Business International Corp., January 1970), p. 210.

We saw that Japanese concentration ratios are not much higher than those in the United States, but the influence of the zaibatsu is a way of managing monopoly control (or oligopoly control) without the kind of monopoly power that the Sherman Act has explicitly outlawed. Bain has concluded that the zaibatsu have not had a significant impact on horizontal seller concentration (which is what concentration ratios measure and antitrust laws tend to outlaw on structural grounds), but the zaibatsu have significantly increased the ease of vertical economic activity, with the result that greater monopoly power develops with a given level of seller concentration within an industry than might otherwise occur.[27] Japan is therefore a good example of the weakness inherent in public policy against bigness that is restricted to or based largely on a definition of monopoly measured narrowly by the percent of the relevant market a firm or several firms control. Not only is the definition of *relevant market* crucial but high concentration ratios are not the only avenue through which firms can achieve market power.

We have seen that in both absolute firm size and company concentration the United Kingdom is most like the United States. Nonetheless, the official view of the British government toward industrial integration prior to World War II has been aptly characterized as one of "guarded approval" by one writer, who perceptively concluded that the British economy has been characterized by considerable industrial concentration throughout the twentieth century.[28] These conclusions are not necessarily incompatible. The British antitrust laws are similar to those of the United States (though probably even less rigorously enforced than in the United States), they have been devised largely in the years since World War II, and industrial power, as we have already seen, can scarcely be said to be widely deconcentrated in the United States.

After World War II the British adopted a structural approach not unlike the one Judge Hand utilized in interpreting the Sherman Act in the 1945 Alcoa case. In 1948 the British set up the Monopolies Commission, which was to investigate industries in which more than one-third of total output was under the control of a single firm or of "interconnected firms." This commission was not particularly successful—it prosecuted very few cases—and in 1956 the government passed the Restrictive Practices Act to tighten the law against monopoly by setting up a registrar of restrictive practices and to curb abuses of monopoly power. The one-third market share structural criterion of monopoly power continued.

Norway's Act on Control of Prices, Profits, and Restraints of Competition includes a structural criterion, but it is weak in operation. Any firm that has 25 percent of the production or distribution of a good or service must register as a "dominant enterprise." Similarly, under the Austrian Cartel Act single firms that control 30 percent of the domestic market must register; if there are more than three firms the rate is upped to a minimum of 50 percent. The law is meaningless, however, as no cases have ever been tried under it.[29]

27 Bain, *International Differences in Industrial Structure,* p. 90.

28 Donaldson, *Guide to the British Economy,* p. 88.

29 See OECD, *Market Power and the Law,* p. 50.

Laws about monopoly in other market-oriented economies can be summarized as follows: "abuses" of monopoly power are to be curbed by laws in Belgium, Denmark, West Germany, the Netherlands, Sweden, and—in certain cases—Switzerland; abuses are "prohibited" in France; but monopolies are allowed in Ireland and Italy.[30] The same general situation prevails with respect to market dominance, for which a good deal less than monopoly power is required.

Laws against Market Conduct and Market Dominance   It has often been said that in the United States the antitrust laws have been more vigorously enforced against the behavior or conduct of *several* firms than against very large firms that can accomplish the same objectives by virtue of the market power which goes with size. Thus a large firm controlling 50 percent of the output of some product clearly sells at a price which it sets. More often than not the firm has no problem with the Department of Justice. However if two firms, each of which controls 25 percent of the product market, make an *agreement* to sell at the same price, all hell breaks loose. The *result* is virtually the same, but the antitrust laws have obviously been interpreted much more strictly against restrictive practices reached through collusion than through mere size.

It is in the area of restrictive practices against agreements, mergers, and the like that the difference in public policy between the United States and many other market-oriented economies becomes sharpest. Section 7 of the Clayton Act, as amended by the 1950 Celler-Kefauver Act, makes mergers illegal "where the effect of such acquisition may be to substantially lessen competition . . . or to restrain . . . commerce, or tend to create a monopoly of any line of commerce."[31]

In the United Kingdom the Monopolies and Mergers Bill of March 1965 broke new ground by requiring that firms which wished to merge would have to show that the mergers were in the public interest *before* they occurred. Criteria for disallowing mergers are not clear, however. In Japan the criteria are

[30] Business International Corporation, *The European Economic Community Today and Tomorrow: New Rules for the Seventies* (Geneva: Business International Research Reports, 1966), p. 54. In most of these countries the abuse of market power is determined by what the OECD has called "substantive criteria." For example, in France market power is based on "monopoly or by the manifest concentration of economic power," in Germany by the "absence of substantial competition," in the Netherlands by "de facto or legal relationship in trade or industry involving a predominant influence on a market for goods or services in the Netherlands." The quotations are all from the relevant national laws and are cited from OECD, *Market Power and the Law*, p. 51. Spain, Sweden, and Switzerland have similar structural criteria for "market dominance." Only Belgium and Denmark define market power in terms of "other criteria." The Danish Monopolies and Restrictive Practices Control Act asks, Do enterprises "exert substantial influence on price, production, distribution or transport conditions throughout the country or into all market areas?" (Ibid., p. 53.) In all these cases the notion of "the relevant market" and power in it are intertwined in defining "monopoly power" or monopolizing activities. Italy is conspicuous by its absence from this listing.

[31] Commerce Clearing House, *The Federal Antitrust Laws*, p. 13. The Clayton Act covered stock acquisitions but not asset acquisitions (outright purchases). The latter loophole in the Clayton Act was plugged by the Celler-Kefauver Act of 1950.

presumably similar to those used in the United States. Will the proposed merger lessen competition?[32] Much the same thing can be said of the antimerger provisions of the Canadian Combines Investigation Act. What of other market-oriented economies? Merger activity has been termed "unrestricted" although certain mergers are sometimes disallowed in West Germany and Spain.[33] In Austria, Belgium, Denmark, France, Italy, the Netherlands, Norway, Sweden, and Switzerland "no prior approval" is required for mergers.[34] In these circumstances the conclusion of the OECD seems eminently justified:

> Compared with the other legislation, . . . the United States has the most advanced practice of merger control, as is reflected by the great number of cases which have been decided involving all types of mergers— horizontal, vertical, conglomerate, and joint ventures—and their effects on competition. The United States also goes much further than any other country in preventing mergers with anti-competitive effects.[35]

On the other hand, we have seen that U.S. plants and firms are much larger than those in other market-oriented economies, and Bain's evidence—considered earlier—suggests that non-U.S. plants are more likely to be inefficiently smaller than those in this country. The same thing might be true at the firm level. Therefore, even if other market-oriented economies were as structure-oriented in their public policy as is the United States in its antitrust laws, they might legitimately be more lax as regards monopoly and merger matters than we are, solely on grounds of promoting greater efficiency. However, the evidence is far too scanty to do more than raise the possibility here.

Restrictive Practices   However one defines *relevant market,* horizontal mergers will affect the level of concentration. Vertical mergers and conglomerate

[32] See Section 15 (i) of the Antimonopoly Act, discussed in OECD, *Market Power and the Law,* p. 79.

[33] In Germany the Act against Restraints of Competition has a 20 percent market share criterion applicable in determining the legality of mergers. This, of course, requires a definition of *market.* The only merger case tried involved the auto industry, for which purpose they divided the industry into small, medium, and large cars. Clearly, what one calls the market will be critical in determining whether or not a proposed merger gives the resultant firm 20 percent of "the market." (See OECD, *Market Power and the Law,* p. 33). Moreover, this law was amended in 1965 to include exceptions to the general restriction on mergers noted above. Firms larger than a prescribed minimum size had to "register" the merger. Accordingly, the amended German law has been termed "less tough" than the 1965 British law. (See Geoffrey Denton, Murray Forsyth, and Malcolm Maclennan, *Economic Planning and Policies in Britain, France, and Germany* [London: George Allen and Unwin, 1968], p. 59.) The Spanish law is next to meaningless—if a merger will give the resultant firm 30 percent of the national market the Spanish Act against Restraints of Competition required that the merger be registered. (Ibid., p. 37.)

[34] Business International Corporation, *The European Economic Community Today and Tomorrow,* p. 54.

[35] OECD, *Market Power and the Law,* pp. 93-94.

mergers are difficult to measure in terms of concentration ratios, because, as we have seen, such ratios tend to measure the share of some predetermined relevant market for a product or service, and this implies some particular stage of a production process—one can speak of raw steel as a product, steel sheeting as a product, fenders as a product, or cars as a product. However, merging plants producing each of these into one firm—hence a vertically integrated firm—would obviously increase market power, though it would not necessarily show up in the kind of concentration ratios we discussed earlier in this chapter. (It would, of course, show up in firm size.) The same comments apply to conglomerate mergers.

Concentration ratios are therefore clearly inadequate as a technique for assessing market power or control. As we noted earlier, there is a whole host of restrictive practices—some involving the behavior of firms horizontally and some their behavior vertically—with which public policy toward business has attempted to cope. Here the U.S. laws must stand as the most severe, with other market-oriented economies taking varying—but mostly more tolerant—views of such competitive restraints.

One of the most interesting approaches is the British. We mentioned that under the Restrictive Practices Act of 1956 the parties to agreements fixing prices or limiting sales were to be required to prove that such agreements were in the public interest. But there, as in the United States, defining *public interest,* let alone what specific actions were or were not in the public interest, is the stuff from which lawyers get rich and economists tear their hair. The British decided to establish "gateways" through which restrictive agreements should be declared in the public interest. So there were two gateways in which restrictive agreements could be approved if they offered consumer protection of some sort. Three gateways suggested that agreements were legitimate if they strengthened competition by permitting several weaker firms to stand up to a larger, stronger firm. Another gateway proposed that restrictive agreements were in the public interest if refusal to approve them could lead to substantial increases in unemployment. Yet another gateway suggested that restrictive agreements were in order if by being disallowed they would lead to a drop in British exports and so endanger the always precarious balance of payments. Of all these gateways, the ones most commonly used to justify restrictive agreements were those which involved fears of increased regional unemployment, endangering of exports, and a catch-all gateway—that the restrictive agreement would be of "specific and substantial benefit" to the public.[36] The March 1964 White Paper, "Monopolies, Mergers, and Restrictive Practices," added a new gateway—that the restrictive agreement "does not deter or restrict competition"—a gateway sufficiently vague to allow almost any agreement to march through.[37] As we mentioned earlier, the case for a given restrictive agreement has to be made before the agreement

[36] For a fuller discussion of the "gateways" see Donaldson, *Guide to the British Economy,* p. 94.

[37] Ibid., p. 95.

goes into effect rather than after. Unscrambling eggs is always difficult, but even so, one does not get the impression that the British system can be very effective in curtailing restrictive agreements.

Unfortunately, we cannot consider market behavior in detail for all the market-oriented economies in which we are interested. The OECD has suggested that various countries in that organization can be grouped by how they determine whether large and powerful firms are abusing their market power by behaving in unacceptable ways. In West Germany and Spain behavior is frowned on if it represents "abuse of a market-dominating position." In the U.K. (as we have seen), Belgium, the Netherlands, Switzerland, and Norway the behavior test is whether "activities (are) contrary to the public interest." In Denmark the criterion is, Does the behavior in question represent "unreasonable prices, unfair business conditions, refusals to sell, and so on"? In France the question revolves around "interference with the normal operation of the market."[38]

What do these various criteria mean when put into practice? The European Economic Community has attempted to summarize the current state of government attitudes toward various restrictive practices. In considering their findings, we should bear in mind that *all* these practices, with one possible exception, are illegal in the United States under one or another antitrust law.[39]

Horizontal agreements under the rubric *horizontal price and marketing agreements* are considered by the EEC as price-fixing, market sharing, market quota setting, exclusion of new firms by erecting barriers of one kind or another to entry into an industry, and cartels (either import or export). We remind you of what U.S. economics principles texts say about the implications of resource allocation when prices are the net result of the interaction of competitive firms with sovereign consumers in free markets—the sort of system that market-oriented, as opposed to command, economies are supposed to exemplify. Then consider this record.

1.   Price fixing. In France, Ireland, Norway, and Spain price fixing is generally not allowed, but in Austria, Belgium, Denmark, the Netherlands, and the U.K. it is allowed with some stipulations (it must be registered, it can be banned in certain cases, and so on). In Switzerland it is "illegal when economically unjustified," and in Italy it is allowed—seemingly with no stipulations whatsoever.

---

[38] OECD, *Market Power and the Law,* p. 105.

[39] The possible exception is resale price maintenance, a system whereby manufacturers can prevent retailers from using their branded products (hence their goodwill) as "loss-leaders"—that is, sell them at a loss in order to lure customers in to purchase other products. The so-called fair-trade laws—the 1937 Miller-Tydings Act as amended in 1952 by the McGuire-Keough Fair Trade Enabling Act—attempted to outlaw these practices, but since the 1950s off-list price selling has flourished in the United States, as any visitor to a discount store can attest. There has been talk of repealing the fair-trade laws on grounds that, like the efforts of the Volstead Act to make prohibition work, these laws are honored more in the breach as things stand and so are "prime candidates for oblivion." (The phrase is Bain's in his *Industrial Organization* [New York: John Wiley & Sons, 1959], p. 623.)

2.   Market sharing. Market sharing is generally prohibited in France, West Germany, Ireland, and Spain but is permissible—within limits—in Austria, Belgium, Denmark, the Netherlands, Norway, Sweden, and the U.K. Again, Switzerland balks if market sharing is not economically justified, and Italy presumably never balks.

3.   Quotas. Once more France, West Germany, Spain, and probably Ireland (where the question has not yet arisen) would object to setting quotas, but the other countries mentioned, though they might require registration of the quota or might "curb them if they are harmful," permit them. Once again, Italy is the most unremittingly permissive economy of all.

4.   Barriers to entry. Utilizing barriers to entry to prevent newcomers from entering an industry is a type of restrictive behavior that market-oriented economies outside the United States (like the U.S. economy) find more difficult to condone. They appear to be either prohibited or looked at with disfavor at least a significant part of the time in Austria, Denmark, France, West Germany, Ireland, the Netherlands, Spain, Sweden, Switzerland, and the U.K. Belgium and Norway will permit them, provided "abuses" are curbed, and once more Italy takes a no-holds-barred attitude.

5.   Import and export cartels. Import cartels are mostly prohibited in France, Ireland, and Spain and are permitted subject to varying restrictions in the other countries. Export cartels are prohibited in Spain but either permitted or actively encouraged in all the other countries.[40]

Vertical Agreements   Turning to vertical price and marketing agreements—that is, agreements which restrain competition by efforts to establish agreements among firms at different stages of the production process, the EEC considers four: resale price maintenance (fair trade laws), discriminatory selling (selling "the same" product to different buyers at different prices—presumably under conditions in which the price differences cannot be justified by cost differences), "refusal to sell" (presumably not treating all potential consumers alike), and exclusive dealing (forcing your buyer to sign an agreement that he will buy from you exclusively as the price of buying from you at all).

1.   Resale price maintenance. Resale price maintenance, interestingly, is forbidden or severely restricted in seven of the countries we are considering and

[40] A cartel is a device permitting importers or exporters to work together in their overseas economic activities, whatever their restrictions in the domestic market may be. European market-oriented economies are prone to encourage export cartels in order to improve their balance of payments positions by reducing competition for foreign markets. The development of the Common Market has, of course, vastly furthered this effort by developing rules designed to reduce international competition within the Common Market area and to "regularize" it with nations outside the Common Market. The only U.S. move to permit export cartellike activity was in the 1918 Webb-Pomerene Act, which attempted to exempt domestic competitors from the operation of the antitrust laws in their international trade activities, the argument being that they had to cooperate to compete effectively with foreign cartels. American concerns still request special concessions for their international trade—e.g., in steel, textiles, etc.

is permitted (sometimes with provisos limiting it) in Austria, Belgium, West Germany, Spain, Switzerland, and Italy.

2.   Price discrimination. Price discrimination is prohibited or sharply curtailed in France, Ireland, Norway, and Spain but is permitted generally in the other countries.

3.   Refusal to sell. A refusal to sell is generally not permitted in Denmark, France, Ireland, Norway, Spain and Switzerland, but it is mostly tolerated in the other countries.

4.   Exclusive dealing. Exclusive dealing arrangements can be foisted onto customers in every single one of the countries under review.

In summary, it would appear that Italy is the most lenient of the market-oriented economies when it comes to permitting agreements which we view as unduly restraining competition; France, West Germany, and Ireland are the most restrictive in their views of these agreements, with the other countries falling somewhere in the middle.[41]

Conclusions

This summary of monopoly law and its enforcement in market-oriented economies has necessarily been brief and far from thorough. The general problem of devising acceptable public policy toward big business is one of the most complex in economics. It is clearly a major arena in the contest between command economies—which abandon the notion that the prices which emerge from their markets should reflect a particular combination of consumer preferences, modern technology, and resource constraints—and entrepreneurial profit maximization activity, which market-oriented economies as a group (though in varying degrees, to be sure) still cling to as optimal. At the beginning of this book we suggested that we would deal with two themes—the similarities which support the general distinction between market-oriented and command economies and the great variety which is nonetheless evident in the way in which the principles of economics are applied in market-oriented economies in the modern world. There is no better example of both themes than current public policy toward industrial structure and conduct.

If the United States has gone furthest in pushing the structuralist approach—the idea that bigness per se might be "bad," particularly if it is associated with control of the bulk of a market by relatively few large firms (concentration)—it is clear that a number of other countries have followed the United States in at least setting up antimonopoly laws. None—not even the United States—has pushed this notion very far (breaking up big firms is

---

[41] This summary of European attitudes toward restrictive agreements is taken from the Business International Corporation, *Today and Tomorrow*, pp. 54-55.

extremely rare in the U.S.), and the structuralist view is always combined with the market conduct notion—if a firm *is* big and does have market power, how does it use that power? How does it behave toward its fellow producers, toward its suppliers and distributors, and toward its customers? Thus in all countries the ultimate test would appear to be, What sort of *performance* is emerging from the industrial or manufacturing sector? Here the differences in the laws, their interpretation in the courts, and their enforcement by public officials can be partially accounted for by differences in the kinds of performance that will be tolerated in various economies. (In the U.S. today many claim that public policy objective is merely "workable competition," which they then define.)

Earlier we asked, Given the large absolute size of American plants and companies, what accounts for the relatively low U.S. concentration ratios (both at the plant and the company level)—comparatively strict antitrust laws, with their greater emphasis on structure per se as an actionable offense, or the vast extent of the market for U.S. goods and services? We can now offer a tentative answer. Despite the strictness of U.S. antitrust laws compared with other market-oriented economies, the lower concentration ratios in the U.S. are the result *more* of the vastness of markets than of the greater severity in law, enforcement, or court interpretation of antitrust laws. At the plant level there is considerable evidence of technological economies, and at the firm or company level there are undoubtedly managerial and other efficiencies. That they are large enough to justify present plant and company size is at the very least a debatable proposition. But that the antitrust laws—which have always been viewed as "conservative" in the literal sense of that word (that is, designed to "conserve" the system we have rather than to alter it to some radically different system)—will very likely never be employed to reform or remake our industrial structure in wholesale style seems a reasonable assumption. We say this despite the fact that some economists and lawyers have for a long time advocated a greater antitrust crackdown on industrial giants.

It must be noted, however, that despite our conclusion that antitrust laws have probably not had a pronounced effect on concentration ratios, they have undoubtedly affected entrepreneurial behavior, and many advocates of greater antitrust enforcement do so precisely for this reason. It appears to us valid to argue that the mere existence of the antitrust laws, coupled with the ever-present threat that their enforcement might be—and frequently is—turned toward flagrant violators of the behavioral proscriptions of the law has acted and continues to act as a "sword of Damocles," preventing many potential and widespread violations of the behavioral illegalities inherent in the law. (The prosecution of the officials in several large electric companies for illegal price fixing agreements in the early 1960s is a clear case in point. That illegal price fixing is not more prevalent is undoubtedly a direct result of fear of antitrust prosecution.) To suggest, therefore, that the laws have not been the primary factor affecting size or concentration in U.S. industry is not to suggest that they have not been of great value on other grounds. By curbing behavioral abuses they have undoubtedly made the overall performance of the American industrial economy more "workably competitive," to use J. M. Clark's term.[42]

That the size of the market rather than the severity of the antitrust laws accounts for U.S. concentration ratios, particularly at the company level, is clear from comparison with Britain, where the antitrust laws are most like ours; the plants—though smaller—are closest to the size of ours, but the concentration ratios are much higher at the plant level due to the smaller size of the markets. Only the existence of relatively fewer multiplant firms puts their company concentration ratios in the same range as those of the U.S.

Generally, all other market-oriented economies place less stress on structure per se in their antitrust laws; the Japanese, with the reemergence of the zaibatsu, appear to be circumventing structure as conventionally viewed as an obstacle to concentrated market power. In Europe the Germans, the Irish, and the French take a sterner view of illegal market behavior than do most of their fellow market-oriented economies, but the influence of the German banks is such that the similarities to the U.S. view of market conduct may be easily exaggerated.

We in the United States take a stricter view of what constitutes illegalities in market behavior by powerful firms because we have attempted to adapt the conventional competitive system to what is technologically and motivationally feasible in a modern industrial society and have also attempted to maintain the largest possible area for a free market in which prices were determined without direct government interference. Others say that we are trying to have our cake and eat it, too. (Certainly command economies argue that such a performance is neither possible nor desirable.)

In earlier chapters we saw that other market-oriented economies, presumably at least partly in order to maintain their viability, have been willing to reduce the area of economic activity which they continue to reserve for the free market. This chapter suggests several conclusions: (1) In the areas which continue to be "free" (not government-owned) both plants and companies are generally absolutely smaller in other economies than they are in the United States, but this can scarcely be attributed to the fact that our antitrust laws place greater stress on structure. Size appears to be a concomitant of industrialization, and as other economies industrialize (for example, Japan), the typical plant and company size can be expected to increase (though as their markets grow, their concentration ratios may decline). (2) Even in the United States no drastic "divorce, dissolution, or divestiture" program designed to reduce all corporations to the minimal size technologically (or even managerially) feasible and justifiable is likely. (3) Those market-oriented economies which are closest to the United States in their attitude toward behavior or conduct which restrains competition (notably France and Germany) do not

---

[42] He introduced the term *workable competition* in an article in the *American Economic Review* 30, (June 1940): 241-46. Reprinted in *Readings in the Social Control of Industry,* American Economic Association, ed. (Philadelphia: The Blakiston Co., 1942), pp. 452-75.

thereby qualify as having similar performance standards, because the French, through indicative planning, permit government intrusion into the allocative and distributive functions of the free market to a far greater extent than would be true here, and in Germany the role of the Banks may allow greater interference with the functioning of the price system than would otherwise be the case.

Karl Schiller has written,

> Competition is and remains the decisive motive force behind the dynamic economic process and economic growth and hence behind stability. No central investment plan, however ingenious it may be, ... can replace the "built-in expansion and stability mechanism" of competition. ...
>
> ... I certainly have nothing against large units as far as they are demanded in the interests of technological and scientific efficacy, and I also have nothing against the demand for elimination of serious artificial distortions in international competition, but this cannot and must not be allowed to lead to a relapse into a cartel-ridden and monopoly-pervaded economy with privileges and shielded positions in an oligarchically structured society.[43]

This is probably valid as a statement of the "credo" of all market-oriented economies today. No one would object to this statement as representative of the guiding principles behind public policy toward business in all market-economies. But we have seen in this chapter that definitions of *monopoly,* of *privilege,* indeed, of *competition* can vary considerably from one market-oriented economy to another. The U.S. has had difficulty agreeing on the goals and objectives of antitrust laws, even though it is generally agreed that we wish to make the minimal changes in conventional market organization that are compatible with modern problems and possibilities for growth and development. It is therefore not surprising that other economies, though desirous of being "oriented" to the market but not to the degree customarily advocated in the U.S., have more lenient antitrust laws. They take a more flexible view of both merger and monopoly on the structural side and of restrictive practices on the behavior side. Their overall performance goals may be similar, as we saw in Chapter 2, but the way in which the price system is expected to contribute to them may vary considerably, as the more limited role of the free market and the greater freedom of firms within the free market underscore.

---

[43] Karl Schiller, "West Germany: Stability and Growth as Objectives of Economic Policy," in J. S. Prybyla, ed., *Comparative Economic Systems,* pp. 169-170.

6

Labor Organizations
in Market-Oriented Economies

"Trade unions and other associations of laborers are designed to protect and advance the interests of the great masses of the working classes."[1] This simple, straightforward definition of the function of trade unions was written almost one hundred years ago, long before economists worried about whether "convergence" of market-oriented and command economies was a possibility, and shortly after Karl Marx had developed communist theory around the premise that capitalist economies were guided exclusively by the profit motive. To Marxists this premise was tantamount to elevating the exploitation of human labor to the pivotal role in the operation of capitalist economies.

In considering the role of trade unions in modern market-oriented economies, it is well to remember that the traditional market system was designed to allocate the factors of production to alternative uses in accordance with the preferences consumers expressed for goods and services. There is something to this simple notion—we still assume that in market-oriented economies increased demand for a particular kind of labor will drive up its return, and decreased demand will drive it down. We still assume that wages in any particular sector of the economy should bear some relationship to what labor contributes to the output of that sector, and so on. But we long ago

[1] Richard T. Ely, *The Labor Movement in America* (New York: Thomas Y. Crowell and Co., 1886), p. 92.

recognized that in industrialized societies there was a basic conflict between large, powerful employers and individual unorganized workers: given the profit motive, workers could get their "fair share" only if they had the muscle to demand it successfully. By 1886, Ely knew that in the factor markets the Invisible Hand could not be relied upon.

In few capitalist economies—certainly not in the United States—was the rise to power of modern trade unionism easy. However, the concentration of business power, discussed in the previous chapter as at least partially a technological consequence of industrialization, preceded the rise of trade unions in all the countries we are considering and therefore made trade union organization necessary if market-oriented systems were to remain viable. It has often been said that modern employment and income theory and policy, associated above all with the name of the great English economist John Maynard Keynes, saved capitalism by devising techniques of coping with economic instability without which socialism or communism could have triumphed as the Marxists predicted. In an even more elemental way, at the level of the firm (what economists call the *micro* level, as opposed to the national, or *macro* level), one can argue that without trade unions no economy could have remained oriented toward the market in basic resource allocation. In this fundamental sense modern trade unions were a conserving institutional force (as were our antitrust laws) rather than the radicalizing force they are sometimes described as.

In short, the same technological and other forces which produced the changes in the operation of the price system described in earlier chapters and which caused the divergence of "market-oriented economies" from "pure capitalist systems," if you will, also created a need for modern labor organizations.

Changing Functions of
Trade Unions in the Modern World

Wages and working conditions may have been the major original motivation for creating trade unions, but the unions soon became concerned with the whole area of welfare, and today they play a considerable role in all market-oriented economies.

The Trades Union Congress (TUC), the major association of trade unions in Great Britain (and therefore like the AFL-CIO in the U.S.) recently commented that trade union objectives were "always changing but always the same." They suggest the following ten objectives of modern trade unions:

1. improved terms of employment
2. improved physical environment at work
3. full employment and national prosperity
4. security of employment and income

5. improved social security
6. fair shares in national income and wealth
7. industrial democracy
8. a voice in government
9. improved public and social services
10. public control and planning of industry[2]

One could easily argue that much on this list—and for the most part it is a list that trade unions in all market-oriented economies would subscribe to—is but an extension of Ely's views of trade union objectives expressed long ago. But there are some significant differences. First, *improved* social security and public and social services suggest that while these remain trade union objectives, they are now part of national welfare programs. It has often been said that U.S. unions have traditionally been "bread-and-butter" unions, whereas European unions were more broadly based and were concerned with fundamental change in the social fabric. To some extent this was true in the formative period (Samuel Gompers, who founded the American Federation of Labor, especially espoused the narrow view of trade union functions). But because all market-oriented economies are now "welfare states" to some degree (see Chapter 3), trade unions everywhere have been concerned with broadening these plans. To this extent, at least, the old distinction between "bread-and-butter" unionism, and "class-conscious" unionism has diminished.

Unions and Political Activity   Closely related is the frequent assertion that European unions have been more political or politically conscious than have their American counterparts. It is true that there are labor parties in a number of countries outside the United States, that trade unions were launched by labor parties (except in the U.K.), and that the labor parties reflected a belief that the kind of objectives trade union leaders sought—even the narrow ones of wages and working conditions—could be achieved only if labor unions were actively involved in the political process. This distinction between trade unions in the Old World and in the United States has become increasingly tenuous since the Second World War, partly because the greater intervention of government in the operation of all market-oriented economies, including the United States, has meant that European trade unions have reached one of their political goals—to get the government to accept responsibility for that social amelioration we spoke of in an earlier chapter. This has lessened the challenge to European trade unions to become more political, but they have remained political in many countries. There is also a counter tendency—a tendency in countries where labor parties exist for trade unions to turn political activities over to the parties. Allan Flanders has commented, "The close association between the British trade

[2] Trades Union Congress, *Evidence of the Trades Union Congress to the Royal Commision on Trade and Union Employers Association* (London: TUC, January, 1967), p. 33.

unions and the Labour Party, which they helped to create, has meant that in the past half century they have relied largely upon the party for the realization of their political objectives. It was not always so."[3]

If other trade union movements have tended to become less political (or in some cases simply no more political), there is evidence that American trade unions, even in the absence of a labor party, have become far more political. From the beginning the CIO philosophy was that labor should be more active politically than Gompers planned for his craft-oriented American Federation of Labor. In the 1940s Sidney Hillman organized the Political Action Committee as the political arm of the CIO, and the AF of L followed suit shortly thereafter. Today, with the two labor organizations combined into the AFL-CIO, political action is viewed as a major way for labor to achieve its objectives, and despite statutory limitations on direct financial participation of trade unions in elections, labor understands the power of the ballot box. "Rewarding its friends" and "punishing its enemies" in political pursuit of its economic objectives is very much a part of trade union philosophy in the United States.

The inclusion of "industrial democracy" on the list of TUC objectives suggests a change from the nineteenth century which trade unions in all market-oriented economies have faced—a change which came with growth, with recognition, and with power. When the unions were fighting for recognition and acceptance they achieved solidarity and cohesion with little effort. Today, as for any other large organization, the problem of how to govern trade unions creates vexing questions. There is a universal tendency for labor leaders to become differentiated from the rank and file (although in Europe the salary differences between union leaders and workers are less extreme). Wildcat strikes are common, and "objectives"—or the next step in achieving them—can be a contentious issue rather than an immediately obvious matter as it was in the days when Tom Girdler, president of Republic Steel, engaged his rebellious workers in bloody warfare at the company gates.

Finally, we must note that the TUC's inclusion of "a voice in government" and "public control and planning of industry" denote change in trade union objectives (certainly early U.S. unions were not concerned with a voice in government, provided they could achieve recognition by management), although from one viewpoint they be viewed merely as a new way to achieve the same objectives unions have always sought. Moreover, the latter objective, certainly as stated by the TUC, suggests a distinction between modern American trade unions and unions in a number of other market-oriented economies.

Unions and National Planning   To the extent that other market-oriented economies have adopted planning, and we saw in Chapter 2 that a very great many have, trade unions have both a voice in government and a means to

---

[3] Allan Flanders, "Great Britain," in *Comparative Labor Movements*, Walter Galenson, ed. (New York: Prentice-Hall, 1952), p. 85.

participate in the public control and planning of industry. In Sweden, Britain, and France for example, the planning commissions are tripartite, involving representatives of trade unions, employer organizations, and the government in the deliberations which produce the plan. However, in considering these structural arrangements we must distinguish between formal arrangements and their actual operation. Thus, despite the tripartite structure in France, trade unions refused to participate in the plans prior to the Fifth Plan; indeed, earlier the unions rejected the plans and published their own programs. Nonetheless, the idea of tripartite planning commissions suggests an avenue through which all three groups can be involved in the planning process in these countries.

The same can be said of the techniques by which national priorities and plans are set in many other countries: trade union organizations in many market-oriented economies are directly involved in the development of national economic objectives and do indeed have a voice in the decision-making process. In the United States the voice is less formalized but no less real. We do not have a plan for trade unions to participate in, but labor leaders extend their influence by testifying before congressional committees and other less structured ways. Alfred Kuhn, for example, has noted that U.S. trade unions have long been active in the battle for free education, civil rights, greater government action in urban renewal, easier financing of housing, and Medicare and other efforts to help the underprivileged in the community.[4] Kuhn argues that this represents an acceptance of "the system," because U.S. trade unions now operate on the national level much as they do at the firm level (where they are also accepted)—they work within the system and so are part of the Establishment. This is no less true of European unions, as we have seen.

The Dilemma of Modern Trade Unions

Earlier we noted that trade unions originated because of the unequal size and power of business firms and individual workers in the market for labor. Setting prices for factors and working conditions for that most important factor, labor, was not a task which a free enterprise price system could accomplish without ignoring some goals of society: it could not set wages and working conditions and assure us that workers would get their "fair share"—an objective which the TUC still states explicitly. But the market system could help us define what a fair share for labor would be. A fair market share would be proportionate to what labor contributed to the value of the output, hence to its selling price. The trick, however, was to measure that fair share accurately, and as trade unions have become stronger throughout the industrialized world, the relatively easy calculations of microeconomic relations between business firms and

---

[4] Alfred Kuhn, *Labor: Institutions and Economics,* rev. ed. (New York: Harcourt Brace Jovanovich, 1967), p. 553.

organized workers have spilled over into the macrocalculations involved in achieving the objectives enumerated in Chapter 2—particularly full employment without inflation.

Cost-push inflation was introduced into the vocabulary of macroeconomic analysis, and as we shall see in a later discussion of inflation and its causes, it involves not the traditional explanation of inflation—too much demand relative to the aggregate supply of goods and services available—but rather the upward pressure on costs (hence prices) produced by excessive increases in wages or profits. It is true that producers can raise prices in an effort to increase their profits and can thus contribute to cost-push inflation, but most analysts rightly or wrongly lay blame on the pressure on costs exerted by organized labor to obtain increases in wages in excess of increases in productivity. This is one of the most vexing policy problems in modern economics, and we shall tackle it in introductory fashion in our later discussion of stabilization policy. Here we wish to note only the dilemma it poses for the modern trade union.

If unions play the role they were designed to play, which originated out of microeconomic considerations, then each union, representing its workers, attempts to improve their lot to the maximum extent possible. This means unremitting pressure on employers for higher wages and better working conditions. If the micro price system is to work at all, this effort on the part of organized workers is comparable to the producer's effort to maximize his profits and the consumers' efforts to maximize their total satisfaction. All operate within certain constraints, but the presumption was that out of the resultant conflict would emerge the ideal resource allocation.

In the previous chapter we saw that business organizations, partly through technological necessity, had become so large that they could not be allowed to operate unfettered, and we raised the question of choosing the appropriate objectives for antitrust policy if we are to maintain competition. The same sort of problems arise in the operation of the labor market, and they arise in more acute form in the United States than in other market-oriented economies because we choose to interfere to the least extent compatible with socially defined "fair" and technologically determined "efficient" operations. This means that Big Business led, as we saw, to Big Labor, and the latter means that when trade unions think only in micro terms—of wage maximization—they can contribute to macro problems—destabilization and inflation—by propelling labor's share of the economic pie faster than the growth of the pie justifies. What does this lead to?

In many market-oriented economies it has led to calls for "labor statesmanship," which means that organized labor must put the public interest ahead of its own interest. Jean Daniel Reynaud has pointed out that while trade union participation in planning efforts requires that they think of their own narrow interests in a broader framework of balanced national advancement, European trade unions are not as eager to push for nationalization now as they were immediately after World War II. Why? If union representatives become involved in the management of nationalized companies, they can no longer think only of the welfare of the unions. For this reason, Reynaud says, experiments in "collective management" in countries like Britain and France have not been very successful.[5]

The dilemma of modern trade unions is that in many countries they have now been sufficiently successful in achieving recognition, size, and power so that they are as influential as business organizations in setting the wages and conditions of work. In consequence, they determine costs of production quite as much as the entrepreneurs. Hence the bargaining process, to which we shall turn shortly, is complicated by the fact that labor leaders, pursuing their self-interest, can no longer be automatically relied on to pursue social welfare. What should labor leaders pursue? The incomes policies developed in other market-oriented economies, like the wage-price guideposts developed during the Kennedy-Johnson days in the United States, are efforts to devise broad, socially acceptable limits within which self-interest can operate at the bargaining table. Incomes policies and wage-price guideposts, discussed in somewhat greater detail in a later chapter, are often declared to have been less than successful, both here and abroad (inflation has become a major international economic problem). But they are an effort to salvage an important part of the functioning of the price system—that in factor markets. As with all tinkering with the price system, successful or not, the changes bring forth more anguish in the U.S. than they do abroad. Shonfield has commented on the "awful doctrinal wrestling" in which Americans tend to engage whenever any part of our previously private system becomes public, and the same can be said of public interference with previously private operations in the system.[6]

It is no doubt true that primarily because Richard Nixon's devotion to untrammeled capitalism was well known was he able in 1971 to persuade the country to go along with his wage-price freeze and the subsequent institution of the Pay Board, Price Committee, and Cost of Living Council during Phase II of his anti-inflation program. These measures were adopted because entrenched inflation seemed to call for extreme measures; they did not appear to represent a fundamental shift in the kinds of interference with the operation of the market system which would be accepted permanently. There were those who maintained that controls over wages and prices would be with us for a long time, but this was a minority view. Business groups embraced controls as a way out of the dilemma which rising factor prices presented to them, but it is not clear that this represented a real break with the basic American predilection for "purity" in its capitalism, which the Europeans, possibly more pragmatic, have seemed to lack for some time.

[5] Jean Daniel Reynaud, "The Role of Trade Unions in National Political Economies (Developed Countries of Europe)," in *International Labor,* Solomon Barkin et al., eds. (New York, Evanston, Ill., and London: Harper and Row, Publishers, 1967), pp. 33-61.

[6] Andrew Shonfield, *Modern Capitalism* (London: Oxford University Press, 1965), p. 298.

This basic difference in outlook accounts for a number of the differences between market-oriented economies outside this country and the United States. It explains why the United States was dragged kicking and screaming, so to speak, to an incomes policy in 1971, where heretofore even "jawboning" (governmental efforts to influence the outcome of collective bargaining negotiations) had not been universally regarded as appropriate. Indeed, jawboning had been denounced by the very groups which were pushed by circumstances to favor the controls enacted in 1971. It does not appear too strong to say that the kind of controls adopted with utmost reluctance as a temporary expedient in the United States had earlier been rather openly embraced in other market-oriented economies. In this difference of attitude lies an important distinction between the U.S. and many other market-oriented economies.

Against this somewhat long but necessary background we will attempt to briefly summarize the major characteristics and important differences among trade union organization and trade union participation in economic decision-making in market-oriented economies.

Characteristics of
Trade Unions in Market-Oriented Economies

In many ways the basic organization of trade unions is similar throughout the Western world. Table 6-1 is an effort to put together some major characteristics of modern trade unions in a form that will underscore both their similarities and their differences. Elsewhere, as in the United States, trade unions are customarily organized at the local level, at the national level, and into federations of national unions. We shall lay stress primarily on the national federations (like the AFL-CIO) because this is the level at which the basic character and economic importance of the unions are determined and most easily seen.

Industry and Craft Unions In the early history of unionism in the U.S. there was considerable controversy over the appropriate organization unit. The old AF of L was organized along craft lines—there was a union for bakers, for painters, for electricians, and so on. This type of organization, sometimes called horizontal organization, is less powerful as the economy becomes more industrialized, and so the CIO employed an industry-wide approach (vertical organization). One organized all the steel workers or all the automobile workers, for example, regardless of where they worked or what they did. In Europe the craft unions were more firmly entrenched than in the United States, but as Table 6-1 indicates (column 7), almost all market-oriented economies have industry-wide trade unions now, although in possibly half these countries there are still, as in the U.S., some unions organized along craft lines. General unions that unite diverse groups of workers are common in Western Europe. In Japan the unions tend to be organized along company lines, although the unions affiliated with the largest national federation (Sohyo) and several other unions appear to cover industries.

Numbers of National Federations   A major difference between unions in the U.S. and elsewhere is that there is a much greater tendency for other market-oriented economies to have several national federations of trade unions, so that workers in given industries (or crafts) have a choice of unions to join. The same industry or craft will often have two or three unions, each of which is affiliated with a different national federation. As is clear from Table 6-1 (column 7), these different national federations are often based either on ideology or religion (or both). This is not the case in the U.S., the U.K., or several other countries included in the list.

Union Membership and Power   Walter Galenson remarked once that "the most obvious index of trade union strength—or weakness—is the degree of organization that has been achieved."[7] He went on to note that obtaining accurate data on union membership was very difficult for both Italy and France and, he might have added, for a number of other countries. Published data on membership vary greatly. Moreover, the number of workers organized in unions is only part of the problem involved in measuring union strength; the other part is the denominator needed to calculate the percentages of workers organized (which we have shown in column 6). In general we have tried to utilize data relating to the civilian labor force, but this has not always been possible. The data on the work force in column 2 and on union membership in column 4 represent our best judgment concerning the most accurate data, and we have calculated the percentages in column 6 from these two sets of information. They do not correspond to some published estimates of union strength.[8]

Neither absolute numbers nor numbers as a percent of the labor force constitute an infallible guide to union influence or power, but it is nonetheless

---

[7] Walter Galenson, *Trade Union Democracy in Western Europe* (Berkeley and Los Angeles: University of California Press, 1961), p. 2.

[8] This was true notably in Japan, in which case Business International Corporation, *Investment, Licensing, and Trading Conditions Abroad* [hereafter *ILT*] (New York: Business International Corp., January 1970) estimates that 32.5 percent of Japanese workers are unionized. Their size estimates for the four major federations are very close to ours. There are a number of unaffiliated locals for which we have found estimates—shown in Table 6-1—of the size of the "major" one only. Another part of the discrepancy lies in the definition of the labor force they employed. Similarly, it is often said that one-third of U.S. workers are unionized (though the percentage has been declining slightly in recent years) but our calculations would put the percentage somewhat lower than this. In general, our estimates are probably on the low side, because splinter unions and small or local unions are not always reported. Their percentages are not apt to affect the relative percentages significantly, however, except possibly in the case noted.

Table 6-1

Major Characteristics of Trade Unions in Thirteen
Market-Oriented Economies, 1969, 1970

Country	Civilian labor force (in thousands)	Trade union federations	No. of members (in millions[d])	No. of affiliated trade unions[d]	Trade unions as a percent of civilian labor force (in percent)	Organizational basis of type
(1)	(2)	(3)	(4)	(5)	(6)	(7)
Japan		Sohyo	4.21[e]	15		Socialist
		Domei	1.87	23		Moderate
		Churitsuroren	1.40	5		
		Shinsambetsu	.70	—		Moderate
			8.18			
		Major nonaffiliated unions	.94[e]	13		(Company unions
	50,150[a]	National councils	4.72[e]	—	27.7[l]	common in all federations)
			13.89			
France		General Confederation of Labor (GGT)	2.4[d]	38		Communist, industry
		Work Force (FO)	1.0	34		Socialist, industry
		French Democratic Confederation of Labor (CFDT)	1.0	4,425+		Catholic, industry
	20,320[a]	Independent groups	?	—	21.7	—
			4.4			
West Germany		German Trade Union Federation (DGB)	6.50[d]	16		Industry or Multi-industry
		Police	.10			
		German Association of Civil Servants (DRB)	.72			
	26,410[a]	German Salaried Workers Union (DAG)	.48		29.6[m]	
			7.80			

Table 6-1 (*continued*)

(1) Country	(2) Civilian labor force (in thousands)	(3) Trade union federations	(4) No. of members (in millions)[d]	(5) No. of affiliated trade unions[d]	(6) Trade unions as a percent of civilian labor force (in percent)	(7) Organizational basis or type
Italy		Italian General Confederation of Labor (CGIL)	3.5[d]	38		Communist, industry
		Italian Confederation of Syndicalist Workers (CISL)	2.4	38		Christian Democratic (Catholic support), industry
		Italian Union of Labor (UIL)	.5	48		Socialist-Social Democratic-Republican, industry
		Other[d]	.4	—		Syndicalists, Neo-Fascist, independent, industry
	19,280[a]		6.8		35.2	
Netherlands		Netherlands Federation of Trade Unions (NVV)	.6[c]	116		Socialist, industry
		Netherlands Catholic Workers Federation (KAB)	.4	19		Catholic, industry
		National Federation of Christian (Protestant) Workers, CNV	.24	24		Protestant, industry (White-collar mostly)
		Independent unions	.31[c]	—		
	4,509[b]		1.55		34.4	

Sweden	3,832[a]	Swedish Federation of Labor (LO)	1.7	29		Industry, some craft
		Central Organization of Salaried Employees (TCO)	.7	—		Salaried employees
		Swedish Professional Association (SACO)	.9[f]	—		Craft (but all white-collar)
		Swedish Customs Officials	.3 / 3.6	—	94.0	
United Kingdom	24,290[a]	Trades Union Congress (TUC)	9.4[d]	150		Industry and craft, multi-industry
		Other	— / 9.4	450[n]	38.7	
United States	80,733[a]	AFL-CIO	14.4[h]	126		Industry and craft
		Alliance for Labor Action[i]	3.3[h]	2		Industry and craft
		Unaffiliated national unions	1.5[h]	62[j]		—
		Unaffiliated local unions	.5[h] / 19.7	—	24.4	—
Austria	3,119[b]	Austrian Federation of Trade Unions (three factions) (OGB)	1.5[d]	16[k]	48.2	Socialist, 66%; Catholic 15%; Communist, 10%; undecided, 9%; industry

Table 6-1 (*continued*)

Country (1)	Civilian labor force (in thousands) (2)	Trade union federations (3)	No. of members (in millions)[d] (4)	No. of affiliated trade unions[d] (5)	Trade unions as a percent of civilian labor force (in percent) (6)	Organizational basis or type (7)
Belgium		Belgian Central Federation of Labor (FGTB)	.8	15		Socialist, industry
		Confederation of Christian Trade Unions (CSC)	.9	17		Catholic, industry
		General Federation of Liberal Unions of Belgium (CSLB)	.1	—		
	3,725[b]		1.8		48.3	Public services (white-collar)
Norway	1,481[b]	Norwegian Federation of Trade Unions (LO)	.6[d]	37	40.5	Industry and craft
Canada		Canadian Labor Congress (CNTU)	1.6[d]	115		
		Confederation of National Trade Unions	.22[d]	900		
		Other (principal)	.14[d]	4		Religious, craft
	8,162[a]		1.96		24.0	
Denmark	2,352[b]	Federation of Danish Trade Unions	.865[c]	60	36.8	Industry and craft

Notes and sources:

a. For these eight industrial countries the *Monthly Labor Review* has attempted to adjust the civilian labor force figures to U.S. concepts. Canadian figures need no adjustment. See Constance Sorrento, "Unemployment in the United States and Seven Foreign Countries," *Monthly Labor Review* 93, No. 9 (September 1970): 14, Table 1. Data are for 1969.

b. All other countries (Netherlands, Austria, Belgium, Norway, and Denmark) are 1968 estimates of the civilian labor force published in *Labor Force Statistics 1957-1968* (Paris: OECD, 1970).

c. Dutch independent union strength is based on a 1966 estimate by John P. Windmuller, *Labor Relations in the Netherlands* (Ithaca N.Y.: Cornell University Press, 1969), Chapter 5. He estimates that 80% of union membership is in the three federations and 20% is in independent unions. We estimated the size of independent union membership accordingly.

d. Union membership and number of affiliated unions (col. 5), except where otherwise indicated, have been calculated from published figures in *The Europa Yearbook, 1971: A World Survey*, vols. 1 and 2 (London: Europa Publications, 1971).

e. In Japan there are eight national councils—coordinating bodies for unions whose members are in the same industry or have the same employer. We have eliminated one (The Liaison Organization of Public Workers Unions—membership 2,5000,000), because it is affiliated with SOHYO. The others appear to be independent. (*Europa Yearbook*, 1971, vol. 2.) (However, see footnote l.) Ayusawa estimated 1962 independent union strength in Japan at 14.9% of the total, "others" at 25%. But there were only three major federations then. (Iwao F. Ayusawa, *A History of Labor in Modern Japan* [Honolulu: East-West Center Press, 1966], p. 363.)

f. 1967 estimate from Everett M. Kassalow, *Trade Unions and Industrial Relations: An International Comparison* (New York: Random House, 1969), p. 89. See also Arne H. Nilstein "White-Collar Trade Unionism in Sweden," in *White-Collar Trade Unions*, Adolph Sturmthal, ed. (Urbana, Ill.: University of Illinois Press, 1967), pp. 261-304.

g. There are approximately twelve national union federations in Italy. "Other" represents membership estimates for only two of these (the size of the others—all small—was not available). Hence seven small national federations are not included in these estimates, but the degree of understatement is believed to be very small.

h. U.S. union membership size based on Business International Corporation, *Investment, Licensing, and Trading Conditions Abroad* (New York: Business International Corp.), as of 1969. Paul A. Samuelson (*Economics*, 8th ed. [New York: McGraw-Hill Book Co., 1970], p. 224) puts the estimate at "one-third" of the nonagricultural working force. Windmuller estimates 28% of organized wage and salary earners (p. 184).

i. Formed in 1968 by the alliance of the independent International Brotherhood of Teamsters and the United Auto Workers (AFL-CIO).

j. Samuelson has estimated that the United States has 190 autonomous national unions (p. 126). Our estimate of the unaffiliated national unions is based on this figure and data in *Investment, Licensing, and Trading Conditions Abroad, 1970.*

k. As of December 1967.

l. The ILT estimate (1970) was that 35.2% of Japanese workers were unionized. Their estimate of the numbers in the four federations agree roughly with the *Europa Yearbook* figures given. Our percentage estimate, as indicated, includes the four federations, the unaffiliated unions, and the national councils, with the exception noted in footnote e. Ayusawa estimated in 1966 that 36.2% of Japanese workers were unionized, with 13.4% in unaffiliated unions and 25% in "other" unions. (He does not mention the councils.) He also suggested that some unions are affiliated with two national federations. He estimated the total membership in all unions in 1966 at about 9 million, indicating that the national councils we have included may represent more duplication than indicated in the *Europa Yearbook* estimates for the information available and presented in footnote e. (See Ayusawa, pp. 370-71.) Our estimate is therefore clearly not exact, but it represents the best available percentage estimate of union strength in Japan.

m. The ILT estimates that the DGB represents 29.7% of "all gainfully employed" workers. Our estimate of total German union strength is reasonably accurate but slightly low because no data are available on the size of the unaffiliated unions other than those shown.

n. Peter Donaldson (*Guide to the British Economy* [Harmondsworth, England, and Baltimore, Md.: Penguin Books, 1965], p. 136), suggests that the total number of trade unions in the U.K. is something under 700, from which the estimate in col. 5 was derived. Membership size is not indicated, but they are all small. The percentage estimate in col. 6 is somewhat low, but not extremely so.

Note: In general, it should be remembered that placing all these percentages, where possible, on a comparable basis with U.S. concepts may cause discrepancies with data published in various national publications.

interesting to note that the percentages indicated in column 6 are, with the exception of Sweden, quite low: no more than one-fifth to one-third of the civilian labor force of the typical market-oriented economy is organized in unions. This understates union power, however, because in many countries (either implicitly or explicitly) trade unions play a pivotal role in determining the wages and working conditions under which nonunionized workers live. Sometimes this happens through the influence of national trade union federations on governmental decisions affecting labor, and sometimes (as in the United States) it is accomplished by the fact that union contracts set patterns which tend to be used to cover nonunion workers as well.

Trade Unions in Action
in Market-Oriented Economies

We cannot possibly review in detail the trade union policies in all the countries considered in Table 6-1, but we can suggest the main kinds of operational techniques employed and their differences from the method utilized in this country, and we can attempt a general assessment of their current status.

Minimum Wages One of the most crucial issues for any trade union involves the pay workers receive. Many economies, including the United States, have now taken this matter out of the hands of employers, at least insofar as minima are concerned, so that collective bargaining revolves around wages in excess of the minimum provided by law and around numerous nonwage matters. The Fair Labor Standards Act of 1938 established minimum wages for workers in U.S. industries that were involved in interstate commerce, and the minimum has been revised upward a number of times since. In France there is a three-zone minimum wage system (skilled, semiskilled, and unskilled workers), and the Netherlands has what they call a social minimum wage, which is revised every two years. In the United Kingdom the tripartite wage councils fix separate minimum wages for different industries.

Wage Agreements The American system wherein each union bargains collectively with each employer is not typically employed in other economies. The AFL-CIO, though much interested in the outcome of wage negotiations, never bargains directly on behalf of any worker. Instead, the negotiations are carried out by representatives of employees and employers in each industry. In many countries (Austria, France, Germany, Belgium, and especially Sweden, for example) collective bargaining is often highly centralized and carried out on an industry-wide basis by representatives of both sides. Other countries now use negotiations between the trade union federations and the employer's associations (with the government involved in varying ways) in which central wage agreements are reached which apply to the workers in all unions. This technique has been particularly prominent in Scandinavia. Italy has a system of nationwide bargaining to set minimum wages, as does Britain. In Britain individual unions are free to bargain for wages higher than the minimum, much as in the U.S., except that the minimum wage here is not the result of economic bargaining. In Italy the minimum wage is tied to the cost of living (for each 6 percent increase in the cost of living there is an automatic increase in wages).

Social Security   The data in Table 6-2 suggest that part of the security which trade unions at one time bargained for has now been institutionalized through social security systems. We have already considered some of the expenditures which national governments make toward the welfare of their citizens (Chapter 3). Here we consider only those social security programs toward which both employees and employers contribute.[9] The United States is the only country in which the government per se makes no contribution to social security. What we shall call paternalism later in this chapter is therefore not a part of the U.S. system, a fact of some importance because collective bargaining procedures in the U.S. are therefore more likely to include efforts to obtain private or company welfare programs to supplement the low social security benefits.[10]

The United Nations source from which the non-U.S. portion of Table 6-2 is derived comments:

> A certain pattern emerges. Where benefits are high, as in Austria, Belgium, France, Western Germany and Italy, . . . the major source of finance was employers' contributions . . . . Where benefits are relatively low, . . . as in Denmark, . . . the Netherlands, . . . and the United Kingdom, social security is financed mainly by Government.[11]

From this statement they exempt the Netherlands, where one finds high benefits but a small percentage of the total financed by the government. The United States is conspicuous both because social security benefits are a small percentage of personal income and because the government does not participate in its financing.

The degree of governmental participation in such schemes, as well as the degree to which employer participation has become structured, reduce the scope required for collective bargaining to augment social security. Clearly such scope is largest in the United States. Concern with fringe benefits in other countries will be commented on in the following discussion.

---

[9] Such programs apply, of course, to nonunionized as well as to unionized employees.

[10] The U.S. figures are not strictly comparable to the others in Table 6-2. See the notes to the table.

[11] United Nations, *Incomes in Postwar Europe: A Study of Policies, Growth, and Distribution* (Geneva: United Nations, 1967), p. 7.

Table 6-2
Social Security Contributions
and Benefits in 1960
(percentages)

	Financing of social security (total receipts = 100)				Employees' contribution as a percentage of personal primary income	Social security as a percentage of personal primary income
	Contributions		General Government	Other Source		
	Employers	Employees				
Austria	50.5	24.4	20.6	4.5	5.3	18.8
Belgium	41.5	18.5	31.4	8.7	3.6	17.2
Denmark	10.6	14.9	74.0	0.5	2.1	13.5
France	61.5	15.4	19.8	3.3	3.0	17.7
West Germany	41.2	24.9	26.1	7.9	6.0	20.7
Italy	59.0	11.9	23.0	6.1	2.4	16.5
Netherlands	39.2	40.3	12.7	7.7	7.1	14.0
Norway	26.5	31.7	40.0	1.7	5.4	15.6
Sweden	11.0	20.5	66.9	1.6	3.3	15.6
United Kingdom	17.0	18.9	59.2	4.9	2.8	13.8
United States	54.9	45.1	—	—	2.1	4.8

Sources:
All non-U.S. data came from United Nations, *Incomes in Post-War Europe: A Study of Policies, Growth, and Distribution* (Geneva: United Nations, 1967), Chapter 6, p. 7. U.S. data on employer and employee contributions to social security and social security benefits paid are for the year 1959 and come from Tax Foundation, *Facts and Figures on Government Finance*, 16th biennial ed. (New York: Tax Foundation, 1971), Table 15, p. 27, and Table 16, p. 28. Social security benefits for 1968 have been related to personal income for the United States in calendar 1968. The percentages do not vary significantly from year to year. However, the U.S. "personal income" is not quite comparable to the U.N. definition of primary personal income, because the latter included depreciation allowances for unincorporated enterprise.

Collective Bargaining in Action We mentioned earlier that union size was no infallible guide to union influence. Some years ago Walter Galenson suggested that Italy and France had rival unions (several national federations with unions competing for the same workers), but the unions in both countries are generally considered to be weak. On the other hand, Belgium, the Netherlands, and Austria have rival unionism but strong trade unions as well. Galenson suggested that the unions in the U.K. and Scandinavia were unified and strong.[12]

Another basic structural difference in these economies enables us to classify unionism in a somewhat different way, on the basis of trade union-government relationships. In countries with no formal planning mechanism there is no official relationship between government and unions. Jean Daniel Reynaud has suggested that the unions in Germany, remembering the 1930s, are wary of government and prefer to keep away from efforts at cooperative planning with government, sticking closer to traditional bargaining techniques (not unlike the system in the United States). In Switzerland, another unplanned economy, the unions are sufficiently close to government that they feel they can make their views known through consultation prior to parliamentary action on matters affecting them, as Big Business, farmers, and other groups do. In some countries (such as the Netherlands, Italy, and the Scandinavian countries) the government draws up a plan and is responsible for ultimate decisions, but the trade unions are consulted in a variety of ways, though not through any channels fixed by law. Finally, the planning mechanism can involve institutionalized mechanisms for government trade union cooperation (often with business as well in the tripartite system we have considered). This is true of French indicative planning, and as well in Belgium and the U.K.[13]

Let us now consider how trade unions function in several representative market-oriented economies. Several patterns in addition to that of the United States can be discerned.

Sweden Sweden was once described as "the organizational society par excellence" in the Western world.[14] In this highly organized society Swedish labor has been described as the best paid in Europe and has been characterized by both high productivity and "exemplary discipline."[15]

The main trade union federations, the Confederation of Swedish Trade Unions (LO), the Central Organization Salaried Employees (TCO), and the Swedish Professional Association (SACO) together represent the highest percentage of workers in any market-oriented economy. The employers in turn are represented by the Swedish Employers Association (SAF), whose main aim is to "safeguard the interests of the employers in questions concerning their relations with

---

[12] Galenson, *Trade Union Democracy in Western Europe*, p. 42.

[13] Reynaud, "The Role of Trade Unions in Developed Political Economies (Developed Countries of Europe)," p. 36.

[14] Galenson, *Trade Union Democracy in Western Europe*, pp. 73-74.

[15] Business International Corporation, *ILT*, Sweden (June 1970).

employees."[16] How centralized the collective bargaining is in Sweden can be seen by the fact that the SAF in 1970 represented 28,650 employers, who in turn employed 1,250,000 workers. Reference to Table 6-1 will show that this represents a good portion of all workers organized in Swedish unions. So both sides of collective bargaining in Sweden are highly centralized, but as Kuhn has pointed out, "Centralization by the unions was a necessary response to the existing strong nation-wide association of employers."[17] This is worth remembering because, as we suggested in another context, most employee organization in market-oriented economies has been in response to employer structure and behavior (a generalization that holds up better than most).

In Sweden, as in Britain, there has long been a labor party with a socialist orientation, but unlike Britain there has been relatively little nationalization in Sweden. We indicated in Chapter 2 the nature of the central wage bargain and the manner in which the LO and the SAF negotiate in determining the national wage system. The resulting contract is for two years. Further evidence of the extreme centralization and coordination of Swedish manpower policy is to be seen in the structure and functions of the national Labor Market Board. This board is composed of two members of the SAF, two from the LO, one from the TCO, one representative each of agriculture and female workers (members of the Women's Liberation Movement in the United States take note!), and three representatives of the government. The board has broad responsibilities in manpower planning and policy, as we shall show, and therefore—because both the SAF and the LO are prominently represented—collective bargaining is forced to remain socially oriented as well as oriented to the special interests of each side of the bargaining process. Kuhn has commented on the "unprecedented dilemma" in the Swedish system of union leaders who want to "do something" for their members and yet not appear to be "economic fools by demanding wage increases."[18] Here in part is the Swedish answer to the dilemma of micro interests and macro interests. Strikes, though not illegal, are little used because Swedish unions realize that in the long run worker incomes depend on increased productivity and that strikes are incompatible with that goal.

The Swedish Labor Market Board is strong and influential. It is responsible for developing techniques to increase employment (by using the investment reserve system referred to in Chapter 2, for example), it operates the public works programs, stimulates both geographic and occupational mobility, and undertakes economic forecasting.[19] In such a milieu collective bargaining and central governmental policy cannot easily diverge too far. Nor is it surprising

[16] *The Europa Year Book, 1971: A World Survey*, Vol. 2 (London: Europa Publications, 1971), p. 1149.

[17] Kuhn, *Labor: Institutions and Economics*, p. 529.

[18] Ibid., p. 530.

[19] For detailed treatment of the Swedish system see Martin Schnitzer, *The Swedish Investment Reserve: A Device for Economic Stabilization?* (Washington, D.C.: American Enterprise Institute for Public Policy Research, July 1967), pp. 13-14.

that many of the nonwage aspects which in other countries become the subject of collective bargaining (job security, vacation, and so on) are paid for by the state out of general taxes. (Note the government's high share of social security in Table 6-2.) Only four fringe benefits are paid for by the employers: workmen's industrial injury insurance, a compulsory pension plan, life insurance for all employees over twenty-one years of age, and health and maternity insurance. Payments for these benefits account for some twenty percent of the total payroll.[20]

In sum, the Swedish system is one of the most impressive collective bargaining systems in the market-oriented world; it appears to combine security, worker freedom, and balance between micro and macro interests. It has not avoided the problem of cost-push inflation, but its inflation problems have been less severe than those of a number of other countries.

The United Kingdom It has been said that labor organization in Sweden and in the United Kingdom is similar to that in the United States. We have seen, however, that while there are resemblances, Swedish union organization, operation, and control is a great deal more centralized than is the case in the U.S. Comparison of the United Kingdom to the United States would appear to be more justified. Collective bargaining is compulsory in nationalized industries—that is, management is required to bargain with unions—but in the rest of the British economy the relations between worker organizations and employers tend to be determined at the industry or plant level, much as they are in the United States. It is true that a centralized wage agreement is worked out between the Trades Union Congress, which "stands unchallenged at the apex of the trade union movement in Great Britain,"[21] and the British Employers Association, and that similar negotiations between, for example, the AFL-CIO and the National Association of Manufacturers would be quite unheard of in the U.S. But the United Kingdom's national wage is not binding on any local union or company unless explicitly ratified; no central authority can impose any wage settlement on any nonnationalized industry. Of this central wage agreement it has been said,

> The United Kingdom is in the almost unique position of permitting collective bargaining agreements to be signed without these contracts becoming legally binding on employers or employees, unless their terms are expressly or implicitly incorporated separately in an individual contract of employment, which is seldom done.[22]

---

[20] Business International Corporation, *ILT* (June 1970), p. 626.
[21] Galenson, *Trade Union Democracy in Western Europe*, p. 43.
[22] Business International Corporation, *ILT* (June 1970), p. 688.

Part of the explanation lies in the fact that the national agreements do not usually reflect local conditions in individual industries or geographic areas.[23] The result is that in practice, wage negotiations tend to be far more localized than in the United States, where industry-wide bargaining is common, and far less centralized than in Sweden.[24]

This situation reflects a traditional British attitude which Shonfield has described as "arms length government," in which the government has pursued in many areas an attitude of letting local units resolve conflict, certainly to a far greater extent than is true in Scandinavia or on the Continent. (It explains, too, why an incomes policy, which may have come naturally to the Scandinavians, has traditionally been almost as alien to the British way of life as it has been to the American.)

Ironically, all this means that despite the fact that trade unions are far stronger in Britain than, say, in France and that there are long-standing ties between trade unions and the Labour party in Britain, as Shonfield has underscored, British workers are far more on their own in achieving the customary benefits of organization (in wages, working conditions, and fringe benefits) than in a country like France, where the state attitude has been far more interventionist than in what Shonfield calls "the Unpaternal State" (Britain).[25] Workers have to achieve whatever wage increases, job security, and fringe benefits they receive via their own local shop steward committees and workshop committees. (It should be remembered, however, that although British workers have to achieve many fringe benefits through collective bargaining with employers, much as in the United States, a number of benefits accrue to British workers which are not available to U.S. workers—for example, the national health system and high social security benefits. Moreover, the state has only recently and reluctantly moved into manpower retraining and similar programs designed to keep the labor force attuned to the changing technological requirements of the economy. Under these circumstances it is not surprising that Britain has had an increasing number of strikes. Many other problems have contributed to labor unrest in Britain, however, including a relatively high unemployment rate.

In sum, it would appear safe to conclude that the British trade union system, despite a number of features which make it appear centralized, is a good deal closer to the U.S. system than to the Scandinavian system. We have seen that the Trades Union Congress has no control over the bargaining activities of its affiliated unions, it has been described as "only a hortatory, advisory, conciliatory body with next to no control over the affairs of the individual unions."[26] Could not this description apply with almost equal accuracy to the

[23] See Peter Donaldson, *Guide to the British Economy* (Harmondsworth, England, and Baltimore, Md.: Penguin Books, 1965), p. 205.

[24] Ibid., pp. 205-6.

[25] Shonfield, *Modern Capitalism*, pp. 112-20.

[26] Donaldson, *Guide to the British Economy*, p. 136.

AFL-CIO? Only in relations with the national government, in which, as we saw in Chapter 2, the TUC is involved through the tripartite principle in the planning mechanism, do the British and American systems diverge sharply. The AFL-CIO can testify before Congress and can occasionally obtain the ear of the president and his advisers, but American unionism is not involved in the development of national policy to the degree that unionism is in Britain. It is at the level of TUC-governmental relations rather than at the level of relations between the TUC and national unions that the differences with the U.S. stand out and the long tradition of close liaison between the trade union movement and the Labour party show up.

> The British Labour party began as a creature of the trade unions, and although it has since gained its independence, relations between the two branches of the labor movement remain close. Seventeen of the eighteen largest national unions are affiliated with the Labour party, and maintain political funds.[27]

Herein lies the crucial difference between the roles played by the trade unions in the U.S. and in the U.K.

The Netherlands   The contrasts between Dutch and U.S. trade union organizations are also great. Not only are there three major national trade union federations, distinguished little by ideology and mostly by religion, but out of this rivalry has come a strong and in many ways responsible trade union movement. The conflict between trade unions' micro interests and the macro interests that inflation has thrust to the fore in recent years has been, if not solved, at least muted in this small but progressive democracy.

As we have already seen, the tripartite principle is firmly established in the Netherlands. The Social and Economic Council (SER), with labor, business, and government represented equally, has divided its fifteeen labor seats by giving five to the Catholic federation (KAB), seven to the dominant NVV (socialist in origin), and three to the CNV (Protestant).[28] These three federations represent 80 percent of all organized workers in the Netherlands; the other twenty percent are scattered in independent unions. The growth of membership in Dutch unions is extremely impressive when one realizes that throughout the entire postwar period collective bargaining has been constrained by these overriding national considerations, or as one writer put it, "Increases in labor costs were centrally limited."[29]

---

[27] Galenson, *Trade Union Democracy in Western Europe*, pp. 65-66.

[28] Ibid., pp. 32-33.

[29] John P. Windmuller, *Labor Relations in the Netherlands* (Ithaca, N.Y.: Cornell University Press, 1969) p. 129.

In the Netherlands collective bargaining between employers and employees is more apt to be bargaining between the interested parties through their representatives on the Social and Economic Council. The constant involvement of Dutch unions in national policy decisions has created a "remarkable system of bargaining," as Galenson has called it, although one in which difficulties have arisen because while the leaders may understand the national issues the rank and file members do not necessarily understand them. All in all, however, Galenson has appropriately characterized it as a system which "has worked."[30] That it has worked without much local union autonomy goes without saying.

Since 1959 the government through the SER has had direct control over wages which make most other moves toward an incomes policy look pale. It has determined the principles to guide wage changes, and it has guided the translation of these principles into actual wage changes. These changes were made by collective bargaining, to be sure, but the results of the bargaining had to be approved by the Board of State Conciliators, which acted under orders from the government. The board also set wages when collective bargaining did not produce results or was not used. Finally, wages paid were (and are) subject to verification—a form of government inspection.[31] This sounds pretty far removed from a free price system and makes the Dutch labor market seem quite remote from the U.S. market-oriented but conflict-ridden system for determining returns to labor.

The Dutch experience is worth pondering because unions are strong, as in the U.S., because there are rival federations that give workers a choice, unlike the U.S., and because industrial peace is impressive despite the overriding macro considerations which rule labor negotiations. One might argue that union choice is relatively meaningless in a nation where unions are strongly supervised. On the other hand, the problems raised by union power and inflation have scarcely been solved either in Britain or the United States. The unemployment rate has remained relatively low in the Netherlands, and inflation, though a problem in the Netherlands, too, is a factor brought relatively easily into the picture in determining wage adjustments. Windmuller correctly characterizes the closeness of micro-economic and macro-economic decisions:

> Macro-economic considerations have always been uppermost in the economic policies of the unions, especially at federation levels. Corrective government intervention in wage setting based on macro-economic agencies, such as the need to reverse the balance of payments from a negative to a positive one, has carried a high degree of conviction with the unions precisely because they themselves have become accustomed to reasoning in these terms.[32]

[30] Galenson, *Trade Union Democracy in Western Europe,* p. 33.

[31] H. A. Turner and H. Zoeteweji, *Prices, Wages, and Income Policies* (Geneva: International Labor Office, 1966), p. 105.

[32] Windmuller, *Labor Relations in the Netherlands,* p. 383. The Dutch, as much as the Swedish labor leaders, wish to avoid looking like "economic fools."

One could scarcely make the same statement about the AFL-CIO, precisely because it has always been an article of faith in the U.S. that a market-oriented economy could work only if prices were mainly determined by self-interest. But self-interest forces crucial limitations on the micro-macro dichotomy, to which the U.S. has clung tenaciously in the field of labor. The Dutch experience suggests that dynamic public labor policy in the modern market-oriented economy will always involve a trade-off between micro and macro self-interest, and that avoiding interference with the collective bargaining process to retain free collective bargaining at the cost of uncontrolled inflation may be too high a price for any economy to pay, however market-oriented or free it hopes to be.

France   France has rival unionism at the federal level, so that workers in similar jobs or industries have a choice (made along ideological or—less often now—religious lines). This situation is therefore not unlike that found in Holland, but unlike the Dutch system, French unions are weak. The percent of organized workers in France is low in comparison with other countries included in Table 6-1. Local organization and discipline is weak and French unions have produced minimal economic impact.

Collective bargaining is not particularly effective, partly because the important decisions are not often left to the collective bargaining process. A generally paternalistic governmental approach has succeeded in guaranteeing workers certain security and some benefits, but these arrangements are outside the normal bargaining procedures. The employers are reasonably well organized in the CNPF (Confédération Nationale du Patrons Français), and they face divided labor unions at the bargaining table. There are currently three major unions; the communist CGT (Confédération Générale du Travail) is the largest, while the FO(CGT-FO—Confédération Générale du Travail-Force Ouvrière) and the CFDT (Confédération Française Democratique du Travail) are smaller and of about equal size.[33] The rivalry among them is intense, and the likelihood of labor unity comparable to employer unity is small.

There is a national minimum wage (SMIG—Salaire Minimum Inter-professionnel Garantie) and it is revised upward periodically, presumably in accord with the dictates of the current plan and the cost of living. The role of collective bargaining is extremely limited—nationalized industries are not subject to the collective bargaining process at all, and basic decisions concerning working conditions and wage adjustments tend to be the result of the negotiations between the government and the employers association. The labor unions are more apt to exert whatever influence they have outside the bargaining process per se. In short, collective bargaining is not yet a primary factor in regulating French industrial relations, a point underscored by Adolph Sturmthal, who adds

---

[33] The CGT has been the leading French union since before World War II, although the splits and reunitings of French trade unions are hard to keep up with. The FO is the result of a split in 1948 from the CGT by more moderate but nonetheless socialist elements. The third union, now known as the CFDT, was formerly known as the Confédération Français des Travailleurs Chretiens, a leftist Catholic union which changed its name in 1964.

that French workers may well end up with more than they would if they were forced to wring concessions from the well-organized and scarcely sympathetic employers associations rather than from the fairly paternalistic state.[34] What recognition the unions have achieved has been the result of state pressure on employers rather than of the strength of the unions.

Although the unions gain relatively little through collective bargaining, social and political pressure can build as the result, say, of declining labor purchasing power during periods of inflation, resulting in explosions such as occurred in 1968. Then the government capitulates to the unions, grants the wage increase, and thus maintains the wage-price spiral. (As we shall see in a subsequent discussion, the French record on stabilization policy is a dreary one.) Strikes are frequent, ineffective, and of a radically different pattern from U.S. strikes. In the U.S. unions tend to strike at the expiration of contracts to force concessions for the subsequent contract; the French stage short-term nuisance strikes to dramatize an issue. The French public seem resigned to these periodic inconveniences, and their ultimate impact is unclear.

As befits a fairly paternalistic system, the state provides workers with much of what they would be forced to obtain through bargaining in other market-oriented economies. Nonetheless, as is shown in Table 6-2, French employers contribute heavily to various fringe benefits (social insurance, family allowances, and so on). Such payments, however, have been generally pushed onto the employers by the government rather than by union pressure, narrowing the necessary scope of collective bargaining. The payments increase labor costs by something approaching 57 percent of basic wages and salaries.[35]

In sum, France is an excellent example of a market-oriented economy in which the economic impact of trade unions through traditional collective bargaining is extremely weak and ineffective, partly because of rivalry among unions, partly because of relatively poor discipline at the local levels, partly because of a generally paternalistic state, and partly because of good organization and relatively little sympathy for unions on the part of the employers association. Galenson has correctly pointed out that in both France and Italy, where unions are in many respects similar to French unions, the character of unionism is as much political as it is economic.[36] Herein lies what power French unions have, and herein lies also a major difference between trade unions in France and in the United States.

West Germany   We shall examine one last example of trade union functioning in market-oriented economies, that of West Germany. There are possibly more similarities in union organization and functioning between the

---

[34] Adolph Sturmthal, "Collective Bargaining in France," in *Contemporary Collective Bargaining,* Adolph Sturmthal, ed. (Ithaca, N.Y.: Cornell University Press, 1957), p. 165.

[35] Business International Corporation, *ILT,* France (November 1970), p. 440.

[36] Galenson, *Trade Union Democracy in Western Europe,* p. 12.

Federal Republic and the U.S. than between the U.S. and other systems, but there are also some crucial differences. Superficially the similarities are apparent. Like the AFL-CIO, the DGB (Deutsch Gewerkschafts Bund) is the sole national trade union federation, and it represents most of the organized workers. There are sixteen trade unions in the DGB, and the largest, I. G. Metall, the metalworkers union, has more than two million members, and is the largest single union in the world. Moreover, in collective bargaining it tends to be a pattern setter, much as the United Steel Workers Union or the United Auto Workers in the United States. The sixteen unions in DGB are very unequal in size and influence: three others at the top with the metalworkers (the transport and public service workers union, the chemical workers union, and the construction workers union) represent three-fifths of all DGB members; eight unions are of intermediate size, and four are very small.[37]

Unlike the United States, strikes are relatively rare. This is attributed by Clark Kerr to the use of pattern-setting arrangements as well as to conciliation and arbitration. It is also due to the fact that the employers associations are very highly organized, and although trade unionism is centralized in Germany, the employers organizations are not only centralized but stronger. In part this may be explained by the fact that the DGB is the end product of a very diverse system of national unions in pre-Hitler Germany, and the socialists and the Catholics "still retain their separate identities within the DGB."[38] It is also due to the fact that collective bargaining is very centralized and coordinated, with the result that employers never bargain with individual unions within the DGB. The unions are becoming multi-industrial rather than industrial (they are never organized along craft lines) in an effort to equalize the bargaining power.

Like the U.S., Germany is "unplanned," and so the tripartite division of political power in some of the economies we have considered, which gave organized labor an avenue through which to influence economic policy, does not exist in Germany any more than in the United States. However, in contrast to the U.S. situation, German unions not only feel themselves economically powerful but have also actively sought to achieve "codetermination," which means that workers want an equal share with business in the management of industrial activities. As Kerr has noted, this battle for codetermination has been fiercely fought in postwar Germany.[39] Codetermination is therefore not unlike the worker-participation plan which de Gaulle advocated, except that the latter was designed to give workers involvement at the rank-and-file level, thus preventing the kind of political eruptions mentioned earlier. The German plan is designed to bring trade unions economic and political power at the top, not at the bottom.

[37] A good summary of postwar German unionism, on which this summary has drawn heavily, is Clark Kerr, "Collective Bargaining in Postwar Germany," in *Contemporary Collective Bargaining,* Sturmthal, ed., pp. 168-209.

[38] Ibid., p. 309.

[39] Ibid., p. 169.

Kerr has remarked that the Nazi interlude has been passed over with remarkably few changes, the status quo ante having reasserted itself in many labor areas. He is in agreement with many other students of recent German history when he notes that the recentralization of power in a relatively short period of time in the hands of the DGB, despite some initial efforts at decentralization of power, is symptomatic of "basic characteristics" in German unionism.[40] Because precisely the same comment has been made about the recentralization of power in the three big German banks, it would appear that centralization of power is a characteristic pattern which comes naturally to the German people.

In sum, while German trade union activity bears more similarity to U.S. trade union activity than that of any other country we have considered, it is also clear that critical differences reflective of basic divergences in the character, history, and traditions of the two countries are apparent in their trade union structure, function, and ultimate economic impact.

Other Market-Oriented Economies   Time and space do not permit even the brief sketches we have thus far given of trade unionism in other market-oriented economies outside the United States. We have not commented on U.S. unionism per se, although it is included in the tables for comparative purposes, and it has been characterized in general terms in this chapter. Suffice it to say that in Galenson's classification of unions, the U.S. belongs with Scandinavia and the U.K.—that is, in the group with unified national federations unrelated to religion or ideology and with strong unions in which collective bargaining is industry-wide. Unlike Scandinavia (of which we have used Sweden as an example), there is no central wage bargaining in the United States, and by the same token, the tendency toward pattern-setting wage and other agreements in major industry bargaining is not prominent in the Scandinavian countries. Collective bargaining for fringe benefits is especially prominent in the U.S.

Among countries with rival unions at the federation level, Italy is very much like France. There are a number of national federations differentiated by ideology, union organization at the local level is weak, and bargaining tends to take place between the top organizations of workers and employers—a situation in which the employers have the advantage because of rivalry among the labor federations. But Galenson points out that rival unionism per se need not be weak, as it is in France and Italy, for it can be strong, as it is in the Netherlands. (He suggests that rival unionism has produced equally impressive results in Belgium and Austria.[41] He might have added Japan, had he been writing a bit later and not concentrating exclusively on Western Europe.)

[40] Ibid., p. 183.

[41] See Galenson's general organization for substantiation of this point and his conclusions: "The French and Italian experience illustrates clearly how dangerous internal division can be to a labor movement which has not gained general acceptance." (*Trade Union Democracy in Western Europe*, p. 88.) "In the Low Countries, and in Scandinavia,

In market-oriented economies in which more or less formalized planning is carried out, there exists a potential political (as well as economic) road to union power and influence. Formal tripartite arrangements appear to be either developed or in the process of development in Belgium, the U.K., and France. In the Netherlands, Norway, Sweden, and Italy planning is emerging and labor organizations are consulted in less formal ways. In Germany (an unplanned economy still, despite some recent developments considered in Chapter 2) trade unions are on their own, as they are in the United States.

The case of Japan is interesting. Its largest and oldest labor federation (SHYO) has been likened to the DGB in Germany.[42] But unlike both the German and British systems, it suffers from much rival unionism. Postwar Japan, like postwar Germany, has been built in the American image, and like Germany, it has had little experience with democratic institutions, so that forming a trade union movement that is both democratic and centralized presents a challenge that is not yet met. The similarities among these three countries (the U.S., Germany, and Japan) are well known. Planning is relatively modest to unknown in all, two are the leading nations in economic growth and development in the period since World War II, and the U.S. is the leading producer. The trade union movement, like much else in Japan, is still finding its appropriate niche, but it appears to be pursuing the path of American unionism, albeit unionism at a less-developed period in U.S. history. Most labor disputes revolve around wages, the next highest number concern conditions of worker dismissal, and relatively few relate to work conditions. The stage of development of the unions is revealed by the fact that relatively few disputes concerned union recognition (a battle won) and relatively few concerned welfare provisions, the latter no doubt reflecting the paternalism that still permeates Japanese economic life.[43]

Conclusions

In general there are two roads to trade union power and influence. The first is through the development of a strong union movement, particularly at the industry level, and the establishment of collective bargaining procedures through which unions can make significant headway in achieving their traditional objectives—higher wages, better working conditions, job security, shorter hours, and various fringe benefits. The development of collective bargaining through strong unions and industry-wide bargaining in market-oriented economies can be viewed as an effort to offset the power of organized business. As such, the

Austria, and Great Britain, trade unions have gained unassailable positions." (p. 89) The latter group includes both the single federation countries and rival federations.

[42] See Iwao F. Ayusawa, *A History of Labor in Modern Japan* (Honolulu: East-West Center Press, 1966).

[43] Ibid., p. 353. The period referred to covers labor disputes from 1955-1962.

argument has always been that organization and strength on both sides of the bargaining table can make the price system work in this important factor market, even in the wake of the requirements of modern industrialism. Without equality of strength factor markets could no longer be subject to allocation by the free prices, but would require heavy government intervention and so could no longer be properly viewed as market-oriented.

The other road to union power depends less on the strength of national unions at the industry level and more on the power of national federations of unions and their ability to represent the interest of workers in the deliberations of councils (usually tripartite) at the highest levels in market-oriented economies where economic planning is advanced. We have seen that this road can be significant whether there is a single federation, as in the United Kingdom, or rival unionism, as in the Netherlands (or Belgium and Austria).

These two roads are by no means competitive. In the United Kingdom both have been pursued with considerable success, whereas in the United States and West Germany the former has been very successful and the latter eschewed (though moves in the direction of tripartite consultation, if not planning, are beginning to be considered in Germany).

Finally, in the area of fringe benefits and job security especially we can see that union development can be either delayed or augmented by the degree of paternalism exercised by the state. Security can be achieved in the face of weak unions if it is provided by the state or if the state can persuade employers to provide it despite weak unions (Italy and France).

Some of our conclusions with respect to labor organization and impact can be summarized in Table 6-3, which brings together relevant information with which to underscore some critical points. The most obvious point is that one must be wary of easy generalizations concerning union size, union impact, and union operations.

Unionization and strikes do not necessarily go hand in hand: Sweden has the highest percent of work force unionized but the lowest strike level. Nor can one conclude that rival unionism leads to more strikes because of jurisdictional disputes. In countries with rival federations the workers join for ideological or denominational reasons, so the situation is radically different from that in the early days of union activity in the United States, where rival unions fought to organize the same group of workers at the plant level.

Unionization is no guarantee against unemployment, either. Neither Germany nor Japan have especially large percentages of the labor force unionized, but their unemployment rates have been low. This is closely related to real economic growth, a major subject to be considered in a later chapter. Suffice it to say that unemployment is related far more to real growth rates than to any relative size of unionization. In this sense the union's micro interests are bound inextricably with the economy's macro interests. For the same reason, no conclusions can be drawn here about the impact on inflation of a larger percentage increase in hourly earnings than in the consumer price index, as was

Table 6-3

Characteristics of Labor Organization and Impact in
Ten Market-Oriented Economies in the 1960s

	Percent of civilian labor force in unions 1969[a]	Average annual increase in hourly earnings 1960-69[b]	Average annual increase in CPI 1964-69[b]	Strikes—working days lost per 1000 wage earners[c] (annual average 1956-65)	Average percent unemployment 1960-69[d]
Belgium	48.3%	7.9%	3.5%	293	NA
Netherlands	34.4	8.8	5.0	27	NA
United Kingdom	38.7	6.0	4.3	174	2.8%
West Germany	29.6	6.5	2.6	28	.6
Japan	27.7	12.9	5.2	NA	1.3
United States	24.4	4.7	3.4	448	4.8
France	21.7	8.2	3.8	167	2.3
Sweden	94.0	8.6	4.0	6	1.7
Italy	35.2	5.7	2.8	722	3.6
Canada	24.0	6.6	3.7	300	5.1

Notes and sources:
a. Table 6-1, p. 111-115.
b. OECD, *The Growth of Output 1960-1980-Retrospect, Prospect and Problems of Policy,* Paris, December 1970. Table F, pp. 46-47.
c. John P. Windmuller, *Labor Relations in the Netherlands* (Ithaca: Cornell University Press, 1969), p. 396.
d. Constance Sorrento, "Unemployment in the United States and Seven Foreign Countries," *Monthly Labor Review,* Vol. 93, No. 9, September 1970, pp. 12-23. Table 1, p. 14. All data adjusted to U.S. concepts. They refer to percent of the civilian labor force unemployed. France publishes no unemployment rate at all. All the other countries (except Canada) include military personnel in their published unemployment estimates.
Note: NA = not available.

clearly the case for all ten countries though the time periods differ and make precise comparison impossible. But the inflation rates, here indicated by the annual average change in the consumer price index, were radically different.

One conclusion which is perhaps striking is that average unemployment rates and days lost through strikes appear positively related. Sweden and Germany have low strike levels and low unemployment rates. Canada, Italy, and the United States have high rates of unemployment and high strike levels. One could perhaps argue that unacceptably high rates of unemployment reflect policies which also lead to worker discontent, which manifests itself in strikes. However, this conclusion must be qualified by noting that strikes are a part of customary institutional behavior in some countries and are not used in others. Strikes, as previously noted, are radically different in character and purpose in the U.S. from those in Italy or France.

The impact of trade unions on the functioning of market-oriented economies is ultimately related not only to the planning techniques and business organizations considered earlier but to the problems of growth and stability, which we shall consider subsequently. In this sense the behavior of factor markets in any economy must be related to both micro and macro considerations. We have seen that trade unionism can make the price system operationally effective through collective bargaining at the microeconomic level, but the important question of the role of trade unions (and business organizations of the sort considered in the previous chapter) on the operational effectiveness of the price system in the macroeconomic level must await our consideration of cost-push inflation and problems of economic growth.

7

Agriculture—Problems and
Policies in Market-Oriented Economies

In Chapter 5 we saw that the requirements of modern technology have played a large role in the structural conversion of "atomistic competition" into large-scale units (which economists call oligopoly) in the industrial sector of all modern economies. The impossibility of producing efficiently with many small units has forced governments to devise new (and only partially successful) policies for achieving efficiency, sensitivity to consumer preferences, and the other objectives an unfettered price system was traditionally thought to guarantee.

One of the supreme ironies of economics is that in all the countries we have been considering, the sector which has conformed most closely to the structural definition of competition—namely, many buyers and sellers, each with no ability to affect the market price by individual price and output decisions—has been agriculture. Yet these very competitive characteristics of agriculture have made it function far less effectively than the industrial sector in almost every country. Moreover, it has required far greater governmental interference. The paradox goes further. While agricultural problems are far from solved, they are gradually becoming less acute in many areas. Why? Because in the past fifty years or so modern technology has begun to affect agricultural production significantly, with the result that efficient production now requires concentration of production on large farms using modern farm machinery. This means that in the long run traditional competition can work no better in agriculture than it could in manufacturing.

The major policy question in Chapter 5 was, How much governmental interference is compatible with a system still appropriately termed *market-oriented?* Our tentative answer was that some nationalization and a good deal of governmental regulation have been adopted in many countries which, in contrast to command economies, may still appropriately be declared market-oriented, even in the manufacturing sector. In the previous chapter we saw that labor organized in response to business organization, and the question became, is uncontrolled concentration of economic power on the part of both labor and management compatible with the functioning of a price system in this important factor market, and if not, how much governmental regulation can be imposed without rendering inappropriate the appellation *market-oriented?* In both these cases concentration of economic power in relatively few hands *preceded* and to this extent presumably justified intervention by government into laissez faire economies. In the case of agriculture the situation has been reversed: the high degree of competition (or low degree of concentration) was a prime factor in *causing* governmental intervention. In the one sector of capitalist economies in which the standard requirements for competition were most closely approximated, the system worked least well and has required extensive governmental intervention to make it work at all.

Agricultural problems are complex, and the possible long-run and short-run solutions can easily fill volumes. Here we can only suggest the nature of the problems and their solutions and underscore one major point. Generally this book is devoted to the themes of the *commonality* of all market-oriented economies which distinguishes them from command economies and to the great diversity in structure and functioning within these economies which make the principles of economics as viewed in the United States less than appropriate for them all. But in the field of agriculture the commonality is far greater than in other areas, and the diversity lies primarily in the gravity of the problems and the degree to which certain common techniques have been used to cope with them. In greater degree than for any other area thus far considered, it is fair to say that the agricultural program adopted in the United States can fairly be described as the prototypical program for all market-oriented economies.

Extent of Agriculture
in Market-Oriented Economies

The economies we have concentrated on in this book have been not only market-oriented but industrialized. We concentrate on them because a major purpose is to explore the similarities as well as the differences among economies which, like the United States, are market-oriented, and "in which the challenges to the traditional functioning of a competitive price system appeared with

Table 7-1
Relative Importance of Agriculture in
Market-Oriented Economies

Country	Percent of national income originating in agriculture (in 1958 prices)		Percent of working population in Agriculture early 1960	Percentage change in agricultural population early 1950s to early 1960s
	1955	1968		
(1)	(2)	(3)	(4)	(5)
Canada	NA	NA	11%	−34%
United States	4.6%	3.1	8	−27
United Kingdom	4.3	3.3	4	−16
Belgium	7.1	NA	9	−39
Netherlands	11.6	7.2	10	−27
West Germany	9.0	4.1	14	−35
Denmark	18.0	9.4	18	−25
Norway	4.6	NA	17	−25
France	12.7	7.0	20	−25
Austria	NA	8.6	23	−30
Japan	NA	11.6	29*	NA
Sweden	NA	6.0*	11	−34
Italy	21.3	NA	29	−28

Notes and sources:
Col. 2: Edward F. Denison and Jean-Pierre Pouillier, *Why Growth Rates Differ: Postwar Experiences in Nine Western Countries* (Washington, D.C.: The Brookings Institution, 1967), Table 16-10, p. 210.
Col. 3: OECD, *Inflation: The Present Problem* (Paris: OECD, 1970), Table 18, p. 99. Figures refer to gross capital picture over a percent of GNP in 1968-69 and so may not be directly comparable to those in col 2. The period of time covered in the percentage changes of col. 5 varies from 1950-54 for the initial measure and from 1960-62 for the terminal measure, but in general represents the percent decline of active agriculture population during approximately a decade.
* Japanese data is from International Information Centre for Local Credit, *Economic Policies in Practice* (The Hague: Matinus Nijhoff, 1968), p. 13, and refers to the late 1960s.

industrialization."[1] Growing industrialization does not reduce the importance of agriculture or agricultural output to an economy, but it changes the character of the problem. It has been said often that the mark of a developed economy is the percent of its economic activity still represented by agriculture—freeing a nation's resources from feeding its population is the first step on the road to industrialization and economic development generally. Some idea of the current status of agriculture in developed market-oriented economies is given in Table 7-1.

[1] Many other problems come with lack of industrialization—hence the great concern nowadays with the problems of developing economies. This, however, is a different topic, and we wish here to compare and contrast the functioning of market-oriented economies operating in roughly comparable economic circumstances, which means that they have a significant industrial sector, without which, say, the problems considered in Chapters 5 and 6 could scarcely be viewed in comparable fashion.

The story revealed in the table is a simple one. It is clear why each country is included among the world's "developed economies": in none does agriculture account for more than about one-fifth of national income or one-third of national employment. Moreover, both percentages are declining. Exact data on the percent of national income originating in agriculture are not available, but column 5 suggests that during a recent decade agricultural employment declined by fully one-quarter to one-third for every country in the table except the United Kingdom, where the decline was somewhat more modest. The agricultural sector of the modern market-oriented economy is thus small and still declining, but it is nonetheless a vital sector and one ridden with problems.

What Is the "Agricultural Problem"?

The problems agriculture faces in all market-oriented economies can be fairly simply stated. The solutions, unhappily, are not so simple. The major problems in this sector, as Richard Caves noted several years ago, include unstable farm income and market prices, redundant resources (particularly labor), and low productivity and inefficiency in many (particularly the many small) agricultural units.[2] These same problems are found in some degree in all market-oriented economies. As we shall see, all too often the solution to these problems that has been tried has involved attempting to bolster the sagging incomes of all farmers rather than adjusting the number of farmers and their production techniques to produce a viable, efficient, self-sustaining agriculture sector. Edward Denison put the problem graphically:

> The nine [Western] countries examined here have had too many agricultural workers. Many farms have been too small or their soil too poor to yield an output for full-time work that would provide an income comparable to that obtained in non-farm activities. Large fractions of the farms produced so little that if they and the workers employed on them had simply disappeared, nearly as much output would have been obtained in each country with many fewer workers.[3]

In the short run the problem has almost always been interpreted as involving programs to provide farmers with an adequate income (defined variously, but inevitably, by extramarket standards—that is, "adequate farm income," unlike

[2] Richard Caves, *American Industry: Structure, Conduct, Performance*, 2d ed. (Englewood Cliffs, N.J.: Prentice-Hall, 1967), p. 78.

[3] Edward F. Denison and Jean-Pierre Pouillier, *Why Growth Rates Differ: Postwar Experience in Nine Western Countries* (Washington, D.C.: The Brookings Institution, 1967), p. 202.

incomes in other professions or occupations, is never defined in the short run to be what even the market forces of supply and demand would determine.) Unfortunately, the emphasis on solving the short-run problem with short-run solutions has merely aggravated the long-run problem and retarded its solution. The long-run problem is to increase modernization of production techniques in agriculture and to adjust the number of farmers to what is required. It has sometimes been said that the problem of agriculture has too often been interpreted in terms of surplus crops, when the real problem is surplus farmers.

The Traditional Solution in Theory

When supply increases at a faster rate than demand, elementary price theory teaches us that price must fall. In the developed parts of the world the demand for food has not increased as rapidly as the ability to increase the supply. The result has been a steady tendency for agricultural prices to fall, and to fall while the prices for other products either remained stable or increased. In the United States there was a feeling that the relationship between farm prices and other prices was "appropriate" in the early years of the twentieth century. It is said that farm and nonfarm prices achieved "parity" in the period 1910-14. This led to the adoption of a number of expedients to keep farm prices higher than a free market would have permitted. The three major short-run plans to affect agricultural price and farm income which have been utilized both in the United States and in other market-oriented economies are illustrated by Figure 7-1.

The supply of agricultural output (for any crop that is subjected to governmental intervention) in any given year is whatever the farmers grow and harvest. In the absence of governmental intervention the market demand (D_m) and the supply of a crop (S_{fm}) will produce a free market price (P_{fm}) which will establish industry equilibrium at E_{fm}. If farmers can persuade their government that selling quantity OS_{fm} at a price per unit of OP_{fm} will yield them an "inadequate income" (one that will not, for example, give them the same purchasing power in nonagricultural markets that they had in some past time when their real purchasing power was in their view "fair") they may succeed, as they have in all market-oriented economies, in obtaining a governmentally supported price (OP_s) higher than the free market price. The most common method for maintaining this artificially high price has been for the government simply to purchase the surplus crop (as indicated in the chart), which the farmers would produce at the support price. Thus for many years the U.S. government acquired enormous stores of wheat, feed grain, and cotton so that the market price would remain at a "suitably high level."

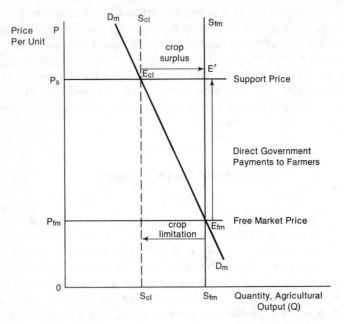

Figure 7.1 Illustration of Three Common Techniques to
Raise Farm Income in Market-Oriented Economies

    The second way to achieve the same goal is to pay farmers not to produce
and so, in effect, to artificially reduce the market supply as indicated by OS_{cl}.
Crop limitation programs (acreage allotments were later called the Soil Bank
Program in the U.S.) at least had the virtue of providing for systematic
revitalization of the soil by letting farmland lie fallow on an organized basis. But
like out-and-out price supports, the crop limitation program had the short-run
defect of forcing the price of the affected crop above what it would have been if
its determination had been left to the free market forces.

    The third technique, known as the Benson-Brannan Plan (after the
secretaries of agriculture during the Truman and Eisenhower administrations
who originally advocated it), lets market price stay wherever free market forces
put it but has the government make a direct payment equal to the difference
between the free market price and the agreed-upon support price on every unit
of agricultural output sold. This was presumably to guarantee a minimal income
to farmers on the basis of their crop sales, and it had the advantage of permitting
lower agricultural prices to consumers and avoiding an unwanted accumulation
of crops in government storage tanks. Its disadvantage was that farmers viewed it
as a handout, which, U.S. farmers made clear through their national organization

was not what they wanted. Moreover, for reasons more complex than we need go into here, it was more expensive for the government than either of the first two plans, and so it was not much favored, though often used by the U.K. and the Netherlands.

All these programs can be criticized on several bases. In the short run, in which the problem is presumably coping with farm poverty, all these programs are subject to the criticism that they are tied to farm output and thus help large farms the most and small farms the least. Indeed, the smaller the farm is, the smaller is the total amount of dollar aid the farmer gets from the government, and if he is inefficiently small and hence poverty-stricken, his condition remains essentially unchanged by these programs. On the other hand, if the farm is huge and capable of taking advantage of all the economies which modern agricultural technology has to offer the farmer's output will be the greatest, his per unit costs the lowest, and his aid from government programs the greatest, too.

The long-run criticism of these programs is even more severe. The basic reason for falling farm incomes all over the Western world (hence in all the market-oriented economies of concern to us) has been that rapidly changing technology has greatly increased agricultural productivity (indeed, as we shall show, agricultural productivity has increased far more rapidly in almost all the countries under consideration than industrial productivity), which has meant that far fewer farmers could produce the same or more output. Too many farmers on too many too small farms—here was the long-run problem—and all the techniques we have enumerated for coping with it simply exacerbated this problem by hindering the amalgamation of small farms into larger and more efficient units, by slowing the exit of redundant farmers from the farms, and meanwhile by forcing higher farm prices onto the consumers.[4]

The Traditional Solution in Practice

In recent years there has been an increasing realization that simple comparison between the prices farmers receive for their products and the prices they must pay for what they buy and how the relationship between them has

---

[4] A somewhat different view of the effect of short-run programs (at least in the U.S.) is that although price supports have been undoubtedly expensive and inequitable in their impact because they helped large farms the most and small—hence poor—farms the least, this very inequity in aid has hastened the movement of redundant labor out of inefficiently small farms. This position may have some merit, but it seems still appropriate to argue that every dollar spent on price supports which went to inefficiently small farms without being matched by manpower retraining programs, soil conservation programs, etc. was a dollar which perpetuated the malallocation of resources. (For a fuller explanation of the view that the traditional solution to the low farm income problem did not hinder the exit of redundant farmers, see James B. Herendeen, "The Farm Income Problem," in *Modern Political Economy: Ideas and Issues*, James B. Herendeen, ed. [(Englewood Cliffs, N.J.: Prentice-Hall, 1968], pp. 257-67.)

changed over time is an inadequate guide to farm programs. It is this simple relationship which lies behind the notion of parity, but it is becoming clear to many that these price relationships are no guide to equity if they are unrelated to the changes in farm productivity relative to nonfarm productivity. Nonetheless, almost all market-oriented economies are concerned with parity. Let us examine this notion for a moment, consider how it has been utilized in formulating agricultural programs in market-oriented economies, and then consider more recent attitudes toward farm legislation.

In its simplest form the idea of parity as developed in the United States argued that if the relationship between farm and nonfarm prices were viewed as "appropriate" in 1910-14, and if nonfarm prices have since increased three times as fast as the price, say of wheat, then the "parity" price of wheat would be a supported price three times the market price, so that the farmer in the later period would have the same real purchasing power as he had in the base period, 1910-14. Later support prices were altered so as to be "flexible" rather than "rigid" and the government might guarantee to support the price of wheat at 70 percent, 80 percent, or some other percent of its "full parity price." Still later price supports were altered to take into account the fact that some product prices declined faster than others relative to all farm prices.

However interpreted, farm price supports, as noted, meant short-run interference with the market mechanism, which, among other disadvantages, had the long-run disadvantage of continuing the malallocation of resources in the agricultural sector. In all fairness, it should be added that during wartime or during crises caused by drought or floods in other parts of the world, farmers would be briefly encouraged to increase their output, only to find that when demand returned to normal their increased harvest forced farm prices even lower than they had been before.

The basic price changes surrounding the notion of parity in the more important market-oriented economies are shown in Table 7-2. The average annual increase in the price of all items included in gross national product increased during the 1960s at the rates indicated in column 2. In view of the relative insensitivity of food purchases to changes in food prices (we all have to eat), one might expect that increasing supplies of foodstuffs would cause food prices to fall faster than prices in general. But column 3 suggests that the average annual increase in food prices was often greater than prices in general. In many countries this is due to the increased role of distribution, processing, and marketing in total food costs. A comparison of columns 4 and 5 shows that in most countries the average increase in prices received by farmers was lower than the increase in prices farmers paid for other items. The decline in German farm prices reflected the impact of entry into the Common Market, whereas entry into the Common Market tended to push up farm prices somewhat in France and Holland and to a lesser degree in Italy and Belgium.[5] Only in Japan, the

[5] For a fuller discussion of the trends, see OECD, *Inflation: The Present Problem* (Paris: OECD, December 1970), pp. 93-99, on which this summary has relied heavily.

Table 7-2
Comparative Price Trends and Imputed Changes in
"Parity," Thirteen Market-Oriented Economies,
1958-60 to 1966-68[1]

(Average annual percent increase)

Country	GNP Prices[2]	Food expenditures	Prices received by farmers	Prices paid by farmers	Imputed change in "Parity"
(1)	(2)	(3)	(4)	(5)	(6)
Canada	2.2	2.0	2.6	3.0	86.7
United States	1.9	1.8	0.9	1.0	90.0
Norway	3.6	4.7	3.4	3.5	97.1
Sweden	4.1	4.4	3.0	3.2	93.8
Denmark	5.1	5.1	2.2	4.6	47.8
United Kingdom	3.0	2.2	0.7	NA	NA
Netherlands	4.0	3.6	3.8	2.6	146.2
Belgium	2.8	2.6	2.6	3.2	81.2
France	4.0	3.5	NA	NA	NA
West Germany	3.1	2.2	0.8	2.1	38.1
Austria	3.5	3.3	2.6	4.8	54.2
Italy	4.3	3.8	3.5	2.9	120.7
Japan	4.3	6.0	7.4	2.9	255.2

Source:
OECD, *Inflation: The Present Problem,* Table 13, p. 93.

Notes:
[1]   These time periods are approximate, and the OECD computed the average annual change to the nearest available period in the initial and terminal years.
[2]   These percentages represent the implicit price deflators in national account series involved in the deviation from GNP in constant dollars. It represents, therefore, an effort to measure the average percent price change in everything included in gross national product.

Netherlands, and Italy did the average annual increase in farm prices exceed the average annual increase in prices farmers paid. Thus, with three exceptions typical agricultural prices would have had to be increased by the percentages implicitly indicated in column 6 if at the end of the 1960s farmers were to have had parity, traditionally viewed, with their real purchasing power in the early 1960s. The United States, for example, would have had to increase average farm prices by ten percent above their market price to give farmers the same real purchasing power at the end of the decade that they had at the beginning.

Hence parity always involves altering the market price to conform to some predetermined idea of equitable real purchasing power for farmers. We can gain little by reviewing in detail the variations in price intervention presented by the agricultural policies of the countries we have been considering. The relevant

Table 7-3

Analysis of Direct Public Expenditures on Agriculture
in Nine Market-Oriented Economies, 1968

Country	Direct public expenditures on agriculture ($ millions)	Percent of GNP	Percent of value of agricultural output	Direct public expenditures for agriculture (as a percent of the value of agriculture) devoted to price and income support		
				1960	1968	Change in % 1960-1968
(1)	(2)	(3)	(4)	(5)	(6)	(7)
United States[a]	$6,221	0.7%	12.9	6.5%	10.4%	+ 3.9%
Sweden	167	0.7	13.0	5.1	4.3	− .8
Denmark	166	1.4	13.0	4.4	9.2	+ 4.8
Austria[a]	145	1.3	13.3	8.4	10.0	+ 1.6
Netherlands	290	1.2	10.3	6.2	2.8	− 3.4
France	1,995	1.6	18.3	2.2	9.2	+ 7.0
West Germany	1,705	1.3	17.7	NA	9.0	−
Japan	2,120	1.5	18.0	2.0	7.0	+ 5.0
United Kingdom	751	0.8	15.7	17.5	13.4	− 4.1

Source:
OECD, *Inflation: The Present Problem,* Table 16, p. 97, and Table 18, p. 99.

Note:
Figures in cols. 2 and 6 refer to 1968 or to 1968-9 (in the case of countries which, like the United States, present budgetary data for the fiscal rather than the calendar year). Column 5 refers to 1968 or 1960-61.
[a] Federal Budget only.

information for a reasonably typical year is summarized in Table 7-3, which indicates for nine countries the amount of direct public expenditure for agriculture in 1968. The U.S., not surprisingly, spent the most—something over $6 billion in fiscal 1969.[6] It should be noted that the $6 billion spent on agriculture compares with slightly over $2 billion spent on resource conservation, a bit under $2 billion spent on community development and housing, and over $81 billion spent on national defense. With the exception of the national defense comparison, the proportions are roughly comparable in the other countries listed.[7] The fact that in no case are the amounts expended on agriculture a very large percent of total GNP suggests primarily how appropriate it is to label these economies *market-oriented*. The entire public expenditure, as noted in Chapter 3, is never more than about one-third of GNP in the least market-oriented of these economies.

The more significant thing to note, however, is that these expenditures for agriculture, viewed as a percent of the value of agricultural output (column 4), add considerably to the total market value of this output. Comparison of the percentages in column 4 with those in column 6 (which indicates the amount of the aid that goes for price or income support programs) suggests that the bulk of governmental expenditures for agriculture in all these countries is still devoted to artificially raising the price or subsidizing the income of farmers. We have not included the column 4 equivalent percentages for 1960, but column 7 suggests that in only three of the countries—Sweden, the Netherlands, and the United Kingdom—among nations for which comparisons can be made has there been any decline in the percentage of aid to agriculture in the form of price and income supports. For the reasons indicated earlier, such aid can be viewed only as temporary stopgap measures designed presumably to improve the income for farmers presently in operation. The aid is invariably tied to the volume of farm output, and so helps most the farms and farmers who need it least, meanwhile postponing or preventing any long-run solution to the problem of agricultural poverty.

An astute observer of agricultural policy in Western economies summarized the situation well a few years ago:

> It has become increasingly difficult to use price support as a means of raising farmers' income. Price guarantees are liable to stimulate

[6] The figures in Table 7-1 refer either to calendar 1968 or to fiscal 1969, which runs from 1968 to 1969. See the note to the table.

[7] Estimates for Britain in 1959 are available. It has been estimated that in that year the total amount spent on agricultural support (price supports and production grants) was £400 to 430 million. In comparison, the British budget called for expenditures of £236 million on roads, £369 million on housing, and £797 million on health. Concluded the author about the size of the payments to agriculture: "It is a large amount of money." (Gavin McCrone, *The Economics of Subsidising Agriculture: A Study of British Policy* [London: George Allen and Unwin, 1962], pp. 56-57.)

unwanted production, and the resulting pressure on the market, while it tends to perpetuate the need for price support, makes this an even more costly procedure for the rest of the community. Further, all the measures have failed—except perhaps in Britain and the Netherlands—to close the gap between farm and nonfarm incomes.[8]

Price and income supports of the sort previously considered are the main type of short-run solution to the problem of low farm incomes, but some countries, typically countries more dependent on foreign trade than the United States, have used a variety of other mechanisms—customs duties to raise domestic prices of food inputs in order to keep foreign foodstuffs from underselling domestic output, import calendars regulating the timing of imports of foreign-grown fruits and vegetables, import levies, minimum import prices for grains (used by the U.K.), efforts among European countries to work out joint agreements on market sharing, export subsidies, and so on.[9] In general the comments on price supports apply with equal accuracy to these devices. A recent survey of agricultural policies in Western Europe during the past one hundred years concluded that the present major problems had been simply the result of a failure to adapt to changed circumstances.[10] Much the same comment could be made of agricultural policies in the United States. What does such adaptation involve?

The Long-Run Solution in Theory and Practice

The OECD is another voice which has been raised in support of the argument that the major cause of continued low incomes in agriculture has been the continued excessive and inefficient employment of manpower in this sector.[11] Here is where adaptation must occur. Because of vastly improved agricultural technology and the consequent increase in productivity, there is much hidden unemployment in agriculture—farmers who are not unemployed, but who, if they left the farms, would not reduce output and consequently would increase income for remaining farmers.

With increased productivity, which is the fruit of modern agricultural technology, the minimum size of a commercially profitable farm has increased greatly. Figures are difficult to come by, but an example from the U.S. indicates

[8] Michael Tracy, *Agriculture in Western Europe* (New York: Frederick A. Praeger, 1964), p. 243.

[9] For a summary of all these plans see OECD, *Agricultural Policies in 1966* (Paris: OECD, 1966), pp. 16-17. For detailed country-by-country analyses see the bulk of the report.

[10] Tracy, *Agriculture in Western Europe*, p. 365.

[11] OECD, *Low Incomes in Agriculture* (Paris: OECD, 1964), p. 10.

the order of magnitude of this problem. It has been estimated that in 1959 farms large enough to sell at least $10,000 a year could provide "a decent living" for their operators, farms between $5,000 and $10,000 "might" provide a decent living, but under no circumstances could farms so small as to yield annual sales below $5,000 be commercially viable. In that year the number of commercial farms large enough to produce $10,000 a year or more in sales came to 21.5 percent of the total number of farms, those yielding $5,000 to $10,000 came to 17.6 percent of all commercial farms, and 26.1 percent of all commercial farms were too small to be successful. What of the other farms? Small farms operated by retirees on a part-time basis and so on represented 34.7 percent, and all had sales far below the minimum of the smallest commercial farms. Only the .1 percent of all farms that were institutional or experimental could be viewed with any sanguinity. In short, 60.8 percent of all the farms in the U.S. in 1959 were too small to be successful, given the minimum requirements of scale attendant upon the use of modern agricultural technology.[12]

This means that modern technology has sounded the death knell for the commercially successful small-size family farm in the U.S. and probably in other market-oriented economies also. It is one thing to farm for your own needs, but quite another to try to operate a successful commercial farm as an independent family venture. (Many large, successful commercial farms are family-owned in the United States.)

The impact of changing farm technology on agricultural productivity can be easily documented. Table 7-3 indicates the average annual increase in productivity (measured as gross domestic product per employed person on constant prices) in agriculture and the rest of the economy in recent years. The fact that in all but a few of these countries agricultural productivity was increasing faster than productivity in other parts of the economy meant that fewer and fewer farmers were needed to produce the amount of food demanded. And the amount of food demanded in these economies increases slowly. Therefore, the first order of business to achieve a healthier long-term balance in the agricultural sector of these economies is to increase the average size of farms, to take advantage of the changing technology which makes these great increases in productivity possible, and to encourage the exit of redundant farmers from agriculture and into other areas where they can contribute more to output.[13]

Modernization of agricultural production processes is at last under way in a number of modern market-oriented economies. The decreases in percent of the working force employed in agriculture shown in column 4 of Table 7-2 suggest that the required reallocation of labor from agriculture to other areas is under way, too, but the rate is far too slow. That the number of farmers working on

---

[12] This information is summarized from Caves, *American Industry,* pp. 80-81.

[13] Increased productivity in agriculture means that it pays to substitute capital for labor in producing agriculture. Wise resource allocation therefore suggests shifting labor to other areas where the labor output ratio is higher (or, if you prefer, the capital output ratio is lower).

Table 7-4
Average Annual Change in Productivity of Agriculture
and Other Sectors, 1957-58 to 1967-68,
Thirteen Market-Oriented Economies

Country	Average annual change in productivity in	
	Agriculture	Other sectors
(1)	(2)	(3)
United States	5.5%	2.4%
Canada	4.8	1.4
Norway	2.8	3.8
Sweden	5.6	3.8
Denmark	6.1	3.0
United Kingdom	6.0	2.4
Netherlands	6.4	3.9
Belgium	3.9	3.4
France	6.5	4.2
West Germany	6.9	4.8
Austria	5.0	4.2
Italy	7.8	4.9
Japan	12.7	12.0

Source:
    OECD, *Inflation: The Present Problem,* Table 14, p. 95.

Note:
    Productivity in agriculture and other sectors has been measured as the average annual
percentage growth rate in gross domestic product per person employed between 1957-58
and 1967-68, or the nearest available period. All are measured in constant 1963 prices
except Japan, which is measured in current prices.

inefficient small family farms was still far too large is indicated by the following
figures, which suggest the ratio of real national income per worker in agriculture
to real national income in other areas of the economy in 1963: United States,
.54; Denmark, .79; France, .49; West Germany, .49; Norway, .20; and Italy, .52.
Only in Belgium, the Netherlands, and the United Kingdom had the decrease in
farmers gone far enough so that the per-worker contribution to real national
income was greater in agriculture than in other sectors.[14]

Agricultural Policies and
the Impact of the Common Market

When the Treaty of Rome establishing the European Economic Community
was signed in 1957, many hoped that the long-held dream of creating a "United
States of Europe," at least for economic purposes, was soon to become a reality.

[14] See Denison and Pouillier, *Why Growth Rates Differ*, Table 16-1, p. 204.

The purpose of the Common Market was to create a free trade area within Europe and to enable European nations to establish common prices for their international trade. Instead of the complex of trade restrictions with which they had been forced to cope before, they would eliminate internal trade barriers and create a single set of tariffs and/or other restrictions governing the trade of Common Market countries with other nations, which would benefit them all.

All the goals of the Common Market are still a long way from full realization in the early 1970s, and progress in agriculture has proved to be even more difficult to achieve than progress in other areas. The difficulties of agreeing on common prices have been particularly intractable in agriculture. We have seen that the presence of many small, economically inefficient farms was a problem in many European countries, as it has been in the U.S., but the degree of inefficiency was not the same, and the incomes farmers gleaned from various crops were disproportionate. In general, French agriculture was the most successful, with prices that were correspondingly lower, and German prices were the highest. If we consider average prices in the EEC as 100 percent, the percents of the major European countries for some representative agricultural products can be compared in Table 7-5.

Table 7-5
Producers' Prices as a Percent of Average EEC Prices,
Representative Crops, 1960-61

Country	Wheat	Barley	Milk	Eggs	Cattle	Pigs
Belgium	100%	90%	99%	97%	96%	86%
France	85	82	100	96	87	110
West Germany	107	132	103	111	102	115
Italy	118	106	103	115	118	95
Netherlands	89	91	95	80	97	94

Source:
Michael Tracy, *Agriculture in Western Europe*, p. 327.

The first step in setting up a free trade area for Common Market countries in agriculture would require that the countries involved agree on a common set of prices for major crops, but Table 7-5 makes it clear that achieving such agreement would be difficult. The more efficient producers (France and possibly Italy) would push for lower prices in order to compete in world markets more effectively and to keep living costs lower at home, whereas the less efficient countries would push for higher prices in order to be able to compete internationally. In the early 1960s, when these countries were attempting to hammer out a set of mutually acceptable agricultural prices, de Gaulle suggested that the prices should be the *average* of the actual prices then being used in the countries involved. Such a policy as Table 7-5 underscores, would obviously work to the advantage of France and against the Germans. In the end the French gave certain industrial concessions to the Germans in return for which the Germans agreed to certain agricultural concessions. These negotiations elicited highly nationalistic and protectionistic responses from the countries involved. This protectionism has been revealed dramatically with the development of the variable import levy, which is applied to all agricultural imports into the Common Market. It is varied daily as prices of agricultural products in the world market vary; the effect is to support prices of agricultural products within the Common Market at a level which is independent of day-to-day changes in world agricultural prices.

More recently, with the revaluation of the Deutsche mark and the devaluation of the franc and other currencies, the German farmers were under even more pressure, and they have obtained an internal tariff to protect German agricultural prices from lower prices in other Common Market countries. This is of course contrary to the principles behind the creation of the Common Market and suggests the power agricultural interests have in that country. That agricultural interests have political influence which is disproportionate to their numerical strength appears to be common in many market-oriented economies.

The entry of Britain into the Common Market has created new agricultural difficulties for the British, because their prices for many agricultural products had been below world prices, and the British had subsidized farmers by means of what were called deficiency payments. The Common Market does not make this kind of payment to farmers, and the result of British entry into the Common Market has been that prices for agricultural products there have been forced up to Common Market levels, with attendant hardships for British consumers.

In short, the Common Market has created for the member countries a number of difficulties arising from the problems of achieving common prices when domestic efficiency and the resultant price levels varied considerably. Agricultural interests have political clout in all these countries, with the result that the development of new agricultural policy has typically lagged behind industrial policies. We have seen, moreover, that many U.S. policies have been copied in various ways in European market-oriented economies, but it is important to note that whereas the U.S. typically has a surplus of agricultural products, many Common Market countries import agricultural products. From this viewpoint the U.S. should have an initial advantage in coping with the Common Market, even though profit margins for particular products might be lowered in certain countries.

Ideally, each Common Market country ought to concentrate in agriculture, as in other kinds of production, on commodities in which it has the greatest comparative advantage and should trade with its partners for other commodities. There may well be advantages to the EEC countries in concentrating on, for example, cattle breeding, for which their relatively scarce land makes them well adapted, and they could then export cattle to other areas, relying on trade with the U.S. for basic crops. This is the direction toward which the virtues of free trade have always pointed, and it constitutes the original rationale for the Common Market as well. However, this kind of international specialization and division of labor, which eschews the attractions of nationalism and economic self-sufficiency, still lies in the distant future.

In conclusion, it is clear that achieving the goals toward which the establishment of the European Economic Community was pointing have proved to be far more intractable in agriculture even than they have been in industry, and the distance left to traverse in achieving these goals remains correspondingly greater.

Conclusions

That we must continue to be conscious of the poverty of many farmers who operate their own farms is immediately apparent to anyone who is unwilling to stand by and let human beings starve to death. But that the traditional techniques for coping with low farm income have tended both to perpetuate the problem and to help the poor the least is also apparent. The long-run solution must be to permit farming to be done on large units, utilizing efficient modern farm technology and encouraging the transfer of excess farmers to areas where they can contribute more to overall productivity. This is true in all market-oriented economies. Far too much effort and expenditure is still devoted to price and income supports, but it is increasingly being realized that application of modern farming methods combined with manpower retraining programs to equip farmers for new occupations must be the long-run solution to low farm incomes.

The U.S. led other market-oriented economies into the quicksand of price-support programs, and it may well be that other countries will now follow the lead of the U.S. toward more realistic farm programs. At least since the early 1960s such a redirection of U.S. farm policy has been in evidence.

> The move to direct payments, low supports, and general land retirement has set the stage for future agriculture policy changes: general land retirement will increase benefits going to smaller farmers and aid the transfer of labor out of agriculture; . . . a growing concern over poverty will bring more attention to the problems of chronic low income in agriculture. [15]

Such, at least, is the direction in which solutions to the farm problem appear to be moving in the United States. In addition, the Common Market has

[15] James B. Herendeen, "The Farm Income Problem," p. 266.

created special problems for some European economies which will require changes in the crop specializations of those countries that cannot produce some crops as efficiently as other countries can. These adjustments may be severe for countries like Denmark, which rely heavily on agricultural exports, and for countries like Britain, which rely heavily on imports. But protectionism is increasingly recognized as a deterrent to economic progress in the long run, both for exporters and importers, in agriculture and in industry.

John Sheahan must have had these factors in mind when he wrote of French postwar agricultural policy, "The magic balance between structural adjustment and short-run protection of farmers has not yet been found."[16] Sheahan's comment is equally applicable to agricultural policy in all market-oriented economies. The magic balance has certainly not yet been found, but there is increasing evidence that at long last the *need* to find it is being recognized. The search for ways out of the endless and futile quagmire of price and income supports is at last under way in the form of fundamental structural reforms of the agricultural sector of market-oriented economies.

[16] John Sheahan, *An Introduction to the French Economy* (Columbus, Ohio: Charles E. Merrill Publishing Co., 1969), p. 9.

8

Stabilization Policies
in Market-Oriented Economies

In their indictment of capitalist economies Karl Marx and Friedrich Engels comment, "It is enough to mention the commercial crises that by their periodical return put the existence of the entire bourgeois society on trial, each time more threateningly."[1] If there was one fatal defect in capitalism, one aspect in which the "seeds of its own destruction" could most surely be counted on to bring the system down, it was the increasingly severe business cycles which were inevitable in any economy where private investment decisions played a prominent role. In short, a stable capitalism was a contradiction in terms.

We have by now made it clear that the kind of capitalism we are talking about when we speak of market-oriented economies is not what Adam Smith was talking about, and it probably is not what Karl Marx was talking about either.[2] The Great Depression, which affected the entire Western world, made everyone aware that no system which produced and tolerated such widespread human suffering could survive. The result was the commitment on the part of all the Western economies to accept full employment and price stability as major economic objectives, which led to the kind of reordering of governmental

[1] Karl Marx and Friedrich Engels, *The Communist Manifesto* (New York: International Publishers Co., 1948), p. 14.

[2] Neither is the system in the USSR, Mainland China, or Eastern Europe precisely what Marx had in mind when he described communist economies, but that is another story—as involved, or more so, than the one with which this book is concerned.

involvement in economic activity which we summarized in Chapter 2. The objectives have not been entirely reached, if success is defined as the complete elimination of business cycles, but a major accomplishment of post World War II market economies has been the taming of business cycles. In *Modern Capitalism* Andrew Shonfield states, "The central thesis of this book is that there is no reason to suppose that the patterns of the past, which have been so ingeniously unravelled by the historians of trade cycles, will reassert themselves in the future."[3]

Business Cycles in the Postwar Period

Even if the "patterns of the past" have not been permitted to reassert themselves, we cannot, unhappily, claim that the problem of economic instability has been eliminated. The chief claim we can make is that in all the economies of the market-oriented world, the cycles which have occurred have been a good deal milder than the kind capitalist economies experienced in their earlier histories. Indeed, one of Shonfield's main contentions is that all market-oriented economies have maintained reasonably full employment, have attained greater stability, and have achieved faster growth rates than they had before World War II. There are exceptions to this statement, and there are qualifications, and, alas, there are some new problems.

The problems of instability, treated in this chapter, and economic growth, treated in the next chapter, are part of the same problem. Economists have more and more tended to view economic change in developed economies not in terms of business cycles, on the one hand, and growth, on the other, but as a single process. The problem is how to achieve rapid growth without undue irregularity in the growth rate. Indeed, viewing business cycles as irregular growth rates seems to conform more closely to economic reality. By a business recession we mean periods when economic capacity is idle, labor is unemployed, output is reduced. That this must also slow the long-run growth rate is clear. However,

---

[3] Andrew Shonfield, *Modern Capitalism* (London: Oxford University Press, 1965), p. 62.

Sources:
Indexes of industrial production are from *Business Conditions Digest,* June 1971, p. 63. Business cycle turning points for Canada, U.S., 1950-61; U.K. 1950-58 are from Keith A. J. Hay, "Early Twentieth Century Business Cycles in Canada," *Canadian Journal of Economics and Political Science* 32, No. 3 (August 1966): 362. (U.S. dates are all originally from the National Bureau of Economic Research and are reproduced monthly in *Business Conditions Digest.*) Italy, Japan, and France are from Martin Bronfenbrenner, ed., *Is the Business Cycle Obsolete?* (New York: John Wiley & Sons, 1969), pp. 179, 73, and 148, respectively. Two dashed recessions in the U.K. are yearly data from J. C. R. Dow in Bronfenbrenner, p. 99. 1950-51 Italian recession was estimated by author. German data are from Ilse Mintz, *Dating Postwar Business Cycles,* National Bureau of Economic Research Occasional Paper 107 (New York: Columbia University Press, 1969), p. 53.

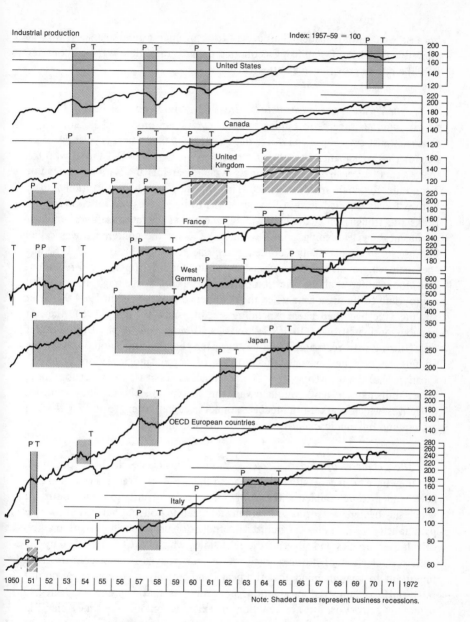

Chart 8-1   Business Cycle Turning Points and Index of
Industrial Production, Seven Market-Oriented Economies,
1950-70.

because we cannot consider all aspects of these problems simultaneously, we will view the problem of stabilizing economic activity first, then we shall consider how the rate of growth can be affected.

Is the Business Cycle Obsolete?   In 1967 a conference was held in London to ask whether success in taming business cycles had proceeded far enough so that capitalist economies could ask the question, Is the business cycle obsolete? One of the participants at the conference was Dr. Geoffrey H. Moore, who for many years had been active in business cycle research at the National Bureau of Economic Research in New York. (This private research organization is best known for its detailed study of cycles in the United States and for choosing the peaks and troughs which are now widely accepted as the most useful chronology of business cycle turning points we have.) Clearly the conference was called because, unlike most of its recorded peacetime economic history, the U.S. was then achieving a sustained economic expansion, uninterrupted by a recession. But Moore noted that the question posed for the conference might have seemed appropriate to its organizers when the conference was planned in 1964-65—after all, the U.S. had then been expanding steadily since February 1961, the last previous business trough. In 1967, however, as Moore put it, the United States was "flirting with recession," and he suggested that "the question posed by the conference may be obsolete, the problem of booms and recessions is not."[4] Clearly Marx was wrong—the "commercial crises" are not getting more severe—but neither have we achieved the lofty, possibly idealistic national objectives which market-oriented economies accepted after World War II—high growth and full employment without instability or inflation.

The Character of Modern Cycles   In short, business cycles have continued, but they have been generally milder than in the pre-World War II period, and they have tended to be coupled with a long-run problem of inflation, the control of which has become a central problem in stabilization policy. Chart 8-1 shows the path taken by the index of industrial production in seven important market-oriented economies and suggests the recessions, which have been marked by the tentative selection of business cycle peaks and troughs in each country. It is important to bear in mind that the peaks and troughs in each country do not refer only to industrial production, important as that measure of aggregate economic activity is, but are based on the examination of many time series. The peaks and troughs finally chosen represent the best judgment of economists about when one can meaningfully say that economic expansion has ceased or economic contraction has been reversed. Business cycles refer to fluctuations in aggregate economic activity, but it is important to note that all measures of

    [4] Geoffrey H. Moore, "Comments," in *Is the Business Cycle Obsolete?* Martin Bronfenbrenner, ed. (New York: Wiley-Interscience, A Division of John Wiley & Sons, 1969), p. 40.

aggregate economic activity are not synchronized. The choice of turning points—as much art as science, perhaps—is designed to help us understand why economies which organize industrial production through systems involving decentralized decision-making have been plagued by fluctuations.[5]

Shonfield has commented of the postwar period, "There have been more recessions in the United States than in Western Europe, and they have been allowed to go further before the government intervened decisively to boost demand."[6] Chart 8-1 does not support this view, although there was a moderately severe recession in the United States in 1948-49 which is not shown (we wished to view the cyclical behavior of postwar market-oriented economies during a period when all the postwar readjustment was over).

Business Cycles—The Recent Record   What does the chart reveal? Significantly, all seven economies had periods of recession between 1950 and 1970. Canadian recessions are very similar in timing to those in the United States, obviously because of the close economic ties between the two countries.[7] The technique used to select the German turning points was sufficiently different from that used for the other countries to make it impossible to conclude that German business cycles were longer than in other countries, but it is clear that West Germany has continued to reflect some cyclical instability (notably in

[5] It must be pointed out that the most widely used technique of choosing turning points was developed by the National Bureau of Economic Research in the U.S. and its application in other countries is in various stages of development. The dates chosen for Chart 8-1 represent the best that are currently available, but they are included largely to make the point that economic fluctuations are very much a part of the postwar scene. They are *not,* strictly speaking, comparable with each other, because they have been chosen by techniques which are not always comparable. For both France and Italy the economists whose dates we have been forced to rely on have utilized "flat periods" at peaks or troughs where they thought this appropriate—and so occasionally we have shown two peaks or troughs in a row—indicating their view that economic activity remained at a high or low level for an extended period between upswings and/or downswings. This procedure is not in accordance with that used by the National Bureau. If French and Italian time series were subjected to procedures comparable to those used in the U.S., the dates chosen would undoubtedly be somewhat different.

Similarly, we have shown the German turning points selected by Ilse Mintz in her recent study of German business cycles, because we consider them to be the most useful dates for analyzing German fluctuations. But she is very careful to note that she has chosen her turning points from "trend-adjusted" data—making her turning points closer to changes in rates of change than to changes in absolute levels. She takes care to note that they are *not* comparable with U.S. turning points as conventionally selected.

Nonetheless, as a rough first approximation, Chart 8-1 makes clear (1) that business cycles have continued to appear in these market-oriented economies and (2) that many of them can be seen in the behavior of industrial production, as discussed in the text.

[6] Shonfield, *Modern Capitalism,* p. 62.

[7] Gideon Rosenbluth has commented, "The important feature of Canadian cycles, both long and short, . . . is their close correspondence to cycles in the United States." (Rosenbluth, "Comments," in *Is the Business Cycle Obsolete?* Bronfenbrenner, ed. p. 68) See also the article by Rosenbluth, "Changes in Canadian Sensitivity to United States Business Fluctuations," *Canadian Journal of Economics and Political Science* 23, No. 4 (November 1957): 480-503.

1966-67) in the postwar period despite the tremendous growth that the "German miracle" represents. France, too, has experienced rapid growth, but not without some cyclical instability. The country with the most remarkable growth rate of all is Japan, and it reveals at least as many cycles as any other country. Moreover, as reflected in the index of industrial production, at least, the Japanese recession of 1957-58 was as sharp as any to be found during the twenty years covered. The United States is frequently charged with greater instability than other market-oriented economies (and it does reveal a rather slower growth rate, as Chapter 9 will make clear), but the instability in the United States, though of greater amplitude than that of a number of countries (as reflected in the movements in the production index), was only slightly greater than that of Japan.

While data are complete enough for the 1970-71 period to demark a recession only in the United States, it is clear from the chart that this U.S. recession was accompanied by a slowdown and possible recession in a number of other countries. This is worth noting because, although a comparable picture for the prewar period would by no means show identical peak and trough dates for cycles in all these countries, the variation in the postwar period has been greater. Almost every country experienced some recession during 1957-58 and there is some rough indication of similar difficulties in 1950-52 (no doubt involving the Korean War), but beyond this the cyclical instability in each country was distinctive. This suggests that the transmission of business cycles from country to country, if it occurs at all, is not a simple phenomenon. It also partly reflects the differences in governmental intervention to stabilize economic activity, to which we shall turn our attention in a moment.

We can conclude that, although postwar cycles have been far less severe than prewar cycles, they have continued to exist since 1950 in all the countries shown in Chart 8-1 and have also been traced in Scandinavia and Austria.[8] Easy generalizations, moreover, must be eschewed. Despite the close relationship between growth and stability and considerable evidence that many postwar cycles are best viewed as variations in growth rates rather than as changes in the absolute direction in which *levels* of aggregate economic activity were moving, much is left unexplained by looking at the growth-cycle process rather than at cycles per se. The United States, for reasons we shall see, has experienced one of

---

[8] At least four cycles have been found for Austria during this period. See Kurt W. Rothschild, "Austria and Switzerland," in *Is the Business Cycle Obsolete?* Bronfenbrenner, ed., especially p. 230 for the Austrian chronology. For Denmark, Norway, and Sweden see the article by Jørgen H. Gelting in the same volume: Some further information on these countries, Belgium, and the Netherlands in the postwar period up to 1960 is found in Angus Maddison, "The Post-War Business Cycle in Western Europe and the Role of Government Policy," *Banca Nazionale del Lavoro Quarterly Review* 13 (June 1960): 104-5, Table 4. Maddison finds two cycles corresponding roughly to those in the U.S. (1948-49) for all these countries except Austria, Denmark, Germany, Sweden, and the U.K. which in his view skipped the 1948-49 recession. His methodology deals with *levels* of activity rather than with rates of change such as Mintz used to date German cycles.

the slower growth rates and also four clear recessions since 1950, in each of which real GNP (that is, GNP in constant dollars) declined. On the other hand, Japan, one of the fastest growing economies, experienced five recessions during the same period, and during at least three of them the index of industrial production turned down. In Germany, again a country with rapid growth, the turning points chosen by Ilse Mintz suggest four periods of recession, though only the 1966-67 recession represented a downturn in real industrial production.

We shall see that the record of instability in market-oriented economies in the postwar period reflects both the inherent pulsation mechanism that has characterized cycles in capitalist economies since industrialization commenced and the modifications in that mechanism produced by monetary, fiscal, and other policies. It is to these policies that we now turn our attention.

Stabilization Policy in Action

There can be no question that the decreased severity of postwar business cycles—the tendency of cycles now to take the form of decreased rates of growth rather than of absolute declines—is bound up with the commitments to optimal growth and full employment which governments in market-oriented economies have undertaken. By the same token, the unwillingness to suffer serious depression, coupled with increased knowledge about ways to maintain economic stability, has contributed to greater stability. In short, it is not so much that the character of business cycles has changed; rather, modern market economies no longer leave cycles to run their course without interference. To the extent that laissez faire was *not* based on ignorance about how to stop instability but on a "natural harmony" attitude toward cycles ("leave them alone and they'll cure themselves"), then classic economic orthodoxy has been replaced by a new orthodoxy—the devout believers in intervention. In the United States, which has generally lagged in intervening, the 1960s saw the growth of the "new economics," led by those who believed in "fine tuning" the economy, which nonbelievers viewed as economic meddling that did more harm than good. (Still later, of course, came President Nixon's New Economic Policy.)

In order to sort all this out and to try to arrive at some conclusions about wise stabilization policy, it is useful to separate the possible kinds of intervention into several types and to consider each in turn. Broadly, stabilization policy can be separated into monetary policy and fiscal policy, and the latter can be viewed in part as "automatic" and in part as "discretionary." Moreover, though we shall not be able to discuss it at length here, we must mention that all modern countries, particularly, of course, the United States, have huge public debts—outstanding bonds which have been sold to the public (in the U.S. almost 95 percent of these bonds are owned by U.S. nationals) and that each year a number of these bonds mature and must be paid off—principal and interest—by the treasury. How these bond payments are handled can affect economic stability, so debt-management policy must be added to the list of modern stabilization tools. Finally, there is the external aspect to stabilization policy. Clearly the larger the role of foreign trade in a country's economic activities, the greater is the possibility that fluctuations in that trade will either produce or intensify internal instability.[9] So we shall have to comment briefly on international trade and exchange rate policy and their impact on domestic stability.

A Perspective on Postwar Stabilization Policy

From what has already been said it is clear that the objectives of public policy in market-oriented economies since World War II have been different, and what has been expected of stabilization policy has been correspondingly different as well. If the cycles have as often as not been growth cycles—that is, variations in the rate of growth rather than absolute declines in income, output, and employment—it is in part because of the goals of economic policy and the interventionism in all market-oriented economies that the goals have led to. Even if interventionism has led to more "doctrinal wrestling" in the United States, as we noted in an earlier chapter, the Employment Act of 1946 signaled a significant change in economic philosophy which paralleled in direction, if not in degree, the interventionism many market-oriented economies were undertaking in economic policy-making.

That the experiences of the Great Depression had much to do with the change in philosophy is clear. Those experiences were coupled with the insight into policy-making from more sophisticated economic techniques, which came partly through John Maynard Keynes' theory of national income determination and partly from the caldron of New Deal experimentation during the Great Depression with what worked and what did not work in raising levels of income, output, and employment. All these elements entered into the determination of all market-oriented economies to strive for the goals we outlined in Chapter 2.

Partly because of the achievement of these objectives to a remarkable degree, stabilization policy in the past twenty-five years has had to cope primarily with mild recessions, or decreased rates of growth against a secular background of containing inflation. The stimulants to overcome periods of recession have been less prominent because the cycles were milder, a condition due at least partially to some of the factors which also created the inflation. This is in sharp contrast to the prewar cycles, when inflation was a phenomenon to be associated with cyclical expansions, particularly the latter part of these expansions. If there was a "silver lining" to prewar depressions, it was that prices

[9] The thoughtful reader who is getting ahead of the story may be wondering why, if unemployment and inflation represent different phases of the conventional cycle, the U.S. in the late 1960s and early 1970s managed to achieve both simultaneously. The answer is that it wasn't easy, and we shall say more about it later.

fell during these periods. This has not been true since World War II; generally prices (wholesale, retail, and for factors of production as well) have risen, and the most one can say for recessions is that prices either rise more slowly or stay at about the same level.

All this has changed the climate in which stabilization policy operates and has also led to a growing controversy about what kinds of stabilization policy are most effective. The pre-Keynesian economist argued that business cycles were best viewed as short-run self-correcting phenomena and that if you did not want to wait for them to cure themselves, a judicious bit of monetary policy would redress the imbalance. The Great Depression and Keynes' theories led economists to doubt the effectiveness of monetary policy to stimulate any badly depressed economy back toward full employment, and this led to the increased advocacy of fiscal policy—direct government stimulation of economic activity through public expenditures or subsidies. But in the past decade or so, in the U.S. particularly, a group of economists called monetarists have become prominent by advocating a return to more conventional means of stabilizing economic activity. They argue that fiscal policy is fatally flawed with political pitfalls, even if in economic theory it could work, and that the most effective stabilization policy would be one in which each economy chooses the growth rate it deems feasible. That stabilization policy should settle, more or less, for following a "simple monetary rule"—increasing the money supply at the same rate. In this way prices would not increase (inflation would cease to be the major problem it now is in all market-oriented economies) because money—the means of payment—would increase no faster than output—the things to be paid for.

It is well to keep these conflicting views in mind in considering the relative usefulness of monetary and fiscal policy in various market economies. There may be reasons for preferring policy governed by automatic rules over policy left to the imperfect foresight of mortal men (a hypothesis which is debatable on its own terms however), but we shall see that a major difference among market-oriented economies at the present time is the political feasibility of diverse policy tools. Accordingly, what may make fiscal policy more difficult to administer in the U.S. need not be a comparable drawback in other countries. Indeed, fiscal policy of the most direct sort—wage or price controls—had been all but ruled out politically in the U.S. (until 1971, when inflation proved especially intractable), but this is not the case in some other market-oriented economies.

Monetary Policy

Monetary policy, simply defined, is policy designed to increase or decrease a country's money supply. If the supply is defined as cash in circulation plus demand deposits at commercial banks, an expansionary monetary policy would encourage an increase in one or both of these components of the money supply.

Because most of the money supply in a modern economy is in the form of demand deposits rather than cash, monetary policy customarily involves primarily having a central bank utilize the flexibility of a fractional reserve system so as to encourage or discourage the creation of demand deposits by commercial banks. Why do this? In expansionary periods it is with the hope that consumers—especially private investors—will borrow and thus expand economic activity. In periods of inflation a "tight money policy" enables the central banks to discourage commercial bank lending through creating demand deposits and so discourages expansions in loans to both consumers and investors.

Because of the system of fractional reserves, the central bank, charged with stabilizing economic activity and promoting growth, can control the lending activities of commercial banks, which are motivated not by concern for stability and growth but primarily by the pursuit of profits. The central bank pursues its goals by affecting the size of reserves and the use to which commercial banks can put excess reserves. By affecting interest rates (the price of borrowing money), the central bank encourages the commercial banks to lean against prevailing economic winds—a policy which can be effective if banks remain willing to part with their liquidity and the public remains willing to borrow at low interest rates. Because of doubts on both scores it is often said that monetary policy can more effectively put a ceiling on lending in inflation than it can put a floor to lending during depression. In recent years, however, monetary policy has faced difficulties in curbing, or helping to curb, inflation. We shall consider below why this has been the case.

From what has been said it is clear that modern monetary policy depends heavily for whatever success it can have on the existence of a strong central bank that has significant controls over the lending activities of commercial banks. The Bank of England, the Bank of France, and the Bank of Holland are all several hundred years old. The U.S. central bank, the Federal Reserve System, was not established until 1914, and its tardy arrival is partly responsible for the chaotic history of bank failures and unstable money which the United States experienced in the nineteenth century. In Germany after World War II a high priority was placed on monetary stability. After the Currency Reform Act of 1948 Germany had a system of decentralized banking—the Deutscher Lander Banks (district banks) were legally independent. In 1957 the Bundesbank was established as a strong central bank to regulate the Lander Banks, and the system in effect now is not unlike that in the United States, where the Federal Reserve Board effectively controls the twelve regional banks which make up the Federal Reserve System. The Bank of Japan shares responsibility with the government, much as the treasury and the Federal Reserve Board do in the United States. Other countries have central banks as well as some special agencies such as the Conseil National du Credit (National Credit Council) in France, but the broad functioning of monetary policy can be characterized without attempting detailed descriptions of the institutional variations found among market-oriented economies.[10]

The major tools of monetary policy—the use of open market operations, the discount rate, changes in reserve requirements, selective controls, and so on are all designed to alter either the size and character of commercial bank assets or what the banks can do with these assets to increase the supply of money. Without attempting to discuss in detail the mechanics by which each of these tools of monetary control operates, we shall attempt a brief survey of their present use in market-oriented economies. We wish to outline the varying emphases, and the uses to which these tools have been put in different countries, and how the flexibility of the monetary authorities is changed from country to country by each country's unique factors.

The Bank Rate   The oldest weapon central banks (sometimes called "bankers' banks") have with which to attempt to influence lending activities is the bank rate, used by every one of the major market-oriented economies we have been considering. In the United States it is more often called the discount rate, and it may be viewed simply as the interest rate which central banks charge to the commercial banks under their control.

One study has termed the *volume* of discounts significant only in Austria, Belgium, France, Italy, and the U.K. However, the rate is varied with considerable frequency also in Japan, West Germany, Denmark, the Netherlands, and the U.S.[11]

The discount rate is significant because it can affect the cost of credit to the ultimate borrower and the availability of credit through the commercial banking system, and because it is an indication of the attitude the central bank takes toward the current condition of the economy (hence, it suggests the kinds of policies apt to be pursued in the immediate future, which will have an impact on interest rates). This latter function of the discount rate has been aptly termed the *announcement effect.*[12]

The usefulness of the discount rate as a tool of stabilization policy depends on the accuracy with which the monetary authorities forecast the immediate future, on their independence in utilizing the discount rate, on the degree to which central bank policies can affect commercial bank lending policies, and on the degree to which private borrowers (for example, corporations) depend on the banks for financing internal expansion or growth, as opposed, for example, to the use of internal funds (retained profits) or the selling of stock. (Nationalized industries may also be insulated from the effects of changes in the discount

---

[10] Details of these arrangements can be found in International Information Centre for Local Credit (hereafter IICLC), *Economic Policy in Practice* (The Hague: Martinus Nijhoff, 1968), and in Geoffrey Denton, Murray Forsyth, and Malcolm Maclennan, *Economic Planning and Policies in Britain, France, and Germany* (London: George Allen and Unwin, 1968).

[11] IICLC, *Economic Policy in Practice,* pp. 17-18.

[12] Lawrence H. Officer and Lawrence B. Smith, *Canadian Economic Problems and Policies* (Toronto: McGraw-Hill Co. of Canada, 1970), p. 22.

rate.)[13] Differences in the institutional structure and the financial habits among market-oriented economies therefore account for many of the differences in the use of the discount rate as a stabilizing tool. In almost all countries where it is employed, however, it is designed to discourage expansion when it is raised and to encourage expansion when it is lowered.

A final observation about the nature of the discount rate is perhaps in order. It is true of many techniques of achieving macroeconomic objectives that pursuit of one goal can conflict with the pursuit of another. In the case of the discount rate, the problem involves internal versus external stability: a high interest rate used to discourage investment at home is also likely to attract capital inflows from abroad (so-called "hot money" seeking greater returns than can be attained at home). Thus since the war a country like West Germany has had considerable difficulty in using the discount rate to offset inflationary pressures because the resultant inflow of capital from abroad offsets or more than offsets the stabilizing effect of higher discount rates on domestic investment activity. The Japanese have had much the same problem and have circumvented it—at least partially—by employing several discount rates simultaneously.[14] Thus in 1965 the discount rate in Japan for commercial bills, 6.205 percent per year, was also the minimum rate employed on loans secured by import trade bills, but the rate for loans secured by export trade bills (in effect the rate to expedite exports) was set at a minimum of 4.380 percent.[15] By using several discount rates this traditional weapon for internal stabilization can at least help to promote external stabilization as well. Of course, as the monetary crisis of the early 1970s showed, such techniques will not restore equilibrium in international money markets when the causes of disequilibrium are fundamental and when they are reflected in international exchange rates that do not reflect the realities of present international currency demands relative to their supplies in international money markets, as must be the case if stable exchange rates are to prevail.

While high export surpluses have caused capital inflows in the case of Japan and Germany, thus adding to domestic inflationary pressures, a country like France, which has a far more modest export surplus, has nonetheless (and for other reasons) been plagued with inflation for many years, and has also had to keep the possibility of capital inflows in mind while coping domestically with inflation. Between 1950 and 1970 the French had several periods of inflation and several recessions, during which they changed the discount rate in the appropriate direction. But the discount rate in France was almost invariably lower than it was in England, which would encourage capital outflows from

[13] See, for example, Peter G. Fousek, *Foreign Central Banking: The Instruments of Monetary Policy* (New York: Federal Reserve Bank of New York, 1957), p. 26.

[14] In the U.S. the discount rate, though nominally set separately by each of the twelve Federal Reserve Banks, rarely differs from one bank to another for more than a few days or weeks at most. When one Federal Reserve rate changes they all change in short order, as indeed they would have to if the principles of the market mechanism are to operate.

[15] IICLC, *Economic Policy in Practice*, p. 154.

France to England although the French could perhaps afford to live with this difference. However, the French discount rate was almost always higher than was the U.S. discount rate until the late 1960s, and the consequences of maintaining this disparity were more compelling. The role of foreign trade in the French GNP is far greater than is the role of foreign trade in the U.S. GNP. The U.S. balance of payments deficits have created considerable concern in the U.S. in recent years. Because of the difference in the relative importance of external economic activities to our internal GNP, U.S. balance of payments disequilibria in one sense create more difficulties for other countries than they do internally, whereas in a country like France, balance of payments difficulties can have a profound direct effect on real GNP. Hence the external consequences of discount rate policy in France must be kept in mind to a far greater degree than in a country like the U.S.

The British have traditionally used the discount rate as a *penalty* rate, raising it to shut off funds to the British capital market, whereas the U.S. discount rate in recent decades has tended more to accommodate the market, so that even when it was high it has not shut off funds to the market. In a sense, therefore, and to the degree that the U.S. rate *follows* the market (that is, other interest rates) rather than *leads* it, the discount rate plays a smaller part in stabilizing economic activity in the U.S. than it does in Britain.

Because of the external consequences of diverse discount rates, it is not surprising that the rates charged by central banks to discount paper from commercial banks tend to move in roughly the same direction in many countries. Thus in January 1971 in most of the countries we are concerned with the discount rate was about 6 percent whereas by January 1972 the rate had fallen to approximately 4 percent. This tendency toward similarity of discount rates reflects the role discounts play in mirroring general short-term interest rates. Also, the fact that "hot money" is inclined to pursue higher interest rates tends to keep these rates more or less comparable among the major market-oriented countries. [16]

One final feature of the discount rate as a stabilizer is worth mentioning, because it is alien to U.S. experience. For a time the Dutch applied a "penalty rate" of 1 percent to discounts to banks lending in what the central bank regarded as "too free" a way. [17] The Japanese have set quotas for each bank and at present are charging a penalty rate for discounts to any bank in excess of this quota. [18] This technique makes the discount rate serve directly as a rationer of credit.

---

[16] The only exceptions to this rise is the case of relatively small economies (e.g., Chile or Vietnam), which have recently maintained very high discount rates, but are of no direct concern to us here. Information on international discount rates is now published in the *Federal Reserve Bulletin*; the information for the paragraph above came from the issue of February 1972, p. A 92.

[17] IICLC, *Economic Policy in Practice* p. 184.

[18] *Federal Reserve Bulletin*, February 1972, p. A 92.

If the discount rate is no longer considered *the* tool of monetary policy, it is nonetheless utilized in all the countries we are concerned with. We have seen that it is not used in the same way, nor even invariably for the same purpose in all countries (in Norway, for example, it is deliberately kept as low as possible to facilitate economic growth, thus emphasizing the accommodation aspect rather than the stabilization role to an even greater extent than, say, in the U.S.).[19]

In the final analysis, therefore, the discount rate can be viewed as a significant tool of monetary policy that is used with reasonable frequency and vigor in Belgium, Denmark, Germany (although it may have been used less purposefully since 1961), Japan, the Netherlands, the U.K., and the U.S. A major reason for the importance of the discount rate in some countries, despite a possibly low volume of total discounts, is that a change in the discount rate is viewed as a guide to the current attitude of the monetary authorities. "The discount rate is regarded in the Netherlands, as in many other places, as a major weathervane of the government's intentions. Moreover, interest rates on commercial bank lending are traditionally tied to the discount rates."[20] This comment is typical of the role played by the discount rate in many of the countries listed. Not only does a rise in the discount rate make commercial bank lending more expensive and so discourage it (the commercial banks, like all middle men able to do so, pass the increased cost on to their customers in the form of higher interest rates) but a rise in the discount rate is a clear signal that the monetary authorities are worried about inflation or excessively rapid growth in liquidity. Commercial banks that ignore this warning are asking for sterner measures from the central bank.

Open Market Operations   Commercial banks in modern market-oriented economies all hold a variety of assets, including, typically, a large volume of securities issued either by the central government or by private companies. These security holdings, mostly bonds, are similar to the securities held by individuals, and there is no reason why they cannot be bought and sold a number of times prior to maturity. Buying securities in the open market is a technique for encouraging commercial bank lending: selling securities (or at least refusing to buy them) is a technique by which central banks can discourage commercial bank lending.

The government (usually through the treasury) creates a goodly volume of securities (the public debt in market-oriented economies consists of securities issued through the government). In the United States the Federal Reserve System held something over $60 billion of such securities in 1970; commercial banks held $63 billion. (Securities are also owned by other kinds of banks, insurance companies, individuals, and so on.) Because of the size of the public

---

[19] IICLC, *Economic Policy in Practice*, p. 15.

[20] Michael Michaely, *Balance-of-Payments Adjustment Policies: Japan, Germany, and the Netherlands*, National Bureau of Economic Research Occasional Paper 106 (New York: Columbia University Press, 1968), p. 106.

debt in the United States, open market operations are widely viewed as the single most important general monetary control available to our central bank. The mark of a genuinely open capital market is that the purchasers and sellers of securities collectively determine the prices of securities and hence also the effective interest rates.[21]

Open market operations can be a powerful tool of monetary policy because the deposits commercial banks have in central banks form the base of commercial bank lending, and in all modern economies the banking systems operate on what are called fractional reserves—they do not need to have as much on deposit in their central bank accounts as the amount of demand deposit accounts they have created through their lending activities. The major limitation to open market operations as a stimulant or depressant to commercial bank operations is that the country must have a well-developed capital market. One can think of a capital market as the sum of institutional arrangements which have been made for the purchase and sale of "used bonds" and the sale of new bonds. In the United States open market operations can be extremely effective because a large volume of securities exists (the public debt was close to $400 billion in 1971). Capital markets here are thus very well developed, so that the sale and purchase of securities can be carried out with facility. Hence the open market policy (decided every two weeks by the Open Market Committee, an important agency of the Board of Governors of our Federal Reserve System) offers the central bank a major channel through which to increase or attempt to decrease the reserve accounts of commercial banks and thus encourage or discourage commercial bank lending activity.

The only other country in which open market operations are significant is Britain. The British capital market is old and well established, and thus the Bank of England regularly purchases and sells securities to affect the volume of cash which will be available.[22]

Japan is a good example of a capital market that is not sufficiently developed to utilize open market operations. Unlike the U.S. system, interest rates are set artificially in Japan and not in a market through the relation of demand to supply for government securities. Very limited types of quasi-open market operations are carried out—for example, the Bank of Japan might buy securities from city banks that are suffering a shortage of liquid funds because of treasury withdrawals, or it might buy securities from local banks to increase their cash position. But when, as in Japan, the purchases and sales are negotiated directly with financial institutions rather than in a market for securities (like our stock market) the central bank activities cannot be called open market operations.[23]

---

[21] When securities sell in the market at prices different from their original selling price, the effective interest rate (determined by the maturity value of the security) is affected. Bond prices and interest rates thus vary inversely.

[22] See IICLC, *Economic Policy in Practice*, p. 260.

[23] Ibid., p. 156.

The Dutch Bank Law of 1948 permits open market operations, but they are relatively little used. In Germany small use is made of open market operations, but thus far the Deutsche Bundersbank deals only with credit institutions, public administrations, and some insurance companies; the public is not yet involved. The Bundesbank does influence the liquidity of local banks to a certain extent by varying the margin between the original selling price of securities and the price at which they will repurchase them. They can decrease liquidity by widening the margin, and increase liquidity by narrowing the margin, thus foregoing their own interest rates. (In 1963 they temporarily gave up altogether their own interest on short-term treasury notes.)[24] Open market operations are also of some importance in Belgium (which has created a special agency, the *Fondes des Rentes,* outside the central bank to carry out the policy) and France. In Italy and Scandinavia the capital market is not yet fully developed.

Open market operations are utilized in Canada along with other general controls, but Canada has special problems because of its close proximity and economic involvement with the U.S. and because of its dependence on international trade. Hence monetary policy generally is sometimes thought to be of greater importance in its external role (that is, in luring capital funds into Canada) than in domestic stabilization. In general, however, open market operations affect a country's external economic relationships less than the discount rate; hence this tool of monetary policy is a flexible weapon for achieving greater domestic stability in countries where it can be effectively employed. It is the most important tool of monetary policy in the U.S., but it is of somewhat less importance in other market-oriented economies; its importance is increasing as the financial structures of other economies grow and mature, however.

Reserve Ratios   As we have suggested, modern commercial banks operate on the principle of fractional reserves—they can create demand deposit accounts for their customers by extending loans to them in amounts which exceed the size of the commercial bank reserves (or accounts, if you like) at the central bank. The relationship between the size of the commercial banks' required reserve accounts at the central bank and their demand deposit accounts outstanding is known as the reserve ratio, and setting this ratio is a third major weapon of monetary policy.[26] When a central bank raises the reserve ratio, it means that with a given volume of reserves, commercial banks are permitted to

[24] Ibid., p. 97.

[25] Ian M. Drummond, *The Canadian Economy: Organization and Development* (Homewood, Ill.: Richard D. Irwin Co., 1966), p. 93.

[26] Reserves had the original purpose of protecting commercial bank depositors from having the banks overextend themselves—i.e., lend more than was prudent—but this purpose has in many countries been taken over by insurance programs such as the Federal Deposit Insurance Corporation in the U.S.—a plan whereby banks pay premiums to the FDIC in return for which their depositors' accounts are insured against loss through bankruptcy up

have a smaller volume of loans outstanding, and so it inhibits monetary expansion. Lowering the reserve requirements has the opposite effect.

Reserve ratio changes are a powerful tool of monetary policy, but this very power is a limitation on their usefulness, because small changes in the required reserves can have very large effects on commercial bank operations. They must therefore be used prudently and many central banks change reserve ratios only as frequently as they feel is consistent with overall stabilization objectives. Some sort of reserve requirement system operates in Austria, Belgium, West Germany, Italy, Japan, the Netherlands, Spain and the United Kingdom as well as the United States.[27] However, in Japan the reserve requirements in the late 1960s were set at about 2 percent of total deposits and thus could scarcely qualify as a major instrument of monetary control.[28] In Norway and France the commercial banks are required to invest some minimum percentage of their assets in public loans instead of being required to hold some minimum percent of their demand deposits outstanding in the form of reserve accounts at the central banks. Presumably the percentage can be varied within limits, and so the effect is similar to (if possibly less effective than) varying the reserve requirement. Reserve requirements as we know them are not part of the monetary controls used in Denmark.

Other General Monetary Controls In addition to the three major methods of regulating the money supply enumerated above, a variety of other techniques are used in certain countries. In general these techniques reveal once again less reticence about direct interference—in this case in credit rationing—than is the case in the United States. It remains to be seen whether the economic crisis which brought about the interventionist policies used by the Nixon administration in 1971 will presage a greater willingness to intervene directly in other areas, as, for example, in credit rationing, presently under discussion. As of this writing, there is no sign that new policies involving direct intervention are being introduced more freely than heretofore.

For example, even in West Germany—the economy Shonfield and others view as most like that of the U.S. in its allegiance to traditional market allocation methods—the Deutsche Bundesbank is permitted (along with its use of the discount rate) to impose specific (and unpublished) quotas on individual Lander Banks limiting the total amount of securities that the commercial banks can sell to the Bundesbank.[29] This enables the Bundesbank to control liquidity within the banking system very directly when it chooses to do so. Similarly, the

---

to $20,000. The U.S. had the highest bankruptcy rate of any major country in the nineteenth century, but the lessons of the Great Depression brought many banking reforms both here and in other countries.

[27] IICLC, *Economic Policy in Practice*, p. 20

[28] Ibid., p. 156.

[29] Ibid., pp. 97-98.

right to invest liquid assets elsewhere than with the Deutsche Bundesbank requires the approval of the Bundesbank; thus the Bundesbank has another means of affecting overall liquidity in the economy.[30]

In several countries the ideal of reserve requirements has been developed and refined into a more explicit control often referred to as *liquidity ratios.* For example, the Austrian National Bank can specify the percentages of deposits which must be kept at the central bank or some other financial institution (for example, a postal saving bank or a credit institution). To these minimum required deposits (on which interest is not paid) the Austrians have added a penalty rate system for commercial banks whose deposits fall below the minimum. In the late 1960s this penalty rate was 7.5 percent of the difference between actual deposits and required deposits at the central bank.[31] Somewhat comparable to this is a French technique introduced in 1963 whereby the Bank of France can specify the particular forms of asset in which commercial banks must cover up to 36 percent of their liabilities. The result is reserve requirements of a more specific sort than in the U.S.[32]

Overall credit ceilings—in effect, a limit on resort to discounts by commercial banks at the central bank—are utilized in France,[33] the Netherlands, and Norway. In the United States there is no absolute limit, but there is also no automatic assurance that all discounts will be granted automatically to commercial banks by the Federal Reserve.

Finally, there is a technique known as *moral suasion,* in which the central bank either by force of logic, by its prestige, or by other means persuades the commercial banks to increase or decrease their willingness to lend. This technique, dubbed by some wags as "open-mouth operations," is used in Austria, Belgium, Japan, the U.K., and the U.S. In Austria the moral suasion takes the form of "recommendations" which the central bank can issue to commercial banks concerning their lending activities, but once again we find a greater willingness to utilize direct intervention. In Austria these recommendations can be made binding—in 1967, for example, the central bank forced the commercial banks to agree to freeze their assets for a period in order to damp inflationary pressures.[34]

As we previously noted, many market-oriented economies have employed various forms of exchange controls from time to time in order to limit access to their exchange markets by foreigners or to limit convertibility of domestic exchange by nationals into other currences. These controls, to which we shall

[30] Ibid., p. 98.

[31] Ibid., p. 58.

[32] Ibid., p. 113..

[33] In France monetary policy includes *plancheurs* (floors), representing minimum amounts in treasury bills which commercial banks are required to hold, and *plafonds* (ceilings), an overall limit on the amount of finance to be discounted by commercial banks at the Bank of France. (See Denton, Forsyth, and Maclennan, *Economic Planning and Policies,* p. 163.)

[34] IICLC, *Economic Policy in Practice,* p. 59.

return, reflect the difference in the importance of external trade in many other market-oriented economies compared to its relatively minor importance in the U.S. economy. Thus overall monetary controls, or the particular mix of policy controls, reflects strategic considerations about the relative importance of external versus internal stability as well as the particular problems faced at home—inflation or deflation, the type of and cause of the inflation or deflation, the extent of capital markets, the size of the public debt, and so on.

Selective Credit Controls In addition to general monetary tools, all of which are designed to affect the *total* supply of money or credit, there are several monetary techniques called *selective controls* because they are designed to affect its growth in selected sectors of the economy instead of attempting to control the growth of the entire supply of money or credit. As is true of other areas we have surveyed, selective controls have generally been used more extensively in other market-oriented economies than in the United States.[35] It can be argued that the use of selective controls to curb the use of credit in sectors of the economy where credit extension threatens to become excessive involves less interference with the overall allocation of financial resources by the market than the use of general controls. Why use a massive, general control when only a small, specific one is necessary? This argument may have considerable merit, but it has not been very persuasive thus far in the U.S.

In the following sections we shall outline the kinds of selective controls currently utilized in the United States and other market-oriented economies. We might note that several techniques considered under general controls, such as differential discount rates, might be viewed more accurately as selective controls.[36]

Consumer Credit Controls The most widely used selective controls are consumer credit controls, under which the maturity and minimum down payment requirements of loans made for the purchase of consumer durables can be set by the central bank or other monetary authority. In the U.S. these controls, known as Regulation W, were employed to prevent the excess demand due to the war-limited supply from inflating the price of automobiles and other consumer durable goods during World War II and again briefly during the Korean War. Since the early 1950s they have not been employed and are now generally viewed as temporary measures to be used only in times of emergency, although some economists advocate their use in more widespread fashion.

Canada utilized instalment credit controls during World War II and again during the Korean emergency. The central bank tried to get agreement from the larger companies to hold down instalment credit in late 1956, when this type of

---

[35] See, for example, Fousek, *Foreign Central Banking*, p. 69.
[36] Fousek considers selective discount rates one of the selective controls (Ibid., p. 70.)

credit was expanding rapidly. The attempt was unsuccessful, although banks did agree to limit the volume of their loans to the more important finance companies to the maximum reached in 1956.[37]

In the U.K. this technique is known as *hire purchase control,* and it is used more or less continuously, depending on the inflationary threat which exists at a given time. It has also been used in Denmark, Belgium, France, and the Netherlands. In both Belgium and the Netherlands the technique takes the form of central setting of minimum down payments and maximum maturities for these loans.[38] Credit controls have been used in the Scandinavian countries, at least in the early postwar period.[39]

Margin Requirements   Margin requirements, designed to limit the amount stock purchasers can borrow from their brokers, were provided for in the U.S. by the Securities and Exchange Act of 1934 to prevent undue speculation of the sort that played so prominent a role in precipitating the 1929 stock market crash. Because of the relatively smaller importance of stock credit in foreign commercial banking, margin requirements are not as important in other market-oriented economies. While no other monetary authorities have the power to set margin requirements, in Canada they have been set by the stock exchanges themselves. In 1956, for example, after conferring with the central bank, these exchanges informed the members that "it would be undesirable for the volume of credit used in stock market trading to increase further under present conditions."[40] This comes pretty close to the U.S. version of margin requirements. In France brokers associations have set margins and varied them occasionally.[41]

Other Controls   Mortgage rates are also controlled in the U.S., both those guaranteed by the Veterans' Administration and those insured by the Federal Housing Administration. A variety of other federal agencies (for example, the Federal National Mortgage Association) are also involved in the control of mortgage credit. "Gentlemen's agreements" concerning various kinds of credit extension are resorted to in Austria, Denmark, France, Germany, the Netherlands, Norway, Sweden, and the U.K.

[37] See ibid., p. 75.

[38] IICLC, *Economic Policy in Practice*, pp. 82, 190; Fousek, *Foreign Central Banking: The Instruments of Monetary Policy,* pp. 74-75.

[39] Maddison reports that they were used in Scandinavia before 1960, but they are not mentioned in IICLC, *Economic Policy in Practice,* on which much of this discussion of monetary policy in recent years is based. (See Maddison, "The Postwar Business Cycle in Western Europe and the Role of Government Policy," pp. 132-33, Table 12.)

[40] Quoted in Fousek, *Foreign Central Banking,* p. 76.

[41] Ibid.

Debt Management Policy

With the advent of the "Keynesian revolution," unbalanced budgets became economically respectable, or at least less unpalatable, and the notion that what balancing there was could well be done over a business cycle rather than a calendar or fiscal year became acceptable, at least in principle. A number of modern market-oriented economies have thus acquired sizable public debts from deficit financing. The U.S. has the largest public debt, and most of it has been necessitated by wars rather than through efforts at stabilizing economic activity. The existence of large public debts can have significant impact on both the internal and external stability of the economy; hence debt management policy has come to be recognized as a type of potential stabilization policy. In order to consider the possibilities and the differences which debt management offers in modern market-oriented economies, it is instructive to examine Table 8-1, which will be of assistance in the subsequent section on balance of payments considerations as well.

Table 8-1
Two Measures of the Impact of Public Debt in Twelve
Market-Oriented Economies, 1969

Country (1)	Public Debt as a percent of gross domestic product (2)	Percent of public debt which is foreign-owned (3)
United Kingdom	75.2%	6.6%
Belgium	52.7	11.0
Canada[a]	48.1	.5
United States	39.6	3.0
Netherlands	30.2	.4
Sweden[a]	18.9	.8
Italy	14.9	NA
West Germany	14.0	5.6
France	13.9	7.5
Austria	13.5	29.3
Japan	4.6	2.1
Denmark	4.1	41.1

Sources:
All data except for the U.S. from *U.N. Statistical Yearbook, 1970,* Tables 179 and 193. U.S. data *Federal Reserve Bulletin*, February 1972, Tables A44 and A70.

Notes:
The definition of public debt varies somewhat from country to country, so the figures must be taken as rough approximations rather than as exact measures.
[a]1968 data.

In the previous discussion of open market operations we noted that to be effective this tool of monetary control requires that the country possess a well-developed capital market—in effect, a market where buyers and sellers of both government and private securities can bid on such securities and so determine their market price, as is done daily on our stock markets, for example. We suggested that one indicator of a capital market is the size of the public debt. In countries where the government has sold a large volume of securities relative to its economic size, one could expect to find well-developed capital markets in which such sales can be made, and Table 8-1 confirms this. The countries where open market operations are important are largely the ones that have the higher public debt-gross domestic product ratios (that is, the U.K., Canada, and the U.S.).

Debt management policy is closely related to monetary policy because both the existence of public debt and how it is handled can have significant effects on the liquidity of an economy. To the extent that commercial banks own government securities (which are, of course, part of the public debt) and to the extent that these securities can always be sold in the open market, commercial banks have a means whereby they can circumvent, at least partially, efforts to restrain their expansion of bank credit. In a real sense, therefore, a large public debt makes the operation of "tight money policy" more difficult. Indeed, in an economy like that of the United States, any holder of a government security can sell it when he wishes if he agrees to the market price and can thereby increase his liquidity. When such activities are carried out in inflation, the net result is destabilizing because increases in aggregate demand relative to aggregate supply are made possible by enabling liquidity to be transferred from those who do not wish to spend it to those who do.

A significant part of debt management policies in modern market-oriented economies involves the manner in which the treasury raises the funds (through the sale of new bonds) to pay off maturing bonds. These operations, called *funding the debt,* increase liquidity in the economy when securities with long maturities are refinanced by securities of shorter maturity (called *shortening the debt*) and decrease liquidity when the debt is "lengthened" by the reverse maneuver. In the U.S., where the debt is largest absolutely, debate has waxed for some time over whether debt should be funded as indicated above, so as to stabilize economic activity; whether it should be funded, so as to keep the interest costs of debt operations as low as possible; or whether the debt should be kept "neutral," so that it has no variable impact of its own on liquidity.

A related effect of debt management on internal liquidity in a number of market-oriented economies outside the U.S. involves the decision to repay foreign-held internal debt with domestically owned debt (to reduce domestic liquidity) or to do the reverse in time of recession—to repay domestically owned maturing bonds with foreign-owned bonds to increase domestic liquidity. That these transactions invariably have balance of payments effects in addition to their effects on the domestic economy should be obvious and will be considered in the next section. For the moment we may content ourselves with noting that only in those economies where a sizable percent of the internal debt is owned by foreigners does this possibility even exist.

The debt has been used in precisely this way in the Netherlands in recent years. Several times after 1958 the Dutch reduced domestic liquidity deliberately during inflationary times by borrowing more domestically than they were expending and by using the surplus to pay off externally held debt. In 1952 they did the opposite—they successfully increased the percent of the total debt held externally so that they could increase economic activity at home.[42] Indeed, the Dutch have been among the most sophisticated in the development of debt management policies. They have reduced internal liquidity by borrowing more than they spent at home and by using the surplus not only to repay externally held debt but also to grant credit to foreign countries and to increase their own governmental accounts at the central bank, all of which would be deflationary in their domestic consequences.[43] The Dutch have also deliberately changed the length of the debt to achieve greater domestic stability. As Table 8-1 indicates, it is those countries that have both a sizable debt relative to their aggregate output and a sizable foreign-owned percentage of their debts which could manipulate their debts in the way the Dutch have. (As the table suggests, relatively little of the Dutch debt is owned externally.) Countries like the U.K. and Belgium could utilize their debt in this way to a far greater extent, but in the U.S. although the debt is relatively large, very little of it is foreign-held. West Germany is another country which has from time to time deliberately altered the percent of its debt held by foreigners, but the Germans have tended to do this more for balance of payments reasons than for reasons of internal stabilization policy.

In sum, debt management is being increasingly recognized as a vital link both in domestic stabilization policies and in external stability, especially for those countries in which the debt is both large and owned to a significant extent by foreigners. In the latter case, debt-management policies can have significant effects on the balance of payments, and it is to this subject that the next section is devoted.

Balance of Payments Considerations

If the world has learned anything in the years since World War II, it is that no country can pursue domestic policies unmindful of their effect on other economies or can hope to remain immune to the impact on its own domestic economic stability of the policies pursued by other nations. If a country has a consistent surplus in its balance of payments (that is, it exports more than it

---

[42] IICLC, *Economic Policy in Practice*, p. 190.
[43] Ibid., p. 189.

imports), this will tend to increase liquidity at home (because the foreigners must pay for what they buy). In the simpler days of a bygone era, imbalances in exports and imports were supposed to lead to corresponding imbalances in the demands and supplies for foreign currencies in international exchange markets. These in turn were supposed to lead, via gold flows, to automatic adjustment in each country's money supply and to changes in price levels which would redress the trade imbalances. But that was before the United States became so important in the economic activities of the Western world that the dollar was considered "as good as gold," and before the European recovery of recent years made other market-oriented economies less dependent on the United States, eliminated the U.S. trade surplus, and lessened the willingness of other countries to pile up dollars.

We cannot hope to examine the myriad ramifications which the intercountry relations among market-oriented economies have on their internal stability, but neither can we survey current stabilization tools without pausing to note that exchange rates—the prices of any currency in terms of another—are no longer permitted to operate as they were in the days before the Great Depression and the war which followed it. Almost every country in the group we have been considering has resorted to both exchange controls and currency devaluation (or revaluation).

Exchange controls are not unlike the price support programs we considered in connection with agriculture. If the British or the French do not want the value of their currency to fall relative to other currencies, they simply buy the excess of their currency out of international money markets and so "support" the official exchange rates. If they suffer a serious imbalance for a long time, so that supporting the official price of their currency would represent an endless drain on their gold supplies, then they devalue their currency—make it cheaper relative to other currencies in the hope, among other things, of stimulating exports (others find their goods cheaper to buy) and depressing imports (their own nationals find it more expensive to buy abroad). Almost all European countries have devalued their currencies one or more times since World War II. (Usually inflation—rising prices—drove them to it because their exports were falling and their imports were rising, with the result that their balance of payments worsened, and maintaining exchange rates became increasingly untenable.)

More recently the great increase in German and Japanese productivity has resulted in a revaluation of both the Deutsche mark and the Japanese yen. German exports were increasing so rapidly relative to German imports that the price of the mark was unrealistically low (the demand for marks was so much greater than their supply in international money markets that there was steady upward pressure on the price), and much the same thing was true of the yen. Finally, in 1971, faced with its first trade deficit since 1893, the U.S. let the dollar "float"—that is, let international money markets determine the dollar price of gold, which had been "fixed" at $35 an ounce since the 1930s. The price of gold was ultimately (1972) set at $38 an ounce, and it was hoped that the devaluation of the dollar coupled with the revaluation of the mark and the yen would improve the U.S. trade balance.

This leads us to return briefly to the possible conflict between domestic stabilization policy and efforts to achieve greater external stability. Efforts to fight domestic inflation with restrictive monetary policy can cause difficulty with two other objectives that all market-oriented economies strive for today. To the extent that restrictive monetary policy drives up domestic interest rates, it can impede real investment and so slow the domestic rate of growth. (We shall return to this problem in Chapter 9.) The second problem is that higher domestic interest rates lure foreign capital, particularly short-run liquid capital, into the domestic economy. Table 8-1 shows the extent to which foreign owners of liquidity have invested in government bonds in twelve market-oriented economies. They may also lend by purchasing bonds of private corporations. A country like Denmark cannot permit interest rates to fall domestically without being mindful of the fact that its debt refunding operations will be thereby complicated.

In 1970 the U.S. coped with the reverse problem. The recession in this country and continuing inflation in European countries caused interest rates to fall because of the easy monetary policy in the U.S. while they continued to climb in Europe, with the result that short-term liquid capital flowed from the U.S. to Europe in massive quantities, thereby contributing to the worst U.S. balance of payments deficit in the twentieth century. This was a classic example of appropriate domestic monetary policy conflicting with balance of payments considerations, and it has led some to advocate coping with domestic recession through tight money and an expansionary fiscal policy. We shall consider fiscal policy in the next section; suffice it to note here that the international financial crisis of 1971, which resulted from the build-up of many factors since World War II, should have been enough to convince everyone that all market-oriented economies—even the United States, which had tended historically to ignore the external consequences of domestic stabilization policy—must remain conscious of the fact that domestic and international economic policies are inextricably related: what seems sound domestically might be disastrous externally. International considerations cannot be avoided in setting domestic monetary policy.

Finally, we should note that it is impossible to consider the problem of appropriate stabilization policy for any economy, internally or externally, without considering fiscal policy, the subject of our next section, along with monetary policy. We have mentioned the possibility, for example, that countries which do not wish to impose exchange controls or to restrict trade might try to utilize monetary policy to achieve external stability (through influencing capital flows via the interest rate) and to utilize fiscal policy to fight domestic inflation.[44] Such possibilities can only be evaluated, however, after we have considered the possible role of fiscal policy in stabilizing economic activity.

Fiscal Policy

Its Origins and Limitations Fiscal policy has been defined as the "deliberate exercise of the government's power to tax and spend in order to dampen the swings of the business cycle and bring the nation's output and employment to desired levels."[45] One of the major contributions made to modern economic theory by John Maynard Keynes (in his *General Theory of Employment, Interest, and Money,* which was published in 1936, when the Western world was still reeling from the aftermath of the Great Depression) was the idea that in times of profound economic collapse there may be no effective way in which monetary policy can adequately stimulate the economy through increased bank lending and hence through increased private borrowing for investment or consumption purposes. Presumably, monetary policy could be more effective in braking inflationary pressures, on the one hand, or in stimulating recovery from mild recessions of the sort that the Western world has experienced since World War II. Ironically, the Great Depression, which pushed fiscal policy for the first time to a position of prominence in the arsenal of stabilization tools utilized by market-oriented economies, also made it appear that monetary policy could be more effective in stopping inflation than in restoring full employment to a sagging economy. Yet the monetarists, to whom we referred early in this chapter, argue that (for reasons we shall discuss) fiscal policy is a clumsy tool for stabilizing economic activity. Whatever the merits of that argument may be, the basic secular problem in the past quarter of a century in most market-oriented economies has been inflation, and monetary policy has not seemed able or willing to cope with it. Why? The monetarists argue that it

[44] See Robert A. Mundell, "The Appropriate Use of Monetary and Fiscal Policy for Internal and External Stability," *International Monetary Fund Staff Papers* 9 (March 1962): 70-79. Reprinted in W. L. Smith and R. L. Teigen, eds., *Readings in Money, National Income, and Stabilization Policy*, rev. ed. (Homewood, Ill.: Richard D. Irwin Co., 1970). Mundell summarizes his position as follows:

> The practical implication of theory, when stabilization measures are limited to monetary policy and fiscal policy, is that a surplus country experiencing inflationary pressure should ease monetary conditions and raise taxes (or reduce government spending), and that a deficit country suffering from unemployment should tighten interest rates and lower taxes (or increase government spending).

(Pp. 611-12.) This will be clearer to the reader after considering the section in Chapter 9 on the rise of Euro-dollars.

[45] Milton H. Spencer, *Contemporary Economics* (New York: Worth Publishing, 1971), p. 689.

has not curbed inflation because it has been mismanaged. They argue that instead of adopting a "simple monetary rule" of the sort explained earlier, market-oriented economies have attempted to use all the discretionary tools of monetary policy previously enumerated, and that men—even sophisticated economists—cannot possibly hope to apply such monetary tools with the appropriate timing to mitigate rather than aggravate economic instability.

But there are other reasons why monetary policy is limited as a technique for stabilizing economic activity in a fundamentally inflationary environment. We have considered some of these changes already; for example, in the United States and elsewhere the existence of a large public debt provides a ready pool of potential liquidity which through the debt-funding process can aggravate inflationary pressures. In market-oriented economies outside the U.S. the huge inflow of "Euro-dollars" (to be discussed in Chapter 9) has made inflation more difficult to curb through monetary policy. Restrictive measures designed to limit domestic monetary expansion can be partially or wholly offset by using Euro-dollars instead. For this reason there is a school in Europe which blames the United States for European inflationary problems. U.S. investment in European business, for example, adds to the aggregate demand pressures in those economies. On the other hand, to the extent that the U.S. payments deficit resulted from loans to European business, for military assistance, or for programs to assist in recovery from the war, the assessment of blame is less appropriate. The fact that inadequate means exist for settling international accounts in the wake of the tremendous expansion of world trade in the postwar period, coupled with the limited increase in gold and the resultant use of dollars as "reserve currency," seems a more likely scapegoat than the simple fact of a U.S. payments deficit.

For many reasons, therefore, monetary policy has consistently been supplemented with fiscal policy (even more in Europe than in the United States) in the effort to achieve greater stabilization as well as economic growth. The major criticisms of fiscal policy as a technique for stabilizing economic activity have been based as much on noneconomic as on economic grounds. Since discretionary fiscal policy refers to deliberate changes in tax rates relative to governmental expenditures, so as to create a net increase or decrease of government spending in the economy, it has been criticized partly in the same terms that discretionary monetary policy has been criticized. Thus, an American team criticized fiscal policy on the grounds that five distinct kinds of lag develop between a change in the basic direction of economic activity and the time the economy might react in response to changed fiscal policy.[46] How serious these

---

[46] For an extended discussion of these lags see Albert Ando, E. Cary Brown, Robert M. Solow, and John Kareken, "Lags in Fiscal and Monetary Policy," in *Stabilization Policies*, the Commission on Money and Credit, Research Study 1 (Englewood Cliffs, N.J. Prentice-Hall, 1963), especially pp. 2-11. As the title of their study indicates, many of these lags are involved in discretionary monetary policy as well and lead to a tendency to urge reliance on either the "simple monetary rule" mentioned earlier or the automatic stabilizers discussed below.

lags are in practice is still a matter for dispute, but some of them at least have been shortened in other market-oriented economies by having the legislative bodies grant stand-by authority to the finance minister or other responsible public official to change the tax and/or spending rates within certain limits when the situation warrants it. (Sweden, as noted below, is a particular case in point.)

In any case, it seems clear that fiscal policy is here to stay, and we shall now briefly summarize the major types utilized in market-oriented economies.

The Underlying Basis   Because fiscal policy involves governmental efforts to alter the net impact of government tax and expenditure programs, it is essential at the outset to consider the basic tax and expenditure systems in different market-oriented economies. The subject of stabilizing fiscal policy is complicated and hampered by inadequate and noncomparable data. We shall content ourselves with commenting on the major differences of emphasis in tax and expenditure systems and their implications for the possibilities for stabilization policy, plus some comments on special programs in certain market-oriented economies.

The basis for what is fiscally possible in stabilizing economic activity is found in the kinds of taxes and expenditures which various market-oriented economies utilize, and this information has been summarized in Tables 8-2 and 8-3.[47] Table 8-2 indicates total tax receipts, by origin, for eleven market-oriented economies. Possibly the most significant revelation is one which we commented on in Chapter 3: the total tax receipts of the United States represent a far smaller percentage of current GNP than is the case for any other country included in the table. Obviously the possibilities for influencing GNP by varying tax rates are increased roughly in proportion to their quantitative significance as a percent of GNP. The European country closest to the U.S. in regard to the relative size of tax receipts is the U.K.

We have already considered the relative size and importance of social security programs in market-oriented economies; hence the relatively small size of tax receipts from this source is no surprise. Of greater significance for the stabilizing potential of tax rate variations are the variations in the percentage of direct taxes and indirect taxes in various countries. By and large, direct taxes paid by households refer to personal income taxes, and the "other" category consists mainly of corporate income taxes. In Chapter 9 we shall refer back to these figures because it has been argued that the relatively large percent of American tax receipts which originate with corporations helps explain the lower growth rates in the U.S. relative to other countries since the Second World War.

---

[47] In general the data refer, so far as is known, only to central governments. The possibilities for utilizing regional or local-unit tax and expenditure systems for discretionary fiscal policy are fairly limited in the U.S., and there is no obvious reason to believe that they would be significantly greater in other countries.

Table 8-2
Tax Receipts of General Government in Eleven
Market-Oriented Economies, 1962-64
(Average Percentages)

Country	Total tax receipts as a percent of GNP at market prices	Share in total tax receipts of:				
		Direct taxes			Social security contributions	Indirect taxes
		Total	Paid by households	Other		
Austria	34.2	34.4	27.2	7.2	20.7	44.9
Belgium	27.9	29.7	23.6	6.1	26.7	43.5
Denmark	27.4	45.5	41.1	4.4	5.2	49.3
France	36.5	16.4	10.8	5.6	36.2	47.4
West Germany	35.2	31.2	23.1	8.1	27.9	40.9
Italy	30.7	19.9	—	—	35.4	44.7
Netherlands	32.0	39.1	30.7	8.4	29.6	31.3
Norway	34.6	38.1	33.4	4.7	19.3	42.5
Sweden	35.9	49.6	43.5	6.1	15.3	35.1
United Kingdom	29.1	38.9	28.9	10.0	14.7	46.4
United States	27.8	50.3	34.8[a]	15.3[a]	15.8[a]	33.9

Sources:
All countries (except the U.S.): *United Nations, Incomes in Postwar Europe: A Study of Policies, Growth, and Distribution,* (Geneva: United Nations, 1967), Chapter 6, Table 6.1, pp. 3-4.
U.S. data from OECD, *National Accounts of OECD Countries, 1960-1970* (Paris: n.d.), Table 1, p. 58 and Table 7, p. 64. Averages and percentages calculated by the author. Total Direct Taxes are on income.
[a] These two percentages have been estimated on the basis of data from the Federal Reserve *Bulletin,* January 1967, p. 146. They refer to personal and corporate taxes.

For stabilization purposes, the relatively large share of total tax receipts originating in indirect taxes in market economies other than the U.S. is noteworthy.

Within the non-U.S. countries there are some differences worth noting with regard to indirect taxes. In some countries indirect taxes are concentrated in relatively few categories—for example, in Britain indirect taxes tend to be found mainly on final goods, especially petroleum products, tobacco, and food and beverages. Denmark and Sweden tax food and alcohol heavily, too, but tend to spread indirect taxes to other products to a somewhat greater extent than Britain does. At the other extreme is France, which collects nearly half of all indirect taxes in the form of a tax on value added (known as TVA), in which each production stage must pay a tax on whatever it has added to the value of final output. (The TVA was being discussed as a possibility for the U.S. in the early 1970s.) In this way the indirect taxes tend to be widely diffused through

Table 8-3

Current and Capital Expenditures (Combined) of General Government by Major Purpose, Ten Market-Oriented Economies, Selected Years (Percentages)

	Belgium	France	West Germany 1959	Italy	Netherlands	Austria 1962	Denmark 1965-66	Norway 1965	United Kingdom 1965	United States 1970
Administration, etc.	10.2	9.1	8.9	12.0	9.7	8.5	—c	8.6	5.9	1.7
Defense	10.5	16.8	10.5	7.7	10.2	2.4	10.1	10.3	15.1	40.8
Transport, communications	9.8	7.6	7.5	6.8	8.8	8.5	6.0	7.7	7.2	4.7
Agriculture, foodstuffs	1.5	2.1	3.8	3.9	4.4	3.3	2.5 }	16.0	2.4	3.2
Industry, services	1.6	6.4	2.6	2.0	3.5	2.5	—c }		7.2	—c
Education, research	12.6	9.9	9.4	9.0	13.1	6.9	16.0	14.2	12.6	3.7
Health, welfare	} 34.9	5.8	6.8	6.7	4.8	8.9	15.9	12.9	10.7	3.7
Pensions, allied items a	}	27.0	31.0	31.0	24.6	31.5	23.7	17.9	17.4	} 28.9
Housing	1.3	5.2	5.2	1.1	8.5	4.5	—c	—c	6.6	1.5
Others b	17.6	10.2	14.3	19.8	12.4	23.0	25.8	12.4	15.0	15.5
Total	100.0	100.0	100.0	100.0	100.0	100.0	100.0	100.0	100.0	100.0

Sources:

European countries: *United Nations, Incomes in Postwar Europe: A Study of Policies, Growth, and Distribution* (Geneva: United Nations, 1967), Chapter 6, Table 6.6, p. 9.

U.S. data: computed from Board of Governors, *Federal Reserve Bulletin*, July 1971, Table A43. Data include operations only of the federal government.

Notes:

a Sickness, invalidity, and old-age pensions; family and children's allowances, unemployment benefits, public assistance (excluding medical care).

b Includes interest on internal debt and internal debt amortization, and in the case of the U.S., expenditures for international affairs, space research, natural resources, veterans' benefits, and an adjustment for intragovernmental transactions (primarily government contributions to employee retirement funds).

c This item cannot be identified and is therefore included with "others."

the economy. The same thing can be said of West Germany, which collects almost a third of its indirect taxes through a general turnover tax (a tax is paid each time products change hands). Austria, Belgium, Italy, and the Netherlands all have fairly diffused indirect tax systems, raising revenues from taxes on food and beverages, petroleum, customs duties, and other general taxes without concentrating on any one or two special types.[48]

We are interested in these variations in indirect and direct taxes because of their potential for variation, either deliberately or automatically, over the business cycle. Before considering this, however, we should consider in the same light the differences in expenditure percentages among market-oriented economies. Here again some of the differences were suggested in our discussion of welfare in Chapter 3. Clearly the similarities among the market-oriented economies in the table (excluding the U.S.) are greater than the differences, and the differences between them all and the United States are striking. The U.S. spends a considerably smaller percentage than any other market-oriented economy in Table 8-3 on administration, on transportation and communications (remember how much of these services are nationalized in other countries), on education, and on health and welfare. On the other hand, the U.S. expends a vastly larger percentage of its total outlay on defense, and also expends somewhat more on agriculture. We commented on the welfare significance of these differences in Chapter 3. What do they mean for stabilizing fiscal policy?

Fiscal Policy in Action

In general, the efficacy of fiscal policy as a stabilizing device depends on the ease and speed with which either the taxes or the expenditures can be changed when the economy appears ready to slip into recession or is threatened with inflation. First we must distinguish two kinds of fiscal policy.

Automatic Stabilizers   Automatic stabilizers refer to built-in features of tax and expenditure policy designed to make disposable income more stable cyclically than personal income. Thus, to the extent that personal and corporate income tax rates are progressive, they alter tax yields automatically as incomes vary over the cycle. In general, direct taxes are more amenable to such automaticity than indirect taxes, although indirect taxes can be stabilizing if they are applied to luxury items, the purchase of which will vary over the

---

[48] For details concerning variations in indirect tax incidence see United Nations, *Incomes in Postwar Europe: A Study of Policies, Growth, and Distribution* (Geneva: United Nations, 1967), Chapter 6, p. 8.

business cycle.[49] To the extent that the U.S. tax system relies more heavily on direct taxes than do the systems of other market-oriented economies, the U.S. potential for automatic stabilization policy may be somewhat greater than that of other market-oriented economies. Unhappily, the same cannot be said of the expenditure side, and the reason should be readily apparent. While certain expenditures vary automatically with cyclical changes in income (unemployment compensation, agricultural price supports, and other kinds of welfare payments) and so can play a part in automatic fiscal stabilization, these are precisely the areas where, in percentage terms, the U.S. expenditures constitute smaller percentages of GNP than in other market-oriented economies.[50] The biggest difference lies in the large percent of the U.S. total expenditures which is committed to defense (and if there is one item that does *not* vary over the cycle, either automatically or because of deliberate governmental action, that is it).

What the net effect of the greater potential for automatic stabilization through tax receipts and the smaller potential through expenditures in the U.S. in comparison with the other market-oriented economies might be is not easy to say. It is certainly safe to say that a larger part of fiscal policy is automatic (rather than discretionary) in the U.S. than in any other country, both because of the factors already noted and because of the greater willingness of other countries to pursue discretionary fiscal policy. Even for the U.S. however, Paul Samuelson was undoubtedly correct when he wrote, "The built-in stabilizers are our first line of defense, but are not by themselves sufficient to maintain full stability."[51]

A recent OECD study suggests that the automatic stabilizers have been most effective in the U.S. and France, where they halved the fluctuations in income,

---

[49] Commenting on the possibility of utilizing a French-style tax, the value-added tax, instead of our present direct corporate income tax, Otto Eckstein concluded, "The value-added tax would be a weaker automatic stabilizer than the corporation income tax, since profits are more sensitive to cyclical changes than value-added. The loss in automatic stabilization would be substantial." (Otto Eckstein, assisted by Vito Tanzi, "Comparison of European and United States Tax Structures and Growth Implications," in *The Role of Direct and Indirect Taxes in the Federal Revenue System: A Conference Report of the National Bureau of Economic Research and the Brookings Institution* [Princeton, N.J.: Princeton University Press, 1964], p. 248.) (Such a tax was, as noted above, nevertheless under consideration by the Nixon Administration in 1971.) This is but a specific example of the general point made in the text concerning the cyclical sensitivity of variations in tax yields from direct and indirect taxes.

[50] One can make a small exception for agricultural price support programs.

[51] Paul A. Samuelson, *Economics*, 8th ed. (New York: McGraw-Hill Book Co., 1970), p. 333. A recent study concluded that automatic stabilizers in the U.S. reduce potential income declines by between 35 and 50 percent of what they would have been in the absence of such stabilizers during the recessions of 1948-49, 1953-54, and 1957-58. They are somewhat less effective during expansions requiring discretionary action in the form of increased tax rates. (See Peter Eilbott, "The Effectiveness of Automatic Stabilizers," *American Economic Review* 56, No. 3 [June 1966].)

and somewhat less effective in Belgium, Italy, Germany, Sweden, and the U.K., where they reduced fluctuations in income by no more than twenty-five percent.[52] As was noted in connection with monetary policy, the Dutch have also been innovative in connection with fiscal policy. They have experimented with an interesting form of automatic stabilizer—relating government expenditures to the trend rate of growth of national output. When the actual rate of growth exceeds the trend rate, as would be the case during a cyclical expansion, government expenditures relative to private expenditures are automatically reduced. When actual growth falls behind the trend rate, as during a recession, government expenditures continue to increase, thereby acting as a stabilizer.[53] In both France and Japan efforts are made to plan government expenditures for fairly long periods into the future. To the extent that such efforts are successful, the constant increase in government expenditures acts as a stabilizing influence.

In any case, it is important to bear in mind that with government expenditures in market-oriented economies now constituting at least 25 percent of total national expenditures (as noted in Chapter 2) government expenditures will ineluctably affect the stability of the economy. This can be accidental or deliberate, stabilizing or destabilizing, depending on how the expenditures are made. All market economies now recognize this and at least attempt to minimize the destabilizing effects of government expenditures.

A major drawback to automatic stabilization policy has been increasingly prominent during the rapid increase in incomes throughout the postwar period. With progressive income taxes, tax revenues take increasingly larger percentages of these income increases, and in the absence of changes in governmental expenditures, create a drag on further expansion in the form of private investment or consumption. This phenomenon, which has been called *fiscal drag*, requires discretionary action in the form of tax reductions (or expenditure increases) if tax rates are not to constitute an increasingly depressing factor on economic development. Between 1955 and 1965, fiscal drag was a problem in all these countries, but was most serious in Italy, Germany, and France. The problem was smallest in Belgium and the United States.[54]

Thus, because of their inherent limitations and the matter of fiscal drag, the OECD study essentially agrees with Samuelson's assessment of the role of automatic stabilizers in a balanced program for stability and growth: "Automatic budgetary responses, at their best, can never by themselves be sufficient to iron out fluctuations in economic activity—and . . . may at times work perversely."[55]

---

[52] The estimates are those of Bent Hansen; they are reported in Walter Heller et al., *Fiscal Policy for a Balanced Economy* (Paris: OECD, December 1968), p. 87.

[53] See IICLC, *Economic Policy in Practice*, p. 26, for a fuller discussion.

[54] Heller et al., *Fiscal Policy for a Balanced Economy*, p. 178.

[55] Ibid., p. 88.

Discretionary Fiscal Policy: Impact of Nationalization   At the outset let us grant that most other market-oriented economies have an initial advantage, with respect to discretionary fiscal policy, over the United States. Discretionary fiscal policy means deliberate changes in tax rates or expenditures to stimulate or depress total spending levels in the economy. To the extent that nationalized industries exist in other market-oriented economies—and we saw in Chapter 2 that this is indeed the case—those governments have a ready-made channel for increasing or decreasing governmental expenditures relative to taxes. The expenditure items marked "transport and communications" and "industry and services" constitute categories of governmental expenditure which are either small or non-existent in the U.S. Beyond this, the deliberate manipulation of tax rates relative to expenditure levels to stabilize economic activity is now employed in all market-oriented economies, including the U.S. Space does not permit extensive examination of these efforts, but we shall comment on some significant types.

Major Types of Discretionary Fiscal Policy   The major techniques by which central governments can deliberately affect the net impact of tax and expenditure flows on economic activity include changing the tax rate structure, changing the timing of tax collections through such devices as accelerated depreciation allowances (which in effect reduce the taxable part of corporate current income), providing investment tax credits (such as the 7 percent reduction in taxes on corporate income reinvested in capital formation which was utilized by the United States to stimulate expansion in 1962-69), and on the expenditure side, deliberately increasing or decreasing the amounts or rate structure involved in unemployment compensation, public works expenditures, agricultural price supports, and so on.

U.S. Policies   In the U.S. discretionary fiscal policy has been used in several ways in recent years. We have already mentioned the 7 percent investment tax credit. A conspicuous example of discretionary fiscal policy was the 1964 tax cut (a reduction in income tax *rates*) enacted in the early days of the Johnson administration and designed to spur expansion and ward off potential recession by stimulating increases in consumption and investment. This is generally viewed as having been effective and having stimulated a sufficiently large increase in the growth rate of national income so that by 1966 the taxes lost through the tax cut had been regained because of the higher income levels achieved. One clear drawback which this episode revealed is the relative inflexibility of discretionary fiscal policy: President Kennedy originally called for the tax cut in 1962, and it took two years to get the measure enacted by Congress. A similar rigidity in fiscal policy was encountered when efforts were made to increase taxes in 1965 after the escalation of the Viet Nam War threatened serious inflation; it was 1968 before Congress finally enacted the 10 percent tax surcharge.[56]

Despite these difficulties, the OECD concluded, "Since the early sixties, the United States has turned from a laggard to one of the leaders in the conscious use of active fiscal policy."[57]

Canadian Policies The Canadians have utilized discretionary fiscal policy in at least two ways in recent years to cope with threats of inflation. They reduced the depreciation allowances which could be claimed for some classes of capital assets between April 1966 and October 1967, in effect to increase tax revenues from corporate sources. Second, they instituted a refundable tax paid by corporations and some trusts during the same eighteen-month period. The 5 percent tax was designed to reduce inflationary pressure through corporate expansion during a period when the Canadians felt that such efforts could lead only to inflation; obviously they hoped that at the end of the eighteen months the refund of the tax could lead toward real capital expansion. Such managed change in the timing of investment constitutes a good example of discretionary fiscal policy in action.[58]

The Swedish Investment Reserve One of the most interesting experiments in discretionary fiscal policy is the Swedish program known as the investment reserve. Unlike many discretionary measures, which depend on direct government expenditures, this one, like depreciation allowance changes, is designed to alter the timing of private investment flows into the economy. Its purpose is to attempt to stabilize private investment over the cycle, and its method is to grant to the Labor Market Board and the Finance Ministry the joint authority (without further action on the part of the legislature) to freeze private investment funds in the latter stages of booms to dampen inflationary pressure and then to release the frozen funds in recession to stimulate economic activity. The basic law enabling the investment fund to operate was enacted as early as 1938, but it has been used for deliberate stabilization purposes only since about 1958. For countercyclical purposes, funds were released during the 1960-61 inflation. The impetus for private companies to cooperate is that they may deduct up to 40 percent of their pretax income as the reserve. Of this sum, 46 percent is deposited in special non-interest-bearing accounts in the Swedish Central Bank while the other 54 percent stays with the company as part of its working capital—the money is still under the control of the company, but the tax advantages keep the private companies from utilizing the finds to feed

---

[56] Taxpayers were required to add ten percent to whatever their tax liability was computed to be. This was later reduced to 5% and was eliminated entirely in 1970.

[57] Heller et al., *Fiscal Policy for a Balanced Economy*, p. 77.

[58] See Martin Schnitzer, *The Swedish Investment Reserve* (Washington, D.C.: American Enterprise Institute for Public Policy Research, 1967), pp. 5-6.

inflation.[59]   Like all discretionary fiscal policies, this plan requires appropriate timing in order to be effective, and the OECD, for one, concluded that while the plan worked reasonably well as a stabilizer in the 1962 recession, it was poorly timed in 1958.[60]

The investment reserve has therefore been very useful in helping to stabilize Swedish economic activity, but it is probably true, as Schnitzer has argued, that the device could not easily be transferred to the United States, where the institutions and traditions are very different. His argument is that the degree of cooperation among labor, business, and government on which this device depends for whatever success it attains has never achieved levels in the U.S. comparable to those in Sweden.[61]   On the other hand, President Nixon's wage-price controls, instituted in 1971, might intensify the drive for greater cooperation among these groups although it is still far too early to tell. Should such cooperation prove to be an outgrowth of these new efforts, a version of the Swedish investment reserve might prove feasible in the U.S. However, in Sweden cooperation among the three groups is an indispensable component of survival in international competition. While the United States has had increasing difficulty maintaining its post-war role in international competition, the reasons lie more with recovery abroad and increased productivity in other countries than in lack of cooperation at home. In any case, the U.S. economy is not nearly as dependent on external trade as is the Swedish, a factor which might retard the growth of the required cooperation in the U.S.

Discretionary Fiscal Policy in Other Economies   In Germany the economy is, at least in Shonfield's view, closer to the U.S. model of a market-oriented economy. Even there, it has been observed that classical *Bedarsdeckungsfinanz* (finance to cover requirements) gave way some time ago to *Ordnungsfinanz* (regulatory finance), and while public opinion has been slow to accept activist fiscal policy, the Germans did pass a Stabilization Law in 1967 which allowed greater discretion for stabilizing fiscal policy. The new policy gave the government authority without further legislation to vary the depreciation rates, to grant an investment premium of 7.5 percent in recession, to vary income tax rates up to 10 percent for "demand management purposes," and to fit budgetary proposals into the current economic situation by varying expenditures within limits beyond those Parliament approved. In these and other ways the new law attempted to grant greater flexibility to German fiscal policy.[62]

[59] The Swedish system is well explained in Schnitzer, *Swedish Investment Reserve*, on which much of this summary is based.

[60] Heller et al., *Fiscal Policy for a Balanced Economy*, p. 57.

[61] Schnitzer, *Swedish Investment Reserve*, pp. 56-57.

[62] For details, see Heller et al., *Fiscal Policy for a Balanced Economy*, pp. 47-48. See also Karl Schiller, "West Germany: Stability and Growth as Objectives of Economic Policy," *German Economic Review* 5, No. 3 (1967): 177-88. Reprinted in Jan S. Prybyla, ed., *Comparative Economic Systems* (New York: Appleton-Century-Crofts, 1969), pp. 161-72.

The British, too, have moved to increase the flexibility of their discretionary fiscal policy by granting the government stand-by authority to increase or decrease industrial taxes by 10 percent without further parliamentary action. The device, known as the Regulator, was put into effect in 1961, but in fact, the Regulator has not been greatly used because the British can usually obtain fairly speedy parliamentary action when it is required. In 1967 the British passed the Selective Employment Tax, designed to facilitate a more efficient allocation of labor by enabling the government to tax business for each employee and then rebate the tax to all employers not in service industries. For certain manufacturing employers the rebate was more than 100 percent of the tax; hence it was in effect a subsidy plan to encourage employees out of services and into manufacturing. This has been called an "important new instrument of demand management."[63]

Finally, the Japanese have a steeply progressive income tax, and they also changed corporate tax rates several times in the 1950s and 1960s, sometimes

Table 8-4
Stabilization of Growth Rates Around Trend
Percentage Stabilization Accomplished

Country	Discretionary measures	Automatic stabilizers	Total effects
Belgium, 1955-65	5	16	21
France, 1958-65	−35	48	13
Germany, 1958-65	14	12	26
Italy, 1956-65	−17	32	15
Sweden, 1955-65	14	17	31
U.K., 1955-65	−10	−8	−18
U.S., 1955-65	17	32	49

Source:
Walter Heller et al., *Fiscal Policy for a Balanced Economy,* (Paris: OECD, December 1968), Table A.6, p. 180.

Notes:
All data refer to central government including public enterprise except for Sweden, which refers to general government. General government data are not available for most countries, and the only significant difference occurs in the case of Italy, in which the total stabilization accomplished rises to 31% with the inclusion of noncentral government. The U.S. percentage rises because, while state and local governments are not very stimulative in recession, they are depressing in expansion, and this was the major problem during this period in the U.S. The figures present the percent of potential short-run fluctuations around trend offset by fiscal action.

[63] Heller et al., *Fiscal Policy for a Balanced Economy,* p. 67. The OECD notes, however, that despite the success of discretionary fiscal policy in Britain, no amount of "demand management" could possibly have coped successfully with the problems faced in recent years by the British economy.

apparently for stabilizing purposes and sometimes simply because the government needed more revenue. Turnover, sales, and excise taxes all are important, and so the potential for discretionary fiscal policy exists.[64]

Fiscal Policy—Summary   The OECD study has attempted to measure the degree to which fiscal policy succeeded in stabilizing economic policy in seven market-oriented economies. Defining *stabilizing effects* as the percentage of the fluctuation around the trend which the measures succeeded in offsetting, they obtained the results indicated in Table 8-4. Table 8-4 suggests that both discretionary fiscal policy and automatic stabilizers had destabilized the British economy and had therefore had "negative effects." In France and Italy central government discretionary policy during the period of the survey appears to have been destabilizing, but the automatic stabilizers were very stabilizing; the latter made the net effect of fiscal policy in these countries stabilizing. In Belgium, Germany, Sweden, and the U.S. both kinds of fiscal policy seem to have been stabilizing. "The strongest stabilization effect occurred in the United States—not always appropriately."[65]   We remind the reader, however, that Chart 8-1 suggested that there was more short-run instability in the U.S. to be stabilized.

Conclusions

What this means is that policy which is successful in stabilizing economic activity in circumstances which include large amounts of unemployment cannot be construed as necessarily appropriate. In the final analysis, stability, which is what we have restricted our attention to in this chapter, is incomplete unless it is related to economic growth, and this involves the rate of unemployment, the rate of increase in productivity, and the rate of inflation as well as the degree of fluctuation in economic activity. Only in these terms, for example, can one consider inflation with unemployment, which was the major economic difficulty in the U.S. by 1970.

As the OECD study appropriately observes of short-run stabilization, "Whether the stabilizing effects thus defined were or were not desirable depends on how far the trend of observed growth can be regarded as an ideal growth path."[66]   The same thing can be said of monetary policy. In order to consider whether growth has been "ideal," all the factors just mentioned must be considered, along with stability, and it is to this important task that the next chapter is devoted.

---

[64] Business International Corporation, *Investment, Licensing, and Trading Conditions Abroad* (New York: Business International Corp., January 1970, December 1970), p. 218

[65] Heller et al., *Fiscal Policy for a Balanced Economy*, pp. 180-81.

[66] Ibid., p. 180.

9

Inflation and Economic
Growth in Market-Oriented Economies

Can rapid growth be sustained in modern market-oriented economies without releasing excessive inflationary pressures? If not, should we settle for slower growth rates and "acceptable" price increases, or should we continue to push for rapid growth and find other ways to contain inflation? Could we, for example, simply accept inflation as an unavoidable price of economic progress? Was U.S. success in containing inflation prior to the escalation of the Viet Nam conflict due to its high unemployment rate? If so, is this an "acceptable" trade-off? If not, is it possible to achieve high employment without inflation? The latter presents the dilemma of the Phillips curve, after the British economist who originally argued that the closer to full employment a market economy moves, the greater is the tendency to inflationary price increases.

These are the difficult questions with which modern market-oriented economies are being forced to come to grips (non-market-oriented economies are suffering some of these problems also!). In order to examine them systematically we must consider separately the rates of real growth and the factors responsible for them and then the factors responsible for inflation in each country. We shall find that the unemployment rate is but one factor contributing to the growth rate. In connection with inflation, we shall see that a crucial modern distinction is between what economists call demand-pull inflation and a newer variety, cost-push inflation, which is far less amenable to control through the monetary or fiscal policy measures considered in the previous chapter. Only after we have considered the elements that determined real growth and caused inflation in the recent past can we attempt a judgment about the prospects for noninflationary growth in the years immediately ahead and consider what appropriate public policies for maximum growth without inflation modern market-oriented economies might encompass.

Real Economic Growth in
Market-Oriented Economies—The Record

"The faster growth experienced after the Second World War is not a temporary or accidental phenomenon. Governments are committed to maintain high levels of employment and utilization of productive capacity, and possess the means to achieve this commitment."[1] So wrote the OECD in considering the objectives of its member countries, and we saw in Chapter 2 that high rates of growth have indeed moved to the forefront of national priorities in recent years. Economic growth is probably defined most simply as the rate of increase in real gross national product, although it is more easily related to economic welfare as reflected in the standard of living if it is defined as the average rate of increase in real per capita gross national product.

That market-oriented economies have achieved some success in attaining higher real rates of growth is indicated in Table 9-1, which summarizes the experience of thirteen market-oriented economies in the years since 1950. Several factors stand out. The spectacular growth rate in Japan and the slow growth rate in the United Kingdom represent the extremes within which the other economies lie. The German growth rate, which was extremely rapid in the 1950s, appears to have slowed somewhat in the 1960s.

Growth and Taxes   There has been much discussion about why the U.S. real growth rate was so much slower than that of most other market-oriented economies. The National Bureau of Economic Research organized a conference to explore the widely held view that the relatively large percent of direct taxes paid by U.S. corporations compared to the percentages in other economies (see Table 8-2) might act as a disincentive to investors in the United States and thus slow the rate of capital accumulation and increased real output. The real growth rates on which that conference was based are shown in Table 9-1, column 1. By 1964-69 the rates in the Netherlands, France, Italy, West Germany, and Japan were all still higher than that in the United States, but the U.S. rate had risen substantially, whereas the countries with the most spectacular high rates of growth in the early period, Japan and West Germany, had both declined. Explaining growth rates in market-oriented economies is clearly not a simple

[1] OECD, *The Growth of Output, 1960-1980: Retrospect, Prospect, and Problems of Policy* (Paris: OECD, December 1970), p. 14.

Table 9-1
Average Annual Increase in Real Gross
National Product, Selected Periods,
1950-69, Thirteen Market-Oriented Economies

(Percent)

	1950-60[a] (1)	1950-64[b] (2)	1950-68[c] (3)	1964-69[d] (4)
Austria	—	—	4.4	4.2
Belgium	—	3.4	4.3	4.1
Canada	—	—	—	5.2
Denmark	—	3.6	4.9	4.3
France	4.2	4.9	—	5.5
West Germany	7.7	7.1	—	4.6
Italy	—	5.6	—	5.5
Japan	9.5	—	—	10.8
Netherlands	4.4	4.9	5.3	5.1
Norway	—	3.8	4.8	4.8
Sweden	—*	—	4.5	3.8
United Kingdom	—*	2.6	—	2.2
United States	3.3	3.5	—	4.6

Sources:
[a] National Bureau of Economic Research, *Foreign Tax Policies and Economic Growth* (New York: Columbia University Press, 1966), p. 1.
[b] Edward F. Denison, assisted by Jean-Pierre Pouillier, *Why Growth Rates Differ* (Washington, D.C.: The Brookings Institution, 1967). p. 17.
[c] OECD, *Economic Outlook,* No. 8, December, 1970, Table 12, p. 61.
[d] OECD, *Economic Surveys: United States* (Paris: OECD, April 1, 1971), Table F. Basic statistics: International Comparisons, pp. 64-65.

Note:
* Real growth rates were "lower than that of the United States during the 1950's." (Source a, p. 1.)

matter, and the conference's conclusion appears justified by later events: growth rates can indeed be affected by tax policies, but very little is known about how tax policies affect savings and investment decisions, and moreover, many other factors can affect growth rates in addition to taxes.[2]

National Policies to Stimulate Growth   Can national governments adopt policies designed specifically to spur economic growth? Many economists believe so. One study has concluded that both Germany and France achieved high rates of growth after World War II, but by employing quite different techniques. This study suggests generally that countries need to adopt some "strategy" to achieve

[2] See the introduction and summary by E. Gordon Keith to National Bureau of Economic Research, *Foreign Tax Policies and Economic Growth* (New York: Columbia University Press, 1966), pp. 1-37, especially pp. 35-37.

growth and that the Germans used "selective intervention" favoring investment and exports and discouraged imports through some import controls and a restrictive monetary policy (to hold down interest rates and encourage investment despite fairly high unemployment rates). France, a good deal more interventionist, resorted to more direct public investment and "guiding" private investment into productive channels through their "indicative planning." The conclusion: "In both Germany and France a virtuous circle was thus established, of a high level of industrial investment, rapid growth of output, buoyant exports, and balance of payments surpluses."[3]

On the other hand, Denton, Forsyth, and Maclennan note that the British could not emerge from their "vicious circle"—slow growth, balance of payments deficits, and so on. Why? These authors appear to have overlooked the major factors, because they insist that Britain's poor performance grew out of

> a failure to accept that faster growth required powerful and consistent policies, such as an adjustment of the value of the currency, or a really rigorous and persistent deflation, combined with a concentration of inducements for the increase of exports and of investments, in order to break the balance-of-payments constraint.[4]

But surely no country has more grimly adjusted the value of its currency when necessary, launched more "austerity programs," or tried harder (albeit with only moderate success) to contain inflationary pressures than Britain. Obviously the factors explaining poor British performance with respect to growth are more complicated than this summary would indicate. What must also be considered are the special circumstances caused by the changing role of Britain in the world economy and the fact that the same factors which gave Germany and Japan such an enormous advantage in the immediate postwar years did not favor either Britain or the United States.

Determinants of Real Growth   What are these factors? A number have been noted in an OECD study which has attempted to explain growth rates in a number of countries between 1955 and 1968. The findings are summarized in Table 9-2, which attempts to indicate the total percentage increase in real output for eleven market-oriented economies.[5] In the course of economic development resources tend to shift out of agriculture (as we saw in Chapter 7) first into

---

[3] Geoffrey Denton, Murray Forsyth, and Malcolm Maclennan, *Economic Planning and Policies in Britain, France, and Germany* (London: George Allen and Unwin, 1968), p. 403.

[4] Ibid.

[5] That there are difficulties in measuring changes in real output is clear if one compares the average annual percentage increase (column 7), which was computed by the author, with the appropriate columns in Table 9-1. The periods covered are not precisely identical, but even so there are unexplained discrepancies, although both come from OECD sources.

industrial activity and then—as economies mature—into the service sector. It is in the last sector that growth rates have been most rapid in the United States recently. (The service area is also the most difficult in which to measure productivity. You can talk about the output of wheat per farmer or even the output of steel or automobiles per worker. But what is the medical service per doctor, the housing per landlord, the uplifted heart or saved soul per minister?)

Table 9-2 suggests that the growth in real output is due to productivity in each of the sectors, to the growth in total employment, and to the change in the sectoral mix. In Chapter 7 we saw that although agricultural productivity has increased tremendously, labor is moving out of agriculture in all market-oriented economies, and the percent which agricultural output contributes to GNP is declining—not because agricultural output is declining so much as because other areas of real output are expanding so much more rapidly. So the growth of agricultural output has contributed very little to the overall increase in real output in all these countries.

Herein lies a fundamental obstacle to greater growth rates for countries like the United States and the United Kingdom: these countries cannot easily increase their growth rates by shifting resources from sectors where they will contribute less to sectors where they will contribute more to total output because they have *already* shifted resources from agriculture to industry or (more recently) services. Moreover, industrial productivity still contributes more to increased output than the services, despite the increasing importance of the latter, and thus increased industrial productivity is a major determinant of real growth in all countries. However, in such countries as the U.S. or the U.K. larger percents of total plant and equipment are in older or less efficient form, which gives new German plants the advantage. The French have made great efforts through their Modernization Commissions to improve industrial productivity (and with considerable success, as Table 9-2 suggests). The failure of Britain to increase industrial productivity in comparison with her Continental neighbors is a major failure and a factor of considerably more significance in explaining poor British growth than those mentioned earlier by Geoffrey Denton, Murray Forsyth, and Malcolm Maclennan (though they do suggest the need to increase investment).

Finally, the growth in employment plays a role in determining general growth rates. Technological developments determine productivity changes (output per worker), but total employment indicates what will in fact be turned out by each sector of the economy. Behind increases in employment are increases in the population and—within this increase—increases in the labor force. Clearly the U.S. achieved a significant increase in total employment, which contributed critically to its growth rate.

Growth Factors and Growth Potential   Table 9-2 does not provide the entire answer; we must still ask, What spurs increases in investment in the several sectors. E. Gordon Keith suggests, for example, that in Japan, Germany and

Table 9-2
Factors Affecting the Growth of Output, Eleven
Market-Oriented Economies, 1955-68
(Percentages)

Country	Sector shift (1)	Growth in employment (2)	Growth in industrial productivity (3)	Growth in productivity of services (4)	Growth in agricultural output (5)	Total percentage increase over period (6)	Average annual increase over period (7)
Canada	11.9	43.9	21.4	-1.2	1.8	77.7	6.0
United States	7.1	27.1	14.7	13.7	0.5	63.1	4.8
France[1]	16.8	8.0	40.4	22.4	4.1	91.7	7.0
Germany[2]	12.6	10.1	44.0	15.8	2.3	84.8	6.5
Italy	36.2	-7.0	34.8	27.4	6.8	98.3	7.6
United Kingdom	2.0	5.0	20.1	10.0	1.4	38.4	3.0
Austria	19.4	2.3	39.2	16.6	3.6	81.2	6.2
Belgium	7.5	5.7	27.7	15.9	1.5	58.2	4.5
Denmark	17.9	21.2	15.4	16.0	4.6	74.9	5.8
Netherlands	9.2	16.1	35.6	23.4	4.5	88.9	6.8
Norway	16.5	6.7	23.7	25.2	-0.4	71.7	5.5

Source:
OECD, "The Growth of Output, 1960-1980," *Retrospect, Prospect, and Problems of Policy* (Paris: OECD, December 1970), Table 9, p. 39.

Notes:
1 1959-68 raised to a thirteen-year period by multiplying the results for each column 13/9.
2 1956-68 raised to a thirteen-year period by multiplying the results for each column 13/12.

Italy "strong investment demand" spurred the growth rates because in these economies "industry had strong incentives to exploit expanding markets at home and abroad."[6] This would lead to investment and thus to the productivity changes shown in column 3 of Table 9-2, and to the encouraging of the sectoral shifts shown in column 1. Keith adds that these three countries were all able to take advantage of immigrant workers or large pools of unemployed workers, which would make growth in employment (column 2) easier to achieve than in countries that were either already at full employment or unable to attract foreign labor. Keith attributes part of the real growth of the Netherlands, France and Germany to particularly rapid growth in export markets, which would encourage increases in all the columns of Table 9-2. Finally, he notes that Japan was "favored by a low capital-output ratio"—that is, it had little industry at the start of the postwar period, and hence had more room to develop, via investment, through capital formation. A highly industrialized economy such as that of the U.S., which already possesses a high capital-output ratio, will have greater difficulty in further increasing its growth rates by this means.[7]

These circumstances—the inability of an economy such as that of the U.S. to increase its growth rates by sectoral shifting (we've already shifted) or through development (we're already developed)—led Edward F. Denison, who has studied real growth rates in the postwar period with greater care and thoroughness than any other scholar, to conclude that the fact that the U.S. growth rate is lower than that of a number of other market-oriented economies is neither surprising nor especially significant of itself. He suggests that this state of affairs will continue for the foreseeable future. Because of differences in institutions and even more, because of differences in the degree to which U.S. resources and capacity are already being exploited, most European economies can attain greater growth than can the United States by using the same means. He goes further, in fact, and debunks the whole notion that U.S. growth rates are slower than European growth rates because somehow the United States is not "trying as hard."[8]

However, American performance has consistently been poorer than European performance in one area—the rate of unemployment that is tolerated. Obviously, lowering unemployment would increase output (provided that the jobs were legitimate, that they contributed genuinely to output and were not "make-work" schemes). But in order to consider the problem of the elimination of unemployment, we must first examine the problem of inflation, because the elimination of unemployment is related to inflation. We shall see that it is not coincidence that the poorer record the U.S. had on the elimination of unemployment was accompanied by a better record on controlling inflation, at least until 1965.

---

[6] National Bureau of Economic Research, *Foreign Tax Policies and Economic Growth*, p. 35.

[7] Ibid.

[8] See Edward F. Denison and Jean-Pierre Pouillier, *Why Growth Rates Differ* (Washington, D.C.: The Brookings Institution, 1967), especially pp. 342-43.

Inflation in
Market-Oriented Economies since 1950

The real growth rates we considered in connection with Table 9-1 do not, of course, reflect what happened to yearly changes in gross national product measured in current dollars. If prices rise, the "same" GNP will be higher, measured in current dollars, in a later year. In Table 9-3 we have summarized the experience with inflation of eleven market-oriented economies since 1950. The measure we have used, average annual changes in the consumer price, is not the only measure of inflation or even the most comprehensive, but it is the one most people are most familiar with and the one consumers are most concerned with.[9] The first factor that stands out in Table 9-3 is that the U.S. record of increases in the cost of living, as reflected in the increases in the consumer price index, was extremely good overall until 1965.

American Inflation and the Rise of Euro-Dollars   It is widely held that a major factor aggravating European inflation problems in the late 1960s and early 1970s was the inflation in the United States, which made the U.S. a better place for other countries to sell and a worse place to buy, which was a major cause of the international deficit in the U.S. balance of payments and the "dollar glut" in European countries. But the postwar dollar shortage began to turn into a dollar glut in the late 1950s, when the U.S, inflation rate was still low by European standards. We cannot undertake an extended examination of the difficulties in international trade, but we can note that even before inflation in the U.S. became a major problem (after 1965), the total represented by American investment in and sales, loans, and gifts to foreign countries far exceeded foreign investment in and sales, loans and gifts to the U.S., the U.S. had a deficit in the payments balance as far back as 1950. The cries from European financial managers that U.S. inflation was the cause of the inflationary pressures in their countries did not begin until the middle to late 1960s. Before that it was U.S. loans to Europe, investments by Americans in foreign business, military and other economic assistance, and so on (all of which economists call capital outflow) that built up the deficits in the U.S. balance of payments.

These deficits often showed up in the form of dollar assets held by banks outside the U.S. and (like other assets of commercial banks operating on

9 The consumer price index (CPI) is a measure of the level of prices consumers must pay for a representative sample of goods and services each year. For each country it is computed with some year as the base year. The figures in Table 9-3 represent the percent change from year to year, summarized into average annual changes. The technique has the limitations of most averages—it obscures significant variations from one year to the next. For example, the 1950-55 and 1955-60 average yearly change for the U.S. are about the same, but there was a fall in rates of increase in the CPI early in the fifties and a rise in 1955-58 which the averages tend to obscure. There are, moreover, criticisms of the consumer price index itself—its composition, the frequency with which its makeup is changed, etc. The picture in Table 9-3 should therefore be taken for what it is worth, but no more—a reasonably accurate summary of general interrelations among countries and changes over time.

fractional reserves) they became the basis for a good deal of foreign bank lending. Because the dollar was a "reserve currency" and presumably "as good as gold," foreign banks held dollars and created loans (just as American banks hold reserve assets and create loans), and the loans took the form of dollar-denominated deposit liabilities of foreign banks. These liabilities, called Euro-dollars, became a prime source of liquidity in Europe, a major means of settling debts, and hence part of European inflation problems.

The impact of Euro-dollars on international financial relations is complex. Suffice it to say here that dollars became an international reserve currency precisely because after World War II other modern market-oriented economies viewed the United States and (to a much lesser extent) Britain as the two strongest currencies in the Western world—in the U.S. case a view founded on the great real strength of the U.S. economy and on the dependence of Europe on the U.S. for assistance in recovery from the war. The loans which helped Europe recover in its agricultural production and the development of its industrial productivity (notably West Germany) in the process also gave Europe a huge supply of dollars. In this sense the development of the U.S. payments deficit, to the extent that it represented capital outflow rather than a deficit on the goods and services account, represented both the strength and the maturity of the U.S. economy rather than the weakness customarily associated with payments deficits. U.S. financial assistance was possible only because of the country's economic strength. U.S. investments represented the belief among U.S. investors that European markets and industry, undeveloped compared to those in the U.S. before the war and badly damaged during the war, represented better investment opportunities than could be found at home.

Thus postwar U.S. loans and investments (1) added to the U.S. payments deficit, which formed the basis for Euro-dollars; (2) materially assisted in the growth of agricultural and industrial productivity in Europe, which was the purpose of the assistance, but also enabled European economies to become less dependent on the U.S. economy than they were immediately after World War II; and (3) led to great growth in world trade, which made increasingly clear the fact that the previous system of settling international obligations, based on gold, was inadequate, which caused dollars and pounds to assume greater importance. Moreover, the stability of the dollar—the only major currency not devalued between 1945 and 1970—therefore became a matter of increasing importance to all market-oriented economies. (The dollar was devalued in 1972.)

The continued deficits in the U.S. payments balance were not the result of U.S. imports exceeding its exports—the customary definition of an unfavorable balance of trade (the U.S. suffered an import surplus only after 1970); rather, they resulted from the factors just mentioned. But, like an unfavorable balance of trade, the deficits did lead to the acquisition by foreign countries of greater supplies of dollars than they had immediate demand for, particularly as their own productivity recovered and began to expand. There was no real concern when they were willing to hold dollars (and the growth of the Euro-dollar market attests to that willingness). However, when they were not willing to hold dollars, as President de Gaulle and some others were not during the 1960s, a gold outflow resulted: the U.S. bought back its excess dollars with the only means then accepted—its gold supply.

It is important to note that the recovery of Europe and the rise of Japanese industry represented healthy growth in the aggregate productivity of all market-oriented economies. At the end of this chapter we shall return to the long-run consequences of U.S. inflation. Here we wish only to emphasize that, except for a brief period in the mid-1950s (before the gold drain even began to be significant), U.S. inflation played only a small role in the European financial situation until after 1965, but because of the size of the U.S. and because the dollar is a reserve currency, inflation in the U.S. causes consternation in other countries because they have so much invested in the stability and ultimate worth of the dollar.

Impact of Inflation on Policy in Other Countries   Michael Michaely has studied the degree to which domestic monetary policies are influenced by balance of payments considerations in Japan, Germany, and the Netherlands— representative countries chosen to start a larger project involving the relationship between international and domestic stability. He found that the Germans have tended to ignore balance of payments considerations in determining domestic monetary policy (although they have more recently been driven to revalue the mark, as previously noted). However, Japan and the Netherlands both tended to gear their monetary policy quite closely to balance of payments fluctuations. When they suffered a payments deficit, they tended to raise the discount rate to prevent expansion in the money supply (which would increase inflationary pressures and so tend to worsen the deficit). In this way domestic and international stabilization can go hand in hand.[10]

How vulnerable are market-oriented economies to domestic instability through changes in the attractiveness of their exports? The answer obviously involves the size of exports relative to GNP. Such considerations will explain why the Dutch must be very sensitive to the inroads which domestic inflation can make on their overall economic progress, because their exports constitute about 51 percent of their GNP. Inflation at home greater than that experienced in other countries will cause a drastic fall in exports and so a great decline in GNP. The percentages exports formed of other market-oriented economies in the late 1960s were: Norway, 40 percent; Belgium, 36 percent; Denmark, 29 percent; Austria, 25 percent; United Kingdom, 24 percent; Italy, 18 percent; West Germany, 16 percent; France, 10 percent; Japan, 9 percent; and the United States, 5 percent.[11]

[10] Michael Michaely, *Balance-of-Payments Adjustment Policies: Japan, Germany, and the Netherlands,* National Bureau of Economic Research Occasional Paper 106 (New York: Columbia University Press, 1968), pp. 3-4.

[11] International Information Centre for Local Credit (hereafter IICLC), *Economic Policy in Practice* (The Hague: Martinus Nijhoff, 1968), p. 14.

Real Growth and Inflation It must be recognized that real economic growth, which has not been as rapid in the United States as in other major market-oriented economies, can mitigate against inflation. It is not an accident that West Germany had one of the most rapid real growth rates in the period 1950-64 (Table 9-1) and one of the lowest inflation rates. If the real goods and services to be bought increase as rapidly or almost as rapidly as the money with which to buy goods and services, there should be little rise in prices from the demand side.[12]

Demand-Pull Inflation The relationship between the aggregate demand for goods and services and the aggregate supply of goods and services is conventionally assumed to determine the price levels reflected in consumer price indexes. The customary view of inflation has assumed, therefore, that appropriate stabilization policy involves "demand management": don't let the money supply increase faster than real output, and inflation can be avoided. If you charge higher prices for goods and services you must pay higher wages with which to buy them, and more money will be required to buy the same output at higher prices. This is demand-pull inflation, and the monetary and fiscal policy discussed in Chapter 8 was designed to cope with it.

Cost-Push Inflation In modern market-oriented economies it has become increasingly apparent that demand management is not enough and that inflationary pressure in the economy can be set off *either* by excessive aggregate demand relative to aggregate supply of goods and services *or* by pressures from the factors of production to increase their monetary return at a faster rate than their real productivity (that is, real rate of increase in output). The latter case, sometimes called cost-push inflation or sellers' inflation, suggests that labor unions can force prices up by demanding greater increases in monetary returns than their contribution to increased output would warrant, or that management can demand greater profits than their managerial talents (which show up in greater rates of real output) would justify. Moreover, the real world has become very complicated indeed. Both labor and management contribute to cost-push inflationary forces, and moreover, demand-pull and cost-push inflation combine in varying proportions.

Inflation in the Real World Let us try to clarify some of the causes and effects of inflation in market-oriented economies in recent years. First, if it is true that cost-push inflation was a factor in the United States briefly in the 1950s, it was brought under control, and the inflation of the early 1960s was within the bounds of what most economists feel is tolerable in a growing

---

[12] This assumes that the habits and institutions affecting the use of money are reasonably stable, so that the "velocity of money" (the average number of times the money supply changes hands in a given period of time) does not change greatly.

Table 9-3
Average Annual Percent Change in Consumer Prices,
Eleven Market-Oriented Economies, 1950-70

Country	1950-55[a]	1955-60[a]	1960-65[b]	1965-68[b]	1969[b]	1970[c]
	%	%	%	%	%	%
United States	2.2	1.9	1.3	3.3	5.4	5.9
Canada	2.9	2.1	1.6	3.8	4.5	3.4
Japan	—	—	6.0	4.8	5.2	7.7
France	6.1	6.2	3.8	3.3	6.4	5.2
West Germany	2.5	1.8	2.8	2.3	2.7	4.7
Italy	4.5	4.3	4.9	2.3	2.6	5.0
United Kingdom	2.0	2.7	3.6	3.7[e]	5.5	6.4
Belgium	.05[d]	1.3	2.5	3.2	3.8	3.9
Denmark	3.6	2.0	5.5	7.4[e]	3.5	5.6
Netherlands	3.2	2.4	3.5	4.3	7.5[e]	4.4
Sweden	5.1	3.0	3.6	4.2	2.7	7.0

Sources:
[a] Computed from OECD, *Statistics of National Accounts, 1950-61* (Paris: OECD, 1964). Reports by country.
[b] OECD, *Inflation: The Present Problem* (Paris: OECD, December 1970) Table 4.
[c] Computed from OECD, *Main Economic Indicators* (Paris: OECD, May 1971). Reports by country.

Notes:
[d] 1953-55 only.
[e] Figures for these years were seriously inflated by changes in indirect taxes and other measures directly affecting consumer prices.

economy. Certainly the average annual increase in the consumer price index of 1.3 percent is modest by the standards of the inflation rates shown in Table 9-3. Beginning with 1965, however, inflation became an increasingly serious problem in the U.S., and by the late 1960s the rate of inflation here was as high as or higher than those in many other market-oriented economies. This American inflation was not a simple matter of demand-pull or cost-push. In the early period, immediately after the build-up of American involvement in Viet Nam, inflation was demand-pull in the sense that the sum of American expenditures on consumption, private investment, and war-swollen government expenditures on goods and services were increasing faster than the real growth in supply of these goods and services. Instead of increasing taxes, thus requiring Americans to give up private goods and services in order to pay for the war, the government tried to have its cake and eat it too. Americans were told that the U.S. was rich enough to maintain customary consumption standards at home, to shoulder its by now usual obligations (military and economic) in other parts of the world, to expand domestic welfare under the Great Society programs, *and* to fight the war in Viet Nam. The result was that the U.S. was trying to spend at a faster rate than it could increase the supply of goods and services; the public debt increased, most notably from 1966-67, and the U.S. fell into demand-pull inflation.

But in modern economies demand-pull inflation is apt to spark "inflationary psychology"—the expectation that prices will continue to increase as they have in the recent past. Thus no union will negotiate a contract without keeping the expected rise in prices very much in the forefront of negotiations, and no corporation will forget the expected rise in prices in determining its own price policies, clearly predicated on trying to maintain, or if possible increase, its profit rate. The longer inflation continues, the firmer the grip of inflationary psychology becomes, and the more vicious the cost-price spiral becomes.

Inflation and Unemployment—The Vicious Trade-Off   In modern market-oriented economies, the closer economic activity approaches full utilization of economic capacity, the greater will be the inflationary pressure. English economist A. W. Phillips tried to quantify this relationship and suggested that pushing the unemployment rate much below three or four percent of the civilian labor force has not been accomplished in the real world without setting off price increases. Chart 9-1 represents a vivid form of Phillips curve. Customarily Phillips curves represent the yearly changes in prices and unemployment for a single country, but we have taken the average yearly percent change in prices and in unemployment over a decade for a number of market-oriented economies and related them to each other. With the exception of Italy, which appears to have achieved more unemployment and inflation than it "should have," the other market-oriented economies clearly indicate the trade-off between higher prices and less unemployment. On the average and very roughly, a reduction in the unemployment rate of one percent appears to have been associated with an annual increase in consumer prices of about 1.5 percent. The decade chosen was 1955-65, because after that the rate of inflation in the U.S. was aggravated by the factors previously considered.

The Phillips curve suggests that it is difficult to decrease unemployment without setting off inflation, but it does not explain why. Nor does it tell us whether the inflation set off is demand-pull or cost-push. Actually, it probably reflects both factors. The closer to full employment an economy comes the greater is the likelihood of bottlenecks, shortages, and so on, which will drive some prices (hence costs) up at a faster rate. Any time prices for any factor increase faster than its productivity the result will be inflation. In general, increasing overall productivity ought to have the effect of shifting the Phillips curve down and to the left—that is, enabling us to eliminate more unemployment without producing inflation. But simply knowing that wages, for example, have increased more than overall productivity tells us nothing about whether the wage increase is the cause or effect of the inflation. Shonfield has commented, "The essential truth about cost inflation is that any policy designed

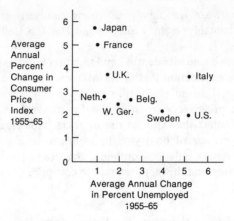

Chart 9-1 Average Annual Percent Change in the Consumer Price Index and in the Percent of the Civilian Labor Force Unemployed, Nine Market-Oriented Economies, 1955-65.

Sources:

All data from Walter Heller et al., *Fiscal Policy for a Balanced Economy* (Paris: OECD, December 1968), Table III. 1, p. 80, except for Japan and the Netherlands. For the latter two countries, the unemployment rates have been computed from Robert A. Gordon, *The Goal of Full Employment* (New York: John Wiley & Sons, 1967), Table i. 3, p. 8, in the case of the Netherlands, and from OECD, *Main Economic Indicators, 1957-1966*, for Japan. For the change in the consumer price index for the Netherlands and Japan, the data were computed from OECD, *Main Economic Indicators, 1957-1966.*

Note:

Data for the Netherlands, 1955-64.
Data for Japan, 1960-65.

to mitigate its effects must concentrate on management of production rather than demand."[13]

Managing production means, among other things, knowing what the factors of production are contributing individually to growth in output, maintaining increases in monetary returns at rates no greater than overall productivity increases, and one final factor, that the existing division of income among the factors of production is considered "fair" by all the factors of production, so that they remain content to divide increase in output and income in the same proportion that factor returns have been divided in the past.

[13] Andrew Shonfield, *Modern Capitalism* (London: Oxford University Press, 1965), p. 223.

Real Growth, Productivity, and Inflation

Measuring Changes in Productivity

It is very difficult to separate the effects of technical progress embodied in new investment, those embodied in intermediate inputs, and those appearing as improvements in skill, organization and managerial efficiency. Without such a separation, however, imputations of productive efficiency to specific factors of production risk becoming meaningless.[14]

Many economists would agree with the truth of this OECD assessment of the difficulties inherent in trying to apportion credit for increased productivity, yet this is precisely what is involved when proponents of cost-push inflation suggest that wage and price restraint is the solution to the problem of inflation in modern market-oriented economies. It is often said that U.S. labor, by making excessive wage demands, is pricing U.S. products out of the world market. Nowhere is this charge more likely to be made than about the steel industry, in which rising prices and falling exports have become a familiar postwar phenomenon. Because labor is the factor of production most often singled out as the culprit, and because the steel industry is basic in most modern major market-oriented economies, Table 9-4 is instructive in understanding the issues involved.

Table 9-4 summarizes some of the factors involved in determining unit labor cost for steel products between 1954 and 1967. It shows unit labor costs for iron and steel computed both in national currencies and in dollars; the latter eliminates the problems raised by currency devaluations and revaluations, which affected France, the United Kingdom, and Germany during the period under review. It is a commonplace by now to note that wage increases cannot properly be related to unit costs of production unless one knows what has happened to labor productivity. If labor in one country is twice as productive as in another country, its wages can be twice as high with no difference in the unit labor costs.

What can we learn from Table 9-4 about "production management" in this basic industry in market-oriented economies in recent years? The Japanese rate of growth in output is the most spectacular, as one would expect of the most recently developed industry. In considering growth rates one must bear in mind that the higher the level from which one begins, the more impressive the *absolute* increments must be to achieve high growth rates. In 1954 the U.S. steel output was the highest among these countries, and therefore maintaining, let

---

[14] OECD, *The Growth of Output, 1960-1980* p. 16. Note that this problem is different from—though of course related to—the problem of measuring productivity changes in sectors of the economy. See the discussion of Table 9-2 above.

Table 9-4
Average Annual Percent Change in Output and Unit Labor
Cost, Iron and Steel Industry, Five Market-Oriented
Economies, 1954-1967

	United States %	France %	Japan %	United Kingdom %	West Germany %
Unit labor cost (national currency)	2.1	4.7	- 2.8	3.1	4.0
Unit labor cost (U.S. dollars)	2.1	1.4	- 2.8	3.0	4.5
Output	1.6	4.8	15.2	1.6	3.8
Output per man hour	1.9	3.7	10.9	2.4	4.0
Total labor cost (nat'l. currency)	3.7	9.8	12.5	4.8	7.9
Hourly labor cost (nat'l. currency)	4.1	8.6	7.8	5.8	8.1
Hourly labor cost (U.S. dollars)	4.1	5.1	7.8	5.7	8.7

Source:
  Patrick M. Jackman, U.S. Bureau of Labor Statistics, *Monthly Labor Review* 93 (August 1969): 17.

alone increasing, growth rates was commensurately more difficult. U.S. output, along with that of the U.K. (the country with the oldest and most thoroughly exploited steel-producing potential), show the slowest rates of increase. Consider now the above picture. So rapidly did Japanese output increase that despite the fact that its total labor costs increased far more than that of any of the other countries, its unit labor costs actually declined.[15] Hourly labor costs increased less in the United States than in any other country,[16] but because output

[15] In technical economic parlance, its average variable costs were still falling—but this is precisely the situation that is typical of large-scale industry in the early stages of development. It is also a situation which cannot continue indefinitely, except in "natural monopolies," which the steel industry definitely is not.

[16] During the entire 1960s the average percent increase in hourly earnings for all workers in the U.S. was lower than for any of the market-oriented economies we have been considering. The average annual percent increase in hourly wage rates or earnings in 1969 were: France, 10.1 percent; Italy, 21.15 percent; Netherlands, 9.7 percent; Canada, 8.2 percent; Japan, 17.9 percent; Germany, 12.5 percent; U.K., 13.1 percent; Belgium, 10.7 percent; Denmark, 12.0 percent; Sweden, 10.5 percent; and the U.S., 5.0 percent. The data are not strictly comparable (for the first three countries they represent hourly rate changes—for others, changes in hourly earnings, etc.), but they give a good approximation of the *relative* inflationary impact of wage changes, unadjusted for the differences in productivity discussed in the text. (Source: OECD, *Inflation: The Present Problem* [Paris: OECD, December 1970], p. 26.)

increased at the rate which was even slower in comparison with the other countries, the unit labor costs increased more in the U.S. than in France or Japan. Significantly, they did not increase more than unit labor costs in West Germany or the U.K.

Clearly, increasing the rate of output in the U.S. steel industry could have improved the unit labor cost situation, and improving productivity in the U.S. steel industry is a factor which is rightly receiving considerable attention. On the other hand, *hourly* labor costs rose less in the U.S. than in any of the other countries, and this leads to the whole complicated question, considered shortly, of the role of an incomes policy in coping with cost-push inflation.

External Instability—Long-Run and Short-Run   The fact that until 1965 inflation was lower in the U.S. than in the other countries in Table 9-4 means that hourly labor costs (that is, wages) did not need to increase at the same rate as in the other countries in order for U.S. steelworkers to maintain their share of national output. The fact that unit labor costs did not increase as fast in the U.S. as in the U.K. and West Germany means that the difficulties of the U.S. steel industry (and by extension, now, all U.S. industry) could not be simply ascribed to labor pushing for wage increases greater than their proportionate contribution to increases in steel output, except in the case of Japan (the differential in the French case is negligible).

So it turns out that many of the difficulties the U.S. has experienced in recent years involve the extremely rapid rate of growth of the Japanese economy—it has hurt steel exports, it has cut into the U.S. trade export surplus (and, indeed, in 1971 was instrumental in turning it into a deficit for the first time since 1893). But before turning to the question of an incomes policy we should note that in part, the difficulties the U.S. has been experiencing in recent years, particularly with Japan, as epitomized by the steel example we have considered, will be at least *partially* self-correcting. There is no reason for complacency with respect to modernizing the U.S. steel (or any other) industry, and the U.S. market economy will have to continue to put as high a premium on increasing efficiency in the use of resources as it has in the past, but it is not a cause for long-run alarm that other market-oriented economies are now putting a high premium on efficiency as well. The great increase in Japanese productivity will in the end benefit all countries engaging in trade with her. Moreover, the rate of increase in productivity in Japanese production (here in the steel industry) will not continue indefinitely at the high rate it has achieved in the recent past. We have seen, too (Table 9-3), that Japan has been plagued increasingly by inflation—its 1970 inflation rate was higher than that of the United States—and this will mean that the relationships shown in Table 9-4 will inevitably alter over the next few years as the rate of productivity decreases and the pressures on prices, which increase in high-growth economies approaching full employment, mount. In these circumstances, Japan, like the other market-oriented economies under review, will have to cope with the problems inherent in maintaining full employment (which means maximum growth), stable prices, and external stability. No market-oriented economy has yet managed all simultaneously, but one partial solution a number of countries have experimented with in recent years is incomes policy.

Can an Incomes Policy Contribute to Stable Growth Rates? Preoccupation with maintaining stable noninflationary growth rates has led a number of market-oriented economies to attempt what has come to be known as an incomes policy. The idea is that overall wage increases should be limited to the overall growth in real output in the economy, which would mean that real income would grow as real output grows, but no faster. In the U.S. the version that was attempted during the Kennedy and Johnson administration was stated as follows:

> The general guide for non-inflationary wage behavior is that the rate of increase in wage rates (including fringe benefits) in each industry be equal to the trend rate of overall productivity increase. General acceptance of this guide would maintain stability of labor cost per unit of output for the economy as whole—though not for individual industries.[17]

In individual industries if overall productivity increased more than the national average, prices should be reduced because unit labor costs would be falling. If overall productivity in a particular industry increased less than the national average prices (and hence wages) should be increased to cover rising unit labor costs.

There was much discussion and criticism of the wage-price guideposts in the U.S., and the program was abandoned early in the Nixon administration on grounds that it had not worked at home and that European versions known as income policies had not worked either. In 1971 intractable inflation and high unemployment rates forced the Nixon administration to order a ninety-day wage-price freeze—a step it found philosophically distasteful but economically necessary. Direct controls of this sort are considered below.

The British pioneered the use of incomes policies. From 1947 to 1950 they attempted "voluntary restraint" to keep wages and other costs from rising faster than productivity increased. In November 1963 the British set up the National Incomes Commission, which has been termed a failure by at least one student because of lack of cooperation from trade unions.[18] In 1965 the National Board

[17] *Economic Report of the President* (Washington, D.C.: U.S. Government Printing Office, 1962), p. 189.

[18] Peter Donaldson, *Guide to the British Economy* (Harmondsworth, England, and Baltimore, Md.: Penguin Books, 1965), p. 22.

for Prices and Incomes was set up under somewhat more auspicious circumstances, but in general the British efforts at curbing price increases through cost increases greater than productivity increases has not been impressive.

The Dutch have been called "the modern pioneers of efforts to guide price and wage developments within the framework of an overall analysis of the economy."[19] Because of the unusually high percentage of the Dutch GNP which originates from exports (see the discussion of this point in Chapter 8), both management and labor have been especially sensitive to the need to keep Dutch export prices competitive with those in other major market-oriented economies. Like much else in the Dutch system, wage decisions are part of the use made of the Planning Bureau and in particular the Social and Economic Council (SER), which is tripartite and has thus become what John Sheahan refers to as "the main arena for the resolution of price-wage issues in the context of the overall economic situation."[20] This means that the government, management, and labor are involved in resolving wage-price questions, and while the government is not bound to do so, it has typically accepted the suggestions emerging from the negotiations in the Labor Foundation and the SER. An effort in 1959 to permit greater decentralization of the wage-price determination process was not particularly successful and led to the same problems of appropriate measurement of productivity changes, and so on that have plagued the use of an incomes policy in other countries. Nonetheless, despite difficulties in maintaining internal and external stability simultaneously (as has been the case in other countries), Sheahan concludes that the incomes policy developed in the Netherlands "seemed to pay off unusually well in terms of high employment, fast productivity, and a strong competitive position in external markets."[21]

The French, too, have attempted an incomes policy (although they have been more apt to try direct wage and price controls). In the Fifth Plan (1966-70), instead of trying to adjust wages to maintain stable prices, the French utilized an assumed increase of 1.5 percent in the general price level. Moreover, the incomes policy developed in France was deliberately designed to alter the proportion of total wages going to different groups of workers so as "to diminish existing inequalities."[22] The reapportionment is indicated by the planned average annual income increases—2.8 percent per capita for wages with no upgrading of skills, 3.3 percent per capita for wages with skill upgrading, 3.3 percent for gross incomes of nonfarm entrepreneurs, and 4.8 percent for farm incomes.[23]

The outcome of French experimentation with an incomes policy has not yet

[19] John Sheahan, *The Wage-Price Guideposts* (Washington, D.C.: The Brookings Institution, 1967), p. 96.

[20] Ibid., p. 98.

[21] Ibid., p. 103.

[22] *The Fifth Plan, 1966-1970* (New York: Ambassade de France, Service de Presse et d'Information, April 1967), p. 8.

[23] Ibid.

been decided; indeed, the French experience raises some fundamental questions about the operation of an incomes policy within the general framework of a market-oriented (and hence still nominally capitalist) economic system. A recent comment concerning French incomes policy experiments is applicable perhaps to many market-oriented economies:

> It is true that the incomes policy which the government has undertaken to draw up is supposed to apply to all categories of incomes, but it can be queried whether the State is likely to succeed in enforcing acceptance of a strict limitation of the growth of profits and even whether such a limitation would be compatible with the maintenance of private enterprise as the motive power behind production.[24]

In market economies, this view asserts, the search for profits presumably makes the system function, and hence it is possible to consider limiting wages but not profits under an incomes policy. This seems to be a serious misreading of what a market-oriented system is all about. As we pointed out earlier, the distinctive feature of market-oriented, as opposed to command, systems is that resource allocation is not dictated by a central body but is determined through a price system by the participants in the economy, *all* of whom are pursuing their own self-interest. So viewed, limiting wages (hence the pursuit of maximum returns by labor) represents no more and no less serious interference with the operation of a market-oriented economy than limiting profits (and hence the pursuit of maximum returns to the entrepreneur). Yet this asymmetry in viewing incomes policies is quite common.

Finally, the French experience makes apparent that proper evaluation of an incomes policy, like many other economic policies, can be clouded by noneconomic factors. Moreover, in France there has been a tendency to use direct controls intermittently, making the evaluation of incomes policies more difficult, and a tendency for the government to grant substantial wage increases based less on economics than on political pressure resulting from periodic social unrest of the kind that erupted in May 1968.[25]

In sum, the difficulties with achieving price stability through an incomes policy can be considerable. An OECD study of the countries which have attempted to achieve price stability plus reasonably full employment (hence growth) with an incomes policy concluded that the results so far have been disappointing. Said the OECD,

---

[24] IICLC, *Economic Policy in Practice,* p. 118.

[25] For an appraisal of French incomes policy see Sheahan, *The Wage-Price Guideposts,* pp. 111-16.

This is not altogether surprising. An effective price-incomes policy implies, almost by definition, that consideration of the common interest has to some degree been injected into individual wage and price decisions; or, more bluntly, that employers and unions are taking different decisions than they would have done if left to themselves.[26]

This is, of course, precisely what President Kennedy asked of the steel industry in his famous intervention in labor-management negotiations in 1962. It is what the whole effort to turn collective bargaining into "labor and management statesmanship" involves, and to this extent it asks that the market system be motivated by principles far removed from the Invisible Hand. But a recurring theme in this book is that such deviations from purism are often the price of preserving a system at all oriented toward the market. Moreover, there are some indications that labor and management statesmanship have had at least partial success in countries where there are centralized tripartite institutions for determining wages and prices (for example, the Netherlands, Sweden, and to a lesser extent possibly the U.K. as well).[27]

Finally, it should be noted that inflationary psychology, a notion introduced earlier in this chapter, is a key factor in the acceleration of cost-push inflation. Merely to know that wage increases have outstripped increases in productivity, in addition to assuming that one can divide productivity increases between labor and other factors in a satisfactory way (a large assumption to begin with), tells us nothing about whether the wage increases are *causing* the price increases or vice versa. If prices are increasing faster than labor productivity, then wage increases that do not exceed labor productivity will mean a smaller share of real income for labor. It is difficult to assume, moreover, as we noted earlier, that labor and other factors of production are satisfied with the current division of the aggregate economic pie. This need not be the case. In assessing the limited success of incomes policies thus far, these difficulties should be borne in mind.

Direct Controls   The most extreme policy tool is the wage or price freeze, and although it had been used only in wartime in the United States until it was forced on the Nixon administration in August 1971, it has been used to implement monetary and fiscal policy during periods of acute inflationary pressure in a number of other market-oriented economies. It has one great advantage in addition to the obvious disadvantage that it contradicts the

[26] OECD, *Inflation: The Present Problem*, p. 8.

[27] Several years ago Hackett concurred essentially in this judgment, declaring that incomes policies had come nearest to being "workable" in the Netherlands, Sweden, and Norway, but were still "in early stages" in France, the U.K., and Italy. (John Hackett, *Economic Planning in France*, the Council for Economic Education (Bombay) [New York: Asia Publishing House, 1965], p. 46.)

principles of a free market system: when inflationary psychology appears to have caught the economy in an unending wage-price (or price-wage) spiral, the freeze can be a dramatic way of stopping the expectations of the participants—in goods but especially in factor markets—from operating in their decision-making processes to accentuate the inflationary spiral. It can serve notice (just as a pool of international liquidity can shore up a currency ravaged by speculative selling based on expectations that it will be devalued) that the expectations cannot possibly be correct and thus can give the economy a chance to adjust to less inflationary conditions.

A number of countries have used both temporary wage and price freezes, and still others have instituted stand-by authority for their central governments to institute wage and price controls should circumstances warrant such measures. In Belgium, for example, the Ministry of Economic Affairs has broad, if rarely used, power to curb inflation by requiring that producers—in principle free to set their own prices—get clearance for price increases from the ministry twenty-one days before they go into effect.

In Denmark companies were required to report certain price increases to the Monopoly Authority, which has the power to investigate "unwarranted price increases," and for about a year (1968-69) a price freeze was in effect in that country to ease inflationary pressure. Simultaneous nationwide collective bargaining makes control of wages somewhat more likely; although wages were not frozen, wage increases were held down.

One of the most famous efforts to control wages and prices came in France in connection with the Plan de Stabilization, which was in effect from September 1963 until the beginning of 1965 (although it was not much enforced toward the end). It began as a general wage and price freeze, brought on by a serious increase in prices in 1962 and 1963. Inflation did decrease in 1964 and early 1965, but the problems in the French economy that were producing both inflation and social unrest were by no means solved. Subsequent efforts at price control took the form of "program contracts," designed to limit price increases, which required manufacturers to sign contracts with the government. Like the Belgian system, the French system requires advance notification for price increases. In 1969 and 1970 nearly one-third of the requests for price increases were turned down as inflationary.[28] While the system of direct wage and price controls has been eased—if not held in abeyance—in many sectors since the crisis of 1968, one view has suggested that

the government would not hesitate to reinstate strict price controls
if necessary, although competition from other EEC and third country

---

[28] Business International Corporation, *Investment, Licensing, and Trading Conditions Abroad* (hereafter *ILT*) (New York: Business International Corp., November 1970), pp. 428-29. Much of this summary of recent experience with direct controls has been drawn from this source.

firms help keep prices in line. It is doubtful that a general and unsupervised liberation of prices will take place for some time.[29]

Italy has price controls over some thirty specific items (mostly basic industrial products and utilities), and these are administered through the Interministerial Price Committee (CTP). In the Netherlands the Ministry of Economic Affairs, as we noted, has considerable control over prices, including the right to freeze them if necessary. As for wages, the government announced a general wage freeze to be in effect during 1971 (it was to limit all wage increases to 7 percent of the 1970 levels).[30]

In Norway, as in the Netherlands, the government has the right to set maximum prices for items in which they feel market forces "cannot regulate prices." Wages have not been frozen, although the tripartite principle of the Price and Cartel Office is designed for "continuing surveillance of prices," among other things, and it could recommend price controls, though it has not yet done so. Swedish labor has been termed the "best paid in Europe," and no wage controls have yet been enacted.[31]

This is by no means a thorough survey of European efforts at using direct controls, but it is sufficient to suggest that they have been tried in many market-oriented economies, at least intermittently. Whatever success they may have achieved, and whatever their failures are, with the exception of Germany there is far greater willingness to utilize either stand-by or direct controls when conditions seem to warrant it in market-oriented economies outside the U.S. It is in this perspective that one should consider President Nixon's ninety-day wage-price freeze instituted in August 1971 (invoking stand-by authority Congress had granted many months earlier). It was a step taken when both inflation and unemployment were very high in the U.S., and in circumstances similar to those in which most other market-oriented economies had already (in the past) adopted similar measures. As such, its use—however infrequent and reluctantly invoked—represented yet another retreat from the principles of the pure market, which seemingly can never be taken in the U.S. without being preceded by lengthy debate of a sort that other market-oriented economies appear to at least minimize (with the possible exception of West Germany).

The ninety-day freeze was followed by Phase II, a period in which the government concentrated its attention on wage and price agreements in large business firms. A new bureaucratic apparatus was instituted—the Pay Board, the Price Commission, and the Cost of Living Council. The authority of the new bureaucracy went considerably beyond the "guidelines" used in the 1960s for wage and price adjustments; for the first time in U.S. peacetime history, prior

---

[29] Ibid., p. 429.
[30] Ibid., p. 588.
[31] Ibid. (June 1970), pp. 619, 626.

approval was required to institute wage or price increases in many large enterprises. This action represented a significant break with past U.S. policy—a move toward direct interference with the market mechanism more in line with what a number of European (for example, the Belgian) market-oriented economies have been attempting for some years. In early 1972 these measures were still being billed as "temporary expedients," although temporary measures have a way of becoming permanent. No one was saying how long they might continue, nor was their long-run success in curbing inflation clear by the early months of Phase II, but their imposition could be viewed as a definite narrowing of the doctrinal differences between Europe and the United States. The fact that European countries have not had exceptional success in containing inflation despite impressive real growth rates suggests that direct controls are no automatic panacea for the problems of inflation. Neither does it suggest that direct controls cannot at times be an effective—even necessary—means of eliminating the inflationary psychology on which cost-push inflation thrives.

Conclusions

Whatever is the answer to the problem of inflation in modern market-oriented economies, one fact is certain: as long as real economic growth in any economy is less than it might be, goods and services are increasing at a slower rate than they could, and to this extent inflationary pressures are increased. *Whatever* aggregate monetary demand may be, the greater the actual supply of goods and services is at any given time, the smaller will be inflationary pressures of the classic demand-pull variety. Hence all countries have much to gain from increasing their real growth rates, although it must always be recognized that if an economy is operating close to full capacity, some of the dangers inherent in cost-push inflation may be greater.

Herein lies a vexing problem for economies beset by inflation: inflation has been worsened from the supply side by idle capacity and can be ameliorated by closing the gap between actual and potential growth, considered below, but dangers of excessive inflationary pressures from the demand side are aggravated as market-oriented economies near full employment. Part of the problem lies in the fact that even the best-coordinated economy cannot hope to reach full employment at an even pace throughout all sectors and all stages of various production processes. Hence the closer an economy comes to attaining full employment and so ameliorating inflationary pressures on the supply side, the greater is the danger that bottlenecks will develop in the form of inadequate facilities at some necessary stage of an otherwise vertically integrated production process, a shortage of some crucial raw material or kind of labor, and so on. Each shortage can lead to rising factor costs, which through the multiplier, accelerator, and so forth cause small disturbances to snowball in market economies. Small price increases can be pressured into excessive increases from the demand side even before aggregate supply has achieved a full employment level overall. How to contain inflation in the face of these two sets of pressures therefore represents a major challenge to the policy-makers in market-oriented economies, but it does not vitiate the major point of the previous paragraph—that striving for increased (or maximal) production through rapid growth can lessen inflationary pressures from the supply side.

During the 1950s and 1960s a number of major market-oriented economies exhibited a gap between the rate of growth they actually achieved and what they could have achieved if they had utilized their capacity to the fullest.[32] Potential growth, in the sense of fully utilizing existing resources and capacity (at some reasonably assumed definition of *fully*), was not achieved in recent years in a number of economies, although the gap was greatest for the United States. The OECD has estimated that there was a gap at one time or another during 1960-68 in Canada, France, the U.K., Austria, Denmark, West Germany, the Netherlands, and Norway as well as in the U.S., although in some cases (especially in Canada, Austria, and the Netherlands) the gaps were small. In Japan and Italy actual growth equalled or exceeded potential growth rates.[33] While eliminating these gaps will increase the rate of growth of real output (by definition) and so eliminate one source of inflation (demand pressures will be smaller relative to the growth of supply), there will be other pressures because of the difficulty in achieving balanced growth throughout a modern economy without precipitating inflation through sectoral factor shortages and so on.

In this chapter we have seen that the problem of achieving full employment, maximum growth rates (based on reasonably full utilization of existing resources and capacity), and stable prices has not yet been solved in any major market-oriented economy. The problem of inflation has been complicated in several ways. First, there is clear evidence that the closer one gets to full employment, the greater is the likelihood of unloosing inflationary pressures. Second, these pressures tend to involve pressures from the supply side, which are less amenable to conventional monetary and fiscal policy than the pressures from the demand side, which have been the primary cause of inflation in earlier

[32] "Potential" growth is a slippery concept. The notion of a gap between actual and potential gross national product most widely used is that devised by Arthur N. Okun ("Potential GNP: Its Measurement and Significance," in *1962 Proceedings of the American Statistical Association,* pp. 98-104; reprinted in *Readings in Money, National Income, and Stabilization Policy,* rev. ed., W. L. Smith and R. L. Teigen, eds. [Homewood, Ill.: Richard D. Irwin Co., 1970], pp. 313-22). This notion of "potential" growth assumes some trend rate of growth based on utilization of capacity at some assumed rate (in the U.S. in recent years about 4% unemployment has been the "targeted rate" of full employment growth). It differs from the maximum possible growth rate, which would have to make additional assumptions about how fast technology can progress and increase productivity, etc. Note, too, that only when there is a gap is actual growth likely to exceed "potential" growth rates for any extended period of time.

[33] This is possible if employment or productivity actually grow faster than anticipated. (See OECD, *The Growth of Output, 1960-1980,* especially pp. 244-48.)

periods. Appropriate stabilization policy based on demand management continues to be a goal of public policy in market-oriented economies, but the problem of cost-push inflation, or supply management, if you will, has been a major new challenge of the past twenty years. Prices and wages are no longer very flexible downward, and to the extent that all factors of production worry about maintaining their real purchasing power, and if possible, *increasing* their share of real income, supply-induced inflationary pressure is built into most of the economies we have been considering.

This situation has led many market-oriented economies to experiment with various voluntary or compulsory wage and price control systems—ranging from actual use to stand-by controls—to augment monetary and fiscal policy. Their results in curbing inflation have been mixed, and opinion is still divided over whether they can be effectively employed or not. That they are fraught with difficulties is clear, but that there are appropriate alternatives which present fewer problems is not so clear. Obviously control of excessive inflation is required, because of the domestic instability it generates and because it makes stable international economic relations impossible. In the latter case, changes in productivity and output, particularly in West Germany and Japan, have created profound difficulties in maintaining stable exchange rates as well as in adjusting domestic production in various countries to the economic realities of increased productivity and efficiency in all countries. [34]

While for the immediate future painful reallocations and structural adjustments would appear unavoidable, it is important to bear in mind that some of the causes of these problems (for example, productivity increases in Japan are greater than elsewhere, and factor costs still lower than elsewhere) will to some extent be self-correcting. For the rest it is crucial to bear in mind that optimal use of the world's resources in producing goods and services has always required free trade, which in the end will benefit consumers everywhere. In such a system the developed world in general and the U.S. in particular would be able to more than hold its own and would have little to fear.

[34] President Nixon's decision in August 1971 to let the dollar "float" in international money markets was merely a long-overdue recognition of changes in *relative* productivity among major market-oriented economies which recovery from World War II (long since accomplished) had led to.

10

Basic Themes of the Book

The previous chapters have been concerned with two themes. First, even though market-oriented economies may now be far removed from pure capitalism and command economies are an equally long way removed from pure communism, it is nonetheless still appropriate to differentiate these two broad approaches to organizing economic activity. The progressive requirements of improved technology, higher standards of minimal welfare levels for all, psychological factors of adequate motivation for participation in economic activity, and increased concern generally with the quality as well as the quantity of economic life have moved both market-oriented and command economies into actions and structural changes which give them more common characteristics than perhaps they once exhibited. Jan Prybyla has argued, for example, that communist economies have been forced by circumstance to pay greater attention to consumption and that growth and maturity have encouraged them to disaffiliate from the rigors of Marxist resource allocation to permit greater differences in income and so on and to increasingly face the complexities of resource allocation in highly industrialized economies, much as market-oriented economies must do. On the other hand, market-oriented economies have been forced to enlarge the public sector and to exempt certain parts of the overall allocation of resources from the operation of the free market. Nonetheless, he has stressed that the differences between these two basic types of economic organization remain large and these differences involve basic philosophy and revolve as much around noneconomic as around economic factors; the likelihood of convergence appears dim for the foreseeable future. This does not mean that *coexistence,* which he carefully distinguished from *convergence,* cannot be encouraged and that the harsh international atmosphere of the cold war years cannot continue to diminish.[1]

The second theme we have attempted to develop is that despite a broad similarity which makes it appropriate to distinguish market-oriented economies from command economies, the market-oriented economies themselves exhibit a great deal of diversity—not so much in their ultimate objectives, which are broadly similar, but in the means they employ to attain their objectives. In the final analysis, one might be tempted to argue that there is little difference even among the means, but that the psychological attitudes with which various means are adopted differ greatly. These differences in attitude toward interventionism are particularly marked, of course, in comparisons between U.S. policy and that of some of the European market-oriented economies. The railroads were long ago nationalized in all other market-oriented economies, but Amtrack, the U.S. version of nationalization, did not appear until 1971. Systems of national health insurance of one sort or another are common in other market-oriented economies, but Medicare and Medicaid were adopted only after much debate, frequently acrimonious, in the U.S. Congress and after more than a decade of effort on the part of its supporters. (Medicare was actually first suggested during the administration of President Truman.) Peacetime wage and price controls, either in practice or on a stand-by basis, were on the books, and not infrequently invoked, in many other market-oriented economies before the inflation and unemployment of 1970-71 finally persuaded the Nixon administration to resort to them.

Are Market-Oriented Economies Converging?

Care must be taken not to carry this notion of convergence among market-oriented economies too far. Vast differences in history, temperament, social and political organization, technological development, resource base, geography, and so on will keep many aspects of economic structure and policy distinct in many of these market-oriented economies. Nationalization of any basic industry, for example, does not appear to be likely in the United States. The British have nationalized, denationalized, and renationalized their steel industry, but while there does not appear to be any strong drive for them to carry their nationalization program further, they do not have the fundamental antipathy to *any* nationalization of industry that is found in the U.S. Similarly,

---

[1] See Jan S. Prybyla, "The Convergence of Western and Communist Economic Systems: A Critical Estimate," *Russian Review,* 23 No. 1 (January 1964): 3-17. Reprinted in Morris Bornstein, *Comparative Economic Systems: Models and Cases* (Homewood, Ill.: Richard D. Irwin Co., 1969), pp. 442-52.

the half nationalized and half private industry—found in Britain but perhaps best typified by the French automobile industry—does not appear to be a likely prospect for the United States.

One could point to other differences. The corporatist form in economic organization seems to be uniquely Italian, where it has had considerable success, but not without difficulties of the sort we have at least briefly considered. Tripartite organization for determining fundamental economic policy, insofar as wages and prices are concerned, appears so far mostly in Scandinavia and Holland, but there is no reason why it could not be adopted in other market-oriented economies as well, as indeed it appears to be.

Kinds of Planning and National Economic Objectives   A major difference between the U.S. and most other market-oriented economies involves the techniques and forms of national economic planning. We have seen that the fundamental objectives of all market-oriented economies today are much the same: full employment; maximum growth; an emphasis on technological development of five-year plans or ten-year plans, while the British and the maintenance of stability, which means keeping the business cycle under control, avoiding both depression and unemployment on the one hand and excessive inflation on the other; guarantees of minimal welfare programs so that all individuals can be assured of some minimum standard of living; concern with the provision of adequate public programs which cannot be provided through resource allocation in private markets—urban development, housing, medical programs, pollution control, resource conservation; and international stability—stable currencies with free trade permitting maximum advantage from international specialization and division of labor. These objectives differ in emphasis and form but have become paramount in all the countries with which this book has concerned itself. But while other economies feel comfortable with the development of five-year plans or ten-year plans, while the British and the French experiment with indicative planning, the Swedes with investment planning, the Dutch with manpower planning, and so on, the United States chooses to pursue these objectives in less structured or formalized ways; in the foreseeable future the U.S. is not likely to establish a national planning commision of participants from various sectors of the economy to help determine reasonable targets for output.

How much of this difference is a matter of form and how much a matter of substance is perhaps a proper subject for debate. The Office of Management and Budget (created by President Nixon in 1970 to expand the old Office of the Budget to encompass coordination of the activities of the federal bureaucracy), along with the Council of Economic Advisers, could perform many of the functions which planning commissions perform in other market-oriented economies. Long-range, middle-range, and short-term forecasting and planning is far more in the forefront in the U.S.—at the corporation level as well as at all levels of government—than it was twenty-five years ago. None of this begins to approach planning in the sense that European market-oriented economies plan, but the same widespread recognition of the need for a more carefully (and centrally organized) coordination of economic activity which led elsewhere to formal planning efforts has also produced institutional and structural changes in the United States.

The Growth of the Public Sector   We shall likely not see an effort at comprehensive planning in the United States, but we shall be likely to see a public sector which grows here as elsewhere to meet the responsibilities which modern objectives have forced on all market-oriented economies. We have seen that the governmental sector has grown in all these economies, but we have also seen that the cries in the U.S. concerning the ever-increasing size of the federal government are capable of somewhat different interpretation when viewed in light of the experience of other market-oriented economies. The percent of gross national expenditures represented by government expenditures is smaller in the U.S. than in other major market-oriented economies. Relative to other economies, the U.S. does not have a big government, nor is the federal bureaucracy relatively larger. (In absolute terms, of course, U.S. governmental activity dwarfs all other efforts.)

If in the final analysis modern market-oriented economies are tests of the ability of decentralizing decision-making systems to function efficiently in the contemporary world, it seems safe to conclude, on the basis of the evidence at hand, that market-oriented economies can perform at least as effectively as command economies, and possibly more effectively. But one must also conclude that the fraction of decision-making which cannot be left to decentralization has grown in all these economies. A major conclusion of our study would seem to be that the public sector must perforce be increasingly strong and interventionist (up to a point) on many fronts.

Functions of the Modern Public Sector

Regulator of the Private Sector   We have seen that none of the major private sectors of market-oriented economies—business, labor, or agriculture—can operate effectively without a good deal of supervision and control. In the case of agriculture, it is only as the private sector acquires sizable units and power that governmental aid has begun to diminish. With size goes power and with power goes the need for regulation, so that antitrust laws, labor laws, and ultimately agricultural laws of comparable scope are required to attain the advantages of modern technology without the disadvantage of uncontrolled power concentrated in private hands, which might be channeled against the public interest.

Provider of Public Goods and Services   But the public sector is now much more than the regulator of the private sector. It is also the provider of public goods and services. It is increasingly clear that modern economies require many outputs from their resources which private markets cannot appropriately accommodate. In the U.S. it was military defense until with the Great Depression came the growing realization that the federal government had the responsibility of providing for minimum standards of living for all Americans—a responsibility which all other market-oriented economies have accepted as well (usually both earlier and to a larger extent than in the United States). The Sherman Act of 1890, the labor legislation of the 1930s, the Social Security Act of the mid-1930s, the Employment Act of 1946, and the growing clamor for a "reordering of national priorities" in the 1970s represent a logical progression indicating the growing importance of the public sector in the U.S., which has been paralleled by developments in other market-oriented economies.

The Economy as a Dynamic Social Institution

In the final analysis it is crucial to remember that the modern economy, like most man-made institutions, must be viewed dynamically. All the institutions which form a market-oriented economy need to be viewed and judged against the perspective of continual change in technology, in resources, in social objectives, and in expectations. While this will require changes in the institutions and operations of the market system, two further conclusions seem justified. First, it seems likely that the general justification for distinguishing market-oriented economies from command economies will continue for the foreseeable future in spite of the changes which circumstances are likely to impose on both. Second, within the broad group of economies we have called market-oriented, in spite of some tendency for them to converge there are also great differences in history, culture, psychology, and economic potential. These factors suggest that under the umbrella *market-oriented* there is room for a good deal of variation in the means with which these economies attempt to achieve their broadly similar national objectives.

A Perspective on Diversity

This last conclusion seems most important for our purposes. Everywhere there is a tendency to judge other systems by the standard of one's own image; the degree to which other systems diverge from ours is the degree to which they are further from "the ideal" than our own. This tendency is perhaps most pronounced in Americans because geography, huge size, great economic success, and other factors make it easy for us to forget that there is much diversity even among market-oriented economies. But it is crucial to remember that what works in one country need not be appropriate in another; there can be more than one acceptable path to the same destination. If this book has convinced the reader of this truth, it has not entirely failed in attaining its objective.

Postscript—January 1973

As this book approached the final stages of production President Nixon announced in mid-January 1973 that under Phase III of the New Economic Policy direct controls will be removed from all wages and prices except for food processing, health care, and the construction industry—all areas where inflation has been especially persistent. For the rest he will rely on voluntary restraint within guidelines not unlike those used during the Kennedy-Johnson years, except that he will ask Congress to extend the Phase II controls for one year on a stand-by basis to be employed (along with fines) for labor unions and managements which flout the guidelines.

We note these developments only to suggest that they corroborate the essential correctness of a theme of this book—and particularly of the last chapter—that the U.S. devotion to an unemcumbered market system is greater than that in most other market-oriented economies and that the New Economic Policy did not represent any major alteration in this devotion. How successful U.S. stabilization policy will be, and whether the role of the Government can be permanently reduced in achieving stable real growth, only time can tell.

Bibliography

Books

Allen, G. C. *The Structure of Industry in Britain: A Study in Economic Change.* 3d ed., London: Longman Group, 1970.

Ayusawa, Iwao F. *A History of Labor in Modern Japan.* Honolulu: East-West Center Press, 1966.

Bain, Joe S. *Industrial Organization.* New York: John Wiley & Sons, 1959.

———. *International Differences in Industrial Structure: Eight Nations in the 1950's.* New Haven, Conn: Yale University Press, 1966.

Barkin, Solomon; Dymond, William; Kassalow, Everett M.; Myers, Frederic; and Myers, Charles A., eds. *International Labor.* New York and London: Harper and Row, Publishers, 1967.

Baum, Warren C. *The French Economy and the State.* Princeton, N.J.: Princeton University Press, 1958.

Berle, A. A., and Means, Gardiner C. *The Modern Corporation and Private Property.* New York: The Macmillan Co., 1932.

Bornstein, Morris. *Comparative Economic Systems: Models and Cases.* Rev. ed., Homewood, Ill.: Richard D. Irwin Co., 1969.

Broadway, Frank. *State Intervention in British Industry, 1964-68.* Rutherford, N.J.: Fairleigh Dickinson University Press, 1970.

Bronfenbrenner, Martin, ed. *Is the Business Cycle Obsolete?* New York: Wiley-Interscience, A Division of John Wiley & Sons, 1969.

Budd, Edward C., ed. *Inequality and Poverty: An Introduction to a Current Policy.* New York: W. W. Norton & Co., 1967.

Business International Corporation. *Investing, Licensing, and Trading Conditions Abroad.* New York: Business International Corp. January 1970.

Clark, John Maurice. *Alternative to Serfdom.* New York: Alfred A. Knopf, 1948.

Cohen, Stephen S. *Modern Capitalist Planning: The French Model.* Cambridge, Mass.: Harvard University Press, 1969.

Commerce Clearing House. *The Federal Antitrust Laws.* New York: Commerce Clearing House, 1949.

Committee for World Development and Disarmament. *Distribution of Population and Wealth in the World.* New York: Committee for World Development and Disarmament.

Denison, Edward F., with the assistance of Jean-Pierre Pouillier. *Why Growth Rates Differ.* Washington, D.C.: The Brookings Institution, 1967.

Denton, Geoffrey; Forsyth, Murray; and Maclennan, Malcolm. *Economic Planning and Policies in Britain, France, and Germany.* London: George Allen & Unwin, 1968.

Donaldson, Peter. *Guide to the British Economy.* Harmondsworth, England, and Baltimore, Md.: Penguin Books, 1965.

Dow, J. C. R. *The Management of the British Economy 1945-60.* London: Cambridge University Press, Students' Edition, 1970.

Drummond, Ian M. *The Canadian Economy: Organization and Development.* Homewood, Ill.: Richard D. Irwin Co., 1966.

Einaudi, Mario; Bye, Maurice; and Rossi, Ernesto. *Nationalization in France and Italy.* Ithaca, N.Y.: Cornell University Press, 1955.

Ely, Richard T. *The Labor Movement in America.* New York: Thomas Y. Crowell Co., 1886.

Ensemble, Jean (pseudonym). *Le Contre Plan.* Paris: Editions du Seuil, 1965.

Espinshade, Edward B., Jr. *Goode's World Atlas.* 13th ed. Chicago: Rand McNally, 1970.

Europa Publications. *The Europa Yearbook, 1971.* Vols. 1 and 2. London: Europa Publications, 1971.

Fousek, Peter G. *Foreign Central Banking: The Instruments of Monetary Policy.* New York: Federal Reserve Bank of New York, 1957.

Fitzgerald, Mark J. *The Common Market's Labor Programs.* Notre Dame and London: University of Notre Dame Press, 1966.

Galbraith, John Kenneth. *The Affluent Society.* Boston: Houghton Mifflin Co., 1958.

–––. *American Capitalism: The Concept of Countervailing Power.* Boston: Houghton Mifflin Co., 1952.

Galenson, Walter, ed. *Comparative Labor Movements.* New York: Prentice-Hall, 1952.

Galenson, Walter. *Trade Union Democracy in Western Europe.* Berkeley and Los Angeles: University of California Press, 1961.

Gitlow, Abraham L. *Labor and Industrial Society.* Rev. ed. Homewood, Ill.: Richard D. Irwin Co., 1963.

Gordon, Robert Aaron. *The Goal of Full Employment.* New York: John Wiley & Sons, 1967.

Gruchy, Allan G. *Comparative Economic Systems: Competing Ways to Stability and Growth.* Boston: Houghton Mifflin Co., 1966.

Hackett, John. *Economic Planning in France.* The Council for Economic Education (Bombay). New York: Asia Publishing House, 1965.

Hackett, John, and Hackett, Anne-Marie. *Economic Planning in France.* Cambridge, Mass.: Harvard University Press, 1963.

Halm, George N. *Economic Systems.* 3rd ed. New York: Holt, Rinehart and Winston, 1968.

Harlow, John S. *French Economic Planning: A Challenge to Reason.* Iowa City, Iowa: University of Iowa Press, 1966.

Harrington, Michael. *The Other America: Poverty in the United States.* Baltimore, Md.: Penguin Books, 1963.

Hayek, Friedrich A. *The Road to Serfdom.* Chicago: The University of Chicago Press, 1944.

Heilbroner, Robert. *The Worldly Philosophers.* New York: Simon and Schuster, 1953.

Hughes, John. *Trade Union Structure and Government.* London: Her Majesty's Stationery Office, 1967.

International Information Centre For Local Credit. *Economic Policy in Practice.* The Hague: Martinus Nijhoff, 1968.

Kassalow, Everett M. *National Labor Movements in the Post-War World.* Evanston, Ill.: Northwestern University Press, 1963.

–––. *Trade Unions and Industrial Relations: An International Comparison.* New York: Random House, 1969.

Kaysen, Carl, and Turner, Donald F. *Antitrust Policy.* Cambridge, Mass.: Harvard University Press, 1959.

Keith, Gordon E. *Foreign Tax Policies and Economic Growth.* A study by the National Bureau of Economic Research and The Brookings Institution. New York: Columbia University Press, 1966.

Kelso, Louis O., and Adler, Mortimer J. *The Capitalist Manifesto.* New York: Random House, 1958.

Kerr, Clark; Dunlop, John T; Harbison, Frederick H.; and Myers, Charles A. *Industrialism and Industrial Man.* Cambridge, Mass.: Harvard University Press, 1960.

Kindleberger, Charles P. *Europe's Post-War Growth.* Cambridge, Mass.: Harvard University Press, 1967.

Kravis, Irving B. *The Structure of Income: Some Quantitative Essays.* Philadelphia: University of Pennsylvania Press, 1962.

Kuhn, Alfred. *Labor: Institutions and Economics.* New York: Harcourt Brace Jovanovich, 1967.

Lindahl, Martin L., and Carter, William M. *Corporate Concentration and Public Policy.* 3d ed. Englewood Cliffs, N.J.: Prentice-Hall, 1969.

Lester, Richard A. *Manpower Planning in a Free Society.* Princeton, N.J.: Princeton University Press, 1966.

Lewis, Ben. W. *British Planning and Nationalization.* New York: The Twentieth Century Fund, 1952.

Loucks, William N., and Whitney, William G. *Comparative Economic Systems.* 8th ed. New York: Harper and Row, Publishers, 1969.

Lydall, H. F. *British Incomes and Savings.* Oxford: Basil Blackwell, 1955.

–––. *The Structure of Earnings.* Oxford at the Clarendon Press, 1968.

McArthur, John, and Scott, Bruce R. *Industrial Planning in France.* Boston: Division of Research, Graduate School of Business Administration, Harvard University, 1969.

McCrone, Gavin. *The Economics of Subsidising Agriculture: A Study of British Policy.* London: George Allen & Unwin, 1962.

Marchal, Jean, and Ducros, Bernard. *The Distribution of National Income: Proceedings of a Conference Held by the International Economic Association.* New York: St. Martin's Press, 1968.

Marshall, Alfred. *Memorials of Alfred Marshall.* Edited by A. C. Pigou. London: Macmillan & Co., 1925.

Marx, Karl, and Engels, Friedrich. *The Communist Manifesto.* New York: International Publishers Co., 1948.

Michaely, Michael. *Balance-of-Payments Adjustment Policies: Japan, Germany, and the Netherlands.* National Bureau of Economic Research Occasional Paper 106. New York: Columbia University Press, 1968.

Mintz, Ilse. *Dating Postwar Business Cycles: Methods and Their Applications to Western Germany, 1950-1967.* National Bureau of Economic Research Occasional Paper No. 107. New York: Columbia University Press, 1969.

Mueller, Bernard. *A Statistical Handbook of the North Atlantic Area.* New York: The Twentieth Century Fund, 1965.

Nelson, Ralph L. *Merger Movements in American Industry, 1895-1956.* National Bureau of Economic Research. Princeton, N. J.: Princeton University Press, 1959.

Officer, Lawrence H., and Smith, Lawrence B., eds. *Canadian Economic Problems and Policies.* Toronto: McGraw-Hill Co. of Canada, 1970.

Prybyla, Jan S., ed. *Comparative Economic Systems.* New York: Appleton-Century-Crofts, 1969.

Robson, William A. *Nationalized Industry and Public Ownership.* London: George Allen and Unwin, 1960.

Reuss, Frederick G. *Fiscal Policy for Growth without Inflation: The German Experiment.* Baltimore, Md.: The Johns Hopkins Press, 1963.

Samuelson, Paul A. *Economics.* 8th ed. New York: McGraw-Hill Book Co., 1970.

Schnitzer, Martin. *The Swedish Investment Reserve: A Device for Economic Stabilization?* Washington, D.C.: American Enterprise Institute for Public Policy Research, July 1967.

Schumpeter, Joseph A. *Capitalism, Socialism, and Democracy.* 2d ed. New York: Harper and Brothers, Publishers, 1947.

Sheahan, John. *An Introduction to the French Economy.* Columbus, Ohio.: Charles E. Merrill Publishing Co., 1969.

Sheahan, John. *The Wage-Price Guideposts.* Washington, D.C.: The Brookings Institution, 1967.

Shonfield, Andrew. *Modern Capitalism: The Changing Balance of Public and Private Power.* London: Oxford University Press, 1965.

Somers, Gerald G. *Essays in Industrial Relations Theory.* Ames, Iowa: Iowa State University Press, 1969.

Somers, Louise, trans. and ed. *Essays in European Economic Thought.* Princeton, N.J.: D. Van Nostrand Co., 1960.

Spencer, Milton, H. *Contemporary Economics.* New York: Worth Publishing Co., 1971.

Storleru, Lionel. *L'Imperatif Industriel.* Paris: Editions du Seuil, 1969.

Sturmthal, Adolph, ed. *Contemporary Collective Bargaining in Seven Countries.* Ithaca, N.Y.: Cornell University Press, 1957.

———. *White Collar Trade Unions.* Urbana, Ill., Chicago, and London: University of Illinois Press, 1967.

Tax Foundation. *Facts and Figures on Government Finance.* 16th Biennial ed. New York: Tax Foundation, 1971.

Tinbergen, Jan. *Central Planning.* New Haven, Conn.: Yale University Press, 1964.

Titmuss, Richard M. *Income Distribution and Social Change.* London: George Allen and Unwin, 1962.

Tracy, Michael. *Agriculture in Western Europe.* New York: Frederick A. Praeger, 1964.

Wright, David McCord. *Capitalism.* Economic Handbook Series. Edited by Seymour E. Harris. New York: McGraw-Hill Book Co., 1951.

Windmuller, John P. *Labor Relations in the Netherlands.* Ithaca, N.Y.: Cornell University Press, 1969.

Articles

Ando, Albert; Brown, E. Cary; Solow, Robert M.; and Kareken, John. *Stabilization Policies.* The Commission on Money and Credit, Research Study 1 "Lags in Fiscal and Monetary Policy." Englewood Cliffs, N.J.: Prentice-Hall, 1962.

Bain, Joe S. "Economies of Scale, Concentration, and the Conditions of Entry in Twenty Manufacturing Industries." *American Economic Review* 44 (March 1954): 15-38.

Blair, John M. "Technology and Size." *American Economic Review* 38 (May 1948): 121-52.

Dooley, Peter C. "The Interlocking Directorate." *American Economic Review* 59, No. 3 (June 1969): 314-25.

Eckstein, Otto, assisted by Tanzi, Vito. "Comparison of European and United States Tax Structures and Growth Implications." In *The Role of Direct and Indirect Taxes in the Federal Revenue System: A Conference Report of the National Bureau of Economic Research and the Brookings Institution.* Princeton, N.J.: Princeton University Press, 1964.

Eilbott, Peter. "The Effectiveness of Automatic Stabilizers." *American Economic Review* 56, No. 3 (June 1966).

Fortune. "The 500 Largest U.S. Industrial Corporations." *Fortune,* May 1970.

–––. "The 200 Largest Non-U.S. Industrial Corporations." *Fortune,* August 15, 1969.

Gilbert, Milton. "The Postwar Business Cycle in Western Europe." *American Economic Review,* 52, No. 2 (May 1962): 93-109.

Hay, Keith A. J. "Early Twentieth Century Business Cycles in Canada." *Canadian Journal of Economics and Political Science,* 32, No. 3, August 1966.

Heredeen, James B. "The Farm Income Problem." In *Modern Political Economy: Ideas and Issues;* Edited by James B. Herendeen, pp. 257-67. Englewood Cliffs, N.J.: Prentice-Hall, 1968.

Johansson, Osten. "Economic Development in Sweden During the 1960's: How Far Has the Long-Term Plan Been Fulfilled?" *Skandinaviska Banken Quarterly Review* 45, No. 4 (1964): 115-23.

Jungenfelt, Karl. "The Methodology of Swedish Long-Term Planning." *Skandinaviska Banken Quarterly Review,* 1964: 4, pp. 11-115 Reprinted in *Comparative Economic Systems,* Jan. S. Prybyla, ed., pp. 193-99. New York: Appleton-Century-Crofts, 1969.

Larner, Robert J. "Ownership and Control in the 200 Largest Nonfinancial Corporations, 1929 and 1963." *American Economic Review* No. 4, Part 1 (September 1966) 779-87.

Maddison, Angus. "The Postwar Business Cycle in Western Europe and the Role of Government Policy." *Banca Nazionale del Lavoro Quarterly Review* 13 (June 1960): 99-148.

Mundell, Robert A. "The Appropriate Use of Monetary and Fiscal Policy for Stability." *International Monetary Fund Staff Papers* (March 1962): 70-79. Reprinted in *Readings in Money, National Income, and Stabilization Policy,* rev. ed. Edited by W. L. Smith and R. L. Teigen, pp. 611-16. Homewood, Ill.: Richard D. Irwin Co., 1970.

National Institute Economic Review. "Leading Indicators for the British Economy." *National Institute Economic Review* No. 24 (May 1963):

Portas, J. H. "United States, Britain, and Austrialia: Some Comparisons." *The Journal of Industrial Relations* 8, No. 2: 111-27.

Rosenbluth, Gideon. "Changes in Canadian Sensitivity to United States Business Fluctuations," *Canadian Journal of Economics and Political Science* 23, No. 4 (November 1957): 480-503.

Schiller, Karl. "West Germany: Stability and Growth as Objectives of Economic Policy." *German Economic Review* 5, No. 3 (1967): 177-88. Reprinted in *Comparative Economic Systems.* Edited by Jan S. Prybyla, pp. 161-72. New York: Appleton-Century-Crofts, 1969.

Svennilson, Ingvar, and Beckman, Rune. "Long-Term Planning in Sweden." *Skandinaviska Banken Quarterly Review* 43, No. 3 (1962): 71-78.

Sweet, Norris L. "Decision Making and French Planning." *Business and Government Review,* University of Missouri, January-February 1967, pp. 21-29. Reprinted in *Comparative Economic Systems.* Edited by Jan S. Prybyla, pp. 200-211. New York: Appleton-Century-Crofts, 1969.

Wiles, P. J. D., and Markowski, Stefan. "Income Distribution under Communism and Capitalism." *Soviet Studies* 22, Issue 3 (January 1971): Issue 4 (April 1971).

Publications of
Governments or International Organizations

Her Majesty's Stationery Office, London

Trades Union Congress. Evidence of the Trades Union Congress to Royal Congress of Trade Union Employers Associations. January 1967.

International Labor Office, Geneva, Switzerland

Measuring Labor Productivity. Studies and Reports, New Series, No. 75. 1969.
Turner, H. A., and Zoeteweij, H. *Prices, Wages, and Income Policies.* 1966.

International Labor Organization (ILO), Geneva, Switzerland

The Cost of Social Security, 1958-1960. 1964.
Minimum Wage Fixing and Economic Development. Studies and Reports, New Series, No. 72. 1968.

Organization for Economic Cooperation and Development, Paris

Border Tax Adjustments and Tax Structures. 1968.
Economic Outlook. December 1970.
Economic Surveys. No. 8, United Kingdom. November 1970.
Economic Surveys. United States. April 1971.
Heller, Walter; Goedhart, Cornelius; Guindey, Guillaume; Halle, Heinz; Houtte, Jean van; Lindbeck, Assar; Sayers, Richard; Steve, Sergio; Dow, J. C. R. *Fiscal Policy for a Balanced Economy: Experience, Problems, and Prospects.* December 1968.
The Growth of Output, 1960-1980: Retrospect, Prospects, and Problems of Policy. December 1970.
Inflation: The Present Problem. Report by the Secretary-General. December 1970.
Labor Force Statistics, 1957-1968. 1970.
Low Incomes in Agriculture: Problems and Policies. Agricultural Policy Reports. 1964.
Main Economic Indicators. May 1971.
Market Power and the Law. 1970. (A study of the restrictive business practice laws of OECD member countries and of the EEC and ECSC dealing with market power.)
National Accounts of OECD Countries, 1958-1967. 1968.
Statistics of National Accounts, 1950-1961. 1964.
Statistics of National Product and Expenditures, No. 2: 1938 and 1947-1955. 1957.

United Nations (U.N.)

Department of Economic and Social Affairs. *Statistical Yearbook*, 1969. New York. 1970.

——. Statistical Yearbook, 1970. New York, 1971.

Secretaries of the Economic Commission for Europe. *Incomes in Post-War Europe: A Study of Policies, Growth, and Distribution.* Geneva, 1967.

United Nations Educational, Scientific, and Cultural Organization (UNESCO)

Statistical Yearbook. Paris, 1968.

United States Government Printing Office (U.S. GPO), Washington, D.C.

Economic Report of the President. February 1971.

Jackman, Patrick M. "Unit Labor Costs of Iron and Steel Industries in Five Countries." *Monthly Labor Review* 92, No. 8 (August 1969): 15-22.

National Resources Committee. *The Structure of the American Economy.*

Readings in Unemployment: Prepared for the Special Committee on Unemployment Problems. U.S. Senate, 86th Congress, 2d Session. 1960.

Sorrento, Constance. "Unemployment in the United States and Seven Foreign Countries." *Monthly Labor Review* 93, No. 9 (September 1970): 12-23.

Temporary National Economic Committee. "The Distribution of Ownership in the 200 Largest Non-Financial Corporations." 1940.

U.S. Department of Commerce, Bureau of the Census. *Business Conditions Digest* (earlier *Business Cycle Developments*).

U.S. Department of Health, Education, and Welfare, Social and Rehabilitation Source, National Center for Social Services (NCSS). "Sources of Funds Expended for Public Assistance Payments for the Cost of Administration, Services, and Training."

U.S. Department of Labor, Bureau of Labor Statistics. *Handbook of Labor Statistics, 1969.* 1969.

U.S. Department of Labor, Bureau of Labor Statistics. *The Social and Economic Status of Negroes in the United States, 1969.* Report No. 375, Current Population Reports, Series P23, No. 29.

United States Federal Reserve Board, Washington, D.C.

Federal Reserve Bulletin (various issues).

Index

7165